HOME COMPUTERS:
2^{10} QUESTIONS AND ANSWERS
Volume 2: Software

HOME COMPUTERS:
2^{10} Questions & Answers
Volume 2: Software

Rich Didday

dilithium PRESS
P.O. Box 92,
Forest Grove, Oregon 97116

HOME COMPUTERS: 2^{10} QUESTIONS AND ANSWERS
Volume 2: Software

Rich Didday

ISBN 0-918398-01-0

©Copyright 1977 by dilithium Press, P.O. Box 92, Forest Grove, Oregon 97116

Library of Congress Cataloging in Publication Data

Didday, Richard L
  Home computers.

  Bibliography: p.
  Includes index.
  CONTENTS: v. 1. Hardware.—v. 2. Software.
  1. Microcomputers—Miscellanea. I. Title.
TK7885.4.D53   001.6'4'04   77-9285
ISBN 0-918398-00-2 (v. 1)
ISBN 0-918398-01-0 (v. 2)

PRINTED IN THE UNITED STATES OF AMERICA

PREFACE

What's in this book

This is the second volume of the two-volume set 2^{10} *Questions and Answers About Home Computers.* This book has two main purposes. First, it's intended to give you a real feeling for what it's like to write programs for home computers. Second, it's intended to give people who come with an interest, but no specialized knowledge, a general background in programming (in general) and in programming microcomputers (in specific). Enough of a background so that you'll have no trouble understanding articles about advanced programming projects and software techniques in the computer hobbyist magazines, ads describing software products, and people who do have specialized software knowledge. There is *no* attempt to push specific products, nor is there an attempt to cover advanced, esoteric software techniques. The whole idea is to get you to the point where you can make your own, informed decisions about what software products you want, and what projects to attempt.

A glance at the Table of Contents and a few minutes of flipping through the book will show you how these purposes are accomplished. The material is expressed in the form of a dialog. One participant (A) has a substantial background in computing and home computing, the other (Q) is a bright, interested newcomer. In addition, an Editor adds occasional fine points and clarifications. Diagrams, Tables, and Appendices are used to provide additional information in a compact form.

Although there is a definite structure to the whole book, so that by reading from start to finish, you will find an orderly progression of material (the organization of specific microprocessors → programming in machine language → programming in assembly language → programming in Basic → generalizations about programming → things you can and can't expect to do with a home computer), the book is also designed to make it easy to skip around, covering topics of special interest to you (see Figure 0). Regardless of your specific background, I'm sure you'll find many topics of interest, simply because computing itself is such a rich, diverse, fascinating, lively activity.

And how I came to write it

I've been interested in computing for a long time (I wrote my first programs in 1964, soldered my first digital logic chips together in 1965), and when affordable computers became available, I jumped at the opportunity to have my own system, free from the constraints imposed by the companies and universities whose computers I had been using. As I went around talking to people, dropping into newly opened computer stores, going to conventions, I was struck by the high proportion of people I met who had substantial backgrounds in electronics and computer hardware — there seemed to be relatively few newcomers. "Why is that?", I wondered. Further investigation revealed what should have been obvious. Although dealing with computers is inherently no more difficult than working on your car, and although programming in a language like Basic is easily and commonly taught to children, the mystique and special jargon built up around computers serves as a barrier. People can't be expected to take a deep interest in computing if they can't really understand what's being said and if they have no way of knowing what they're in for.

My first plan was to produce a short book of answers to questions like "What is a buffer?", "What is an array?", "What is the difference between machine and assembly language?", "What is flip-flop?", etc. That failed because the terms, although each one is simple in itself, are densely interconnected and make little sense out of context. The solution was to write a more extensive book consisting of coherent conversations involving the terms to be explained. But now another problem arose. If enough material was included to make the book of real use to people with wide differences in background, that is, if it was to cover both the hardware *and* the programming aspects of home computing, the cost to the purchaser would be objectionably high. Fortunately, the material lent itself quite naturally to a division in two, so the person who is interested mainly in hardware aspects of home computing as well as the person who is interested mainly in programming can each find the material they want in a moderately priced book (Vol. 1 and Vol. 2, respectively).

Overall, it turned out to be much more work than I'd bargained for, but I feel it will be well worth the effort if it succeeds in helping people over the initial barriers, enabling them to discover the joys and excitements of computing.

Thanks to . . .

Many, many thanks to "Nick" Nichparenko, Dan Ross, Dennie Van Tassel, John Craig, the Byte Shop of Santa Cruz, Merl Miller, Rob Walker of Intel, Margaret Kinstler, Raymond Langsford, the late Walter Orvedahl, Rex Page, the lady in Albuquerque, and William Makepeace Thackeray.

December 19, 1976
Santa Cruz, California

Rich Didday

EDITOR'S INTRODUCTION

This book and the companion volume 2^{10} *Questions and Answers About Home Computers:*
Vol. 1 represent a heavily edited transcription of nine days of conversation focusing on home/hobby computing. Among the steps taken to create a useful book from the raw recordings are these:

—each Day's conversation has been grouped into sections, and each section given a title.

—presentable figures have been drawn from the rough sketches provided by the participants.

—the material has been cross-referenced to aid the reader in quickly finding related material.

—editorial insertions (denoted by [square brackets]) have been made to explain fine points or to correct potentially misleading statements.

—an extensive set of Appendices, a Bibliography, and an Index have been provided.

—much of the conversation has been condensed. Some has been converted into tabular form. Portions of questionable relevance have been deleted. In other cases, material representing qualifications of previous statements has been made into parenthetical phrases and inserted at the appropriate points.

—a numbering scheme has been placed on the material. Questions are numbered only where either the question or the answer (or both) add substantively to the discussion. Unnumbered material has been retained where necessary for continuity or where it gives an indication of the nature of the interaction between the participants.

The conversations divided into two self-sufficient volumes very naturally, with a few minor exceptions. The switch from a concern with hardware issues to a concentration on software occurs very gradually during Day 5, so gradually that there seems to be no single point at which the change can be said to occur. For this reason, the first three sections of Day 5 have been included in both volumes. In addition, some material, notably the discussion of binary, octal, and hexadecimal number systems, is needed in both volumes. Hence, a summary of the relevant information from the First Five Days has been included in the Last Five Days. In addition, there is a duplication of some of the Appendices, the Bibliography, and the Index. This last duplication is intended to aid those readers who possess both volumes.

The Editor

TABLE OF CONTENTS

SUMMARY OF RELEVANT INFORMATION FROM VOL. 1

The conceptual computer

There are two main aspects of computer systems: **hardware** and **software**. The term **hardware** refers to those parts of the computer system that you can touch — the integrated circuit components, the wires, switches, lights, keyboard, power supply, the chassis the subassemblies are mounted in, so forth. **Software** refers to entities that exist as patterns, i.e. programs, data, stored values.

All digital computers have a hardware organization that fits the conceptual framework shown in Figure E1. Programs, data, and temporary values are stored in **memory.** Memory is organized as a number of **locations,** each of which has a unique **address.** On most microcomputers, each location in memory stores one 8-bit binary pattern (a **byte**), and each address is a 16-bit binary value.

The **controller** (alternate names: **processor, microprocessor, central processing unit, cpu**) takes instructions (i.e. statements in a program) from memory and carries them out. Each command in a microprocessor's **instruction set** (see Appendices for the 8080 and 6800 instruction sets) causes the controller to take a specific action (e.g. store a value in a specific place in memory, get a value from a specific place in memory, perform a test on a value and if the test succeeds take the next instruction from some specific place in memory, halt, send a value to a specific input/output device, etc.).

Figure E1 The Conceptual Computer

The **input/output (i/o) devices** are used to communicate values from and to the computer. Typical i/o devices are front panel switches and lights, terminals (such as Teletypes, keyboards and TV interfaces, video terminals, etc.), and external storage devices (such as cassette tape recorders, discs, etc.).

Figure E2 is an elaboration of Figure E1 and shows how the parts of the conceptual computer are tied together in most microcomputer systems.

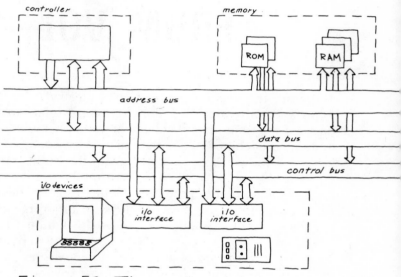

Figure E2 The various component parts communicate through busses

Two different types of memory (ROM and RAM) are shown in the memory block. ROM is random access **read-only memory;** RAM is random access **read-write memory.** (**Random access** means that any location in memory can be accessed in the same amount of time; an example of a memory device which is not random access is cassette tape in which values are accessed **sequentially.**)

The controller consists of a microprocessor chip plus any necessary support chips (e.g. circuitry to provide synchronization signals, devices which serve to connect the microprocessor to other parts of the conceptual computer, etc.). Most microprocessors (8080, 8085, 6800, Z-80, 6502, etc.) are **general purpose, byte-oriented, variable instruction length, sequential machines.**

general purpose: intended for use in a wide range of applications; able to compute anything that is **computable** (see Q982).

byte-oriented: the basic unit of storage is one **byte** (8 binary digits); basic machine commands are one byte long; memory is accessed one byte at a time.

variable instruction length: although each basic machine command is one byte long, a complete instruction may require additional information, thus instructions can be one, two, or three bytes in length. For instances, a Jump instruction is (typically) three bytes long — one byte to specify the command Jump and two additional bytes to specify a (16-bit) memory address (i.e. two additional bytes which specify where to Jump to).

sequential: a sequential computer carries out one instruction at a time. Computer systems which contain more than one processor and can therefore carry out more than one instruction at a time are said to be capable of **parallel processing.**

The three major components of the computer shown in Figure E2 are interconnected by groups of wires called **busses.** The **address bus** communicates 16-bit values from the controller to memory and i/o. The **data bus** communicates 8-bit values from any component to the others. The **control bus** is used to communicate control and synchronization signals among the components. For example, if the controller is carrying out an instruction which says to store a value in a specific spot in memory, the busses are used in the following way: The controller places the address of the desired memory location on the address bus. All devices on the address bus receive the signal, and it is up to circuitry on each device to determine if it should respond. Thus, only the block of memory which contains the specified address will allow the signals on the other busses to affect it. The controller places the value which is to be stored on the data bus and it too is communicated to all devices on the busses, including, of course, the block of memory previously mentioned. In addition, the controller places a signal on the control bus which specifies that a **memory write** (as opposed to **memory read**) operation is to take place, and this causes the specified memory location to store the value appearing on the data bus in the memory location whose address appears on the address bus. Since (most) microprocessors use **synchronous busses,** no further communication is necessary (i.e. in an **asynchronous bus,** the controller would wait until it received a signal informing it that the memory operation had taken place). (For a description of what happens if the memory used in the system responds so slowly that the controller can demand another memory operation before the first is completed, see Q97-99 in Vol. 1.)

Number Systems

There are four number systems in common use among people who program in machine and assembly language — **decimal, binary, octal,** and **hexadecimal.** All are **positional** number systems, which means that the position of a symbol in the number determines its value (the "3" in 13 means three, but the "3" in 327 means three hundred).

In the **decimal** number system (base 10), there are 10 different symbols,

0 1 2 3 4 5 6 7 8 9

and each column in a number is associated with a different power of 10.

In **binary** (base 2), there are 2 different symbols,

0 1

and each column in a number is associated with a different power of 2.

In **octal** (base 8), there are 8 different symbols,

0 1 2 3 4 5 6 7

and each column is associated with a different power of 8.

In **hexadecimal** (base 16), there are 16 different symbols

0 1 2 3 4 5 6 7 8 9 A B C D E F

and each column is associated with a power of 16.

Binary is used for the obvious reason — computers are built of two-state elements. **Octal** and **hexadecimal** are used because they provide a compact (hence easily re-memberable) representation for binary values, and the conversion to and from binary to octal or hexadecimal is extremely simple.

The notation y_x indicates that the string of digit symbols y represents a number expressed in base x. Thus 11_2 means "the binary value 11" ($11_2 = 3_{10}$).

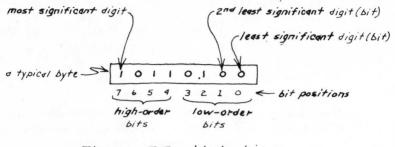

Figure E3 Notation

Conversions

binary to decimal

The rightmost digit of a binary number (also called the **least significant digit**) tells how many (i.e. either 0 or 1) 2^0's there are in the number. The next digit to the left tells how many 2^1's there are. Thus, to convert a binary value to decimal, start with the rightmost digit. If it's a 1, write down 1_{10} ($=2^0$), otherwise go to the next digit to the left. If the second digit from the right is a 1, write down 2 ($=2^1$), otherwise go on. If the third digit from the right is a 1, write down 4 ($=2^2$), otherwise go on. After repeating this process until all digits in the binary number have been dealt with, add up the numbers you wrote down — their sum is the equivalent decimal value. (For powers of 2, 8, and 16 see Appendix — Powers.)

$$32 \leftarrow \text{from } 2^5 \text{ column}$$
$$\underline{4} \leftarrow \text{from } 2^2 \text{ column}$$
$$36_{10}$$

octal to decimal, hexadecimal to decimal

The procedures for converting from octal or hexadecimal to decimal are the same as for binary except that the value in each digit position is multiplied by the corresponding power of 8 (for octal) or 16 for (hexadecimal) instead of 2.

$$8^2 8^1 8^0 \qquad 16^2 16^1 16^0$$

$$123_8 \qquad\qquad 140_{16}$$

$$3 \times 1 = 3 \qquad\qquad 0 \times 1$$

$$2 \times 8 \quad = 16 \qquad 4 \times 16 \quad = 64$$

$$1 \times 64 \ = 64 \qquad 1 \times 256 = 256$$

$$83_{10} \qquad\qquad 320_{10}$$

decimal to binary

Repeatedly divide the decimal value by 2, writing down the remainders from *right to left* as you go, stopping when you are left with zero as the next dividend.

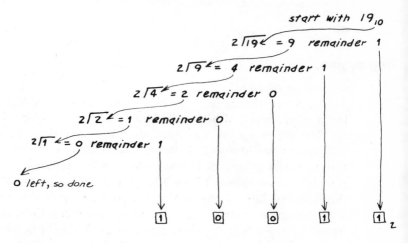

decimal to octal, decimal to hexadecimal

Follow the same procedure as for converting decimal to binary, but repeatedly divide by 8 or 16.

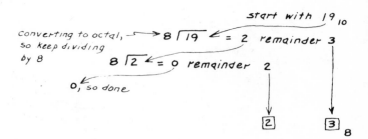

binary to octal

Each octal digit corresponds (exactly) to three binary digits. Starting from the right, mark off each set of three binary digits, convert each set (in place) to the equivalent octal digit.

3-bit binary value	equivalent octal digit
000	0
001	1
010	2
011	3
100	4
101	5
110	6
111	7

octal to binary

Replace each octal digit (in place) by the equivalent three digit binary value.

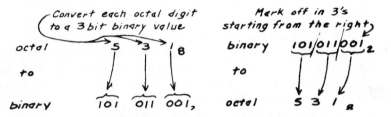

binary to hexadecimal

Each octal digit corresponds to (exactly) four binary digits. Starting from the right, mark off each set of four binary digits, convert each (in place) to the equivalent hexadecimal digit:

4-bit binary value	equivalent hexadecimal digit
0000	0
0001	1
0010	2
0011	3
0100	4
0101	5
0110	6
0111	7
1000	8
1001	9
1010	A
1011	B
1100	C
1101	D
1110	E
1111	F

hexadecimal to binary

Replace each hexadecimal digit (in place) by the equivalent four digit binary value.

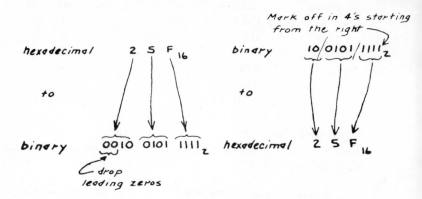

Numbers used in everyday arithmetic have this property: if you add a number to the negative version of itself (i.e. 5 + -5), the result is zero. Signed numbers used in computers have the same property, but use a trick to obtain it. Assuming that we are dealing with 8-bit binary values, let us consider the following addition:

$$00000001$$
$$+11111111$$

The rightmost column has two 1's in it, so the sum is 0 carry 1 (see Figure E4). The next column to the left (and all succeeding columns) have 0 plus 1 with a carry, giving 0 carry 1. Thus, the result is

$$00000001$$
$$+11111111$$
$$\overline{1\ 00000000}$$

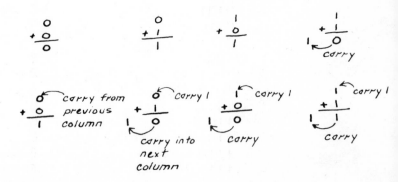

Figure E4   All possible one column binary additions

However, since we are dealing with 8-bit numbers, there is no room to store the 1 which resulted from the carry out of the leftmost column, so it is lost, giving 00000000 as the result. Since 00000001 is the obvious way to represent the decimal value 1, and since 00000001 added to 11111111 gives zero, 11111111 is the natural choice to represent -1. The negative numbers obtained in this way, and arithmetic involving such numbers, go under the name **two's complement.** There are two equivalent ways to find the two's complement of a given binary value:

method 1: subtract the value from 00000000, ignoring any borrow which might arise in the leftmost column.

method 2: change all 0's in the original number to 1's and vice versa, then add 1.

(A gives a somewhat sloppy proof of the equivalence of these two methods in Q297-299 in Vol. 1.) Using the two's complement representation, additions and subtractions (to subtract, take the complement of the number to be subtracted and then add) may be performed without worrying about the signs of the numbers involved — the result will automatically have the correct sign.

The following **logical operators** are available on all microcomputers.

operation	symbol	meaning	examples
and	∧	result is 1 if both the first operand and the second operand are 1	$C \wedge 0 = 0$ $0 \wedge 1 = 0$ $1 \wedge 0 = 0$ $1 \wedge 1 = 1$
or	∨	result is 1 if the first operand is 1 or if the second operand is 1 or if both are 1	$C \vee 0 = 0$ · $0 \vee 1 = 1$ $1 \vee 0 = 1$ $1 \vee 1 = 1$
exclusive-or	⊕	result is 1 if exactly one of the two operands is 1	$0 \oplus 0 = 0$ $0 \oplus 1 = 1$ $1 \oplus 0 = 1$ $1 \oplus 1 = 0$

The basic machine commands for the logical operators perform the **bit-wise** operations, that is, if two 8-bit values are (say) **and**ed together, each bit in the resulting 8-bit value is obtained from the **and** of the corresponding two bits in the operands.

bit-wise and

00001111
01010101
00000101

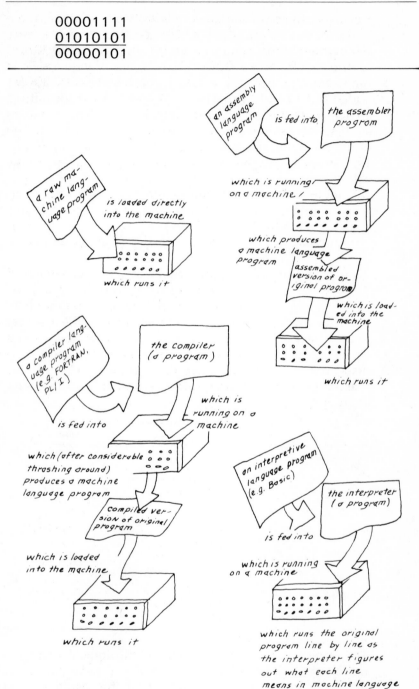

Figure E5 The steps involved in running
different kinds of languages

Programming

A **program** is a sequence of instructions to the controller, expressed as a sequence of statements in some computer language. If a program is expressed in anything except the machine language of the computer it is to be run on, a translation must be performed. If the program is expressed in a computer language (assembly language, or a higher-level language such as Basic, Fortran, PASCAL, etc.), then another program carries out the translation into machine language. In the case of assembly language, the program which performs the translation is called an **assembler**. In the case of a language like Basic, this program is called an **interpreter**. In the case of languages like Fortran, this program is called a **compiler**. (See Figure E5.)

An **algorithm** is a statement of a solution to a problem. More formally, an **algorithm** is a set of rules which, when carried out, solve a (specified) problem in a finite number of steps. There is a distinction between a **program** and an **algorithm**. The bottle in Figure E6 describes a ''program'' for washing one's hair, but since it requires an infinite number of steps to complete, it is not an algorithm. (The reader who is already familiar with these ideas may enjoy reconsidering the definitions of **program** and **algorithm** in light of the material covered in Q981-993).

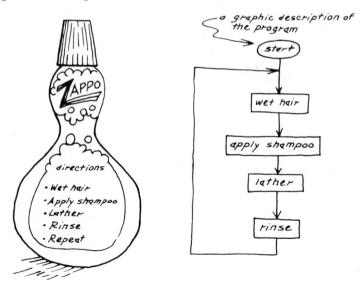

Figure E6   A household program

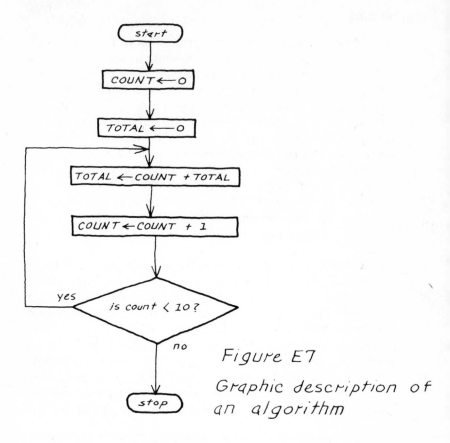

Figure E7

Graphic description of an algorithm

LOOP :
store Ø in memory location COUNT
store Ø in memory location TOTAL
add the value of COUNT to the value of TOTAL
store the result in TOTAL
add one to COUNT
if the value of COUNT is less than 10, repeat from
  "LOOP", otherwise,
stop

Figure E7 Verbal description of an algorithm

Figure E7 shows two different ways of describing an algorithm. To the left is a **verbal description**, to the right is a graphic description (called a **flowchart**). Writing or drawing one or both is an important, extremely useful step in developing any program. The shapes of the boxes in the flowchart conform to a set of standards — **rectangles** for computations which change values, **diamonds** to indicate tests, and **ovals** to indicate entry to and exit from the program. The **arrow** in the computation boxes signals the assignment of a value to the memory location named on the left. Thus,

$$COUNT \quad COUNT + 1$$

means "get the value stored in memory location COUNT, bring it into the controller, add one to it, and store the result in memory location COUNT".

Designing a program is like planning a task. Successful programmers have found it advantageous to follow a systematic procedure when writing programs. First, write down a general, high-level description (in English) of the task your program is to carry out. Then, gradually refine your problem statement, taking care to keep clear notes, and to organize your solution so that each subpart is small enough to be easily understood. Make sure you have a clear understanding of what values each subpart will need, what computation it must perform on them, and what outputs it will produce. After you have a solution to your initial problem, code (translate) your solution into whatever computer language you happen to be using. The chore of making your program work after you have gone through the steps mentioned above is called **de-bugging.** It is a rare program that works properly the first time you run it, and if you have not been careful in the first phases of program design, de-bugging may prove to be difficult. These general principles are illustrated in the context of programming in machine language, assembly language, and Basic in Days 6-9 of this volume.

DAY 5:
SOME SPECIFIC
MICROPROCESSORS

The organization of specific microprocessors

A   Here's my plan for today. I know you want to know, in detail, what a microprocessor is really like to program, how it's organized, and so on. Instead of taking one specific microprocessor chip and going over it inside and out, I thought it would be better to cover two chips, each in a little less detail. That way . . .

Q 612   Why?

A   The most important thing is for you to be able to read the manufacturer's literature for whatever chip you wind up with. Although the basic ideas are similar, it seems like each manufacturer uses slightly different terminology. There's no reason for you to completely memorize all the details of one specific microprocessor . . . then you'd be lost when the next one comes along.

Q 613   Go on. I'll see how it goes . . . my hunch is that I'll want more specifics. You have a tendency to go off into outer space with your generalizations.

A   Let's start from the outside in.
Microprocessors like the 8080 (designed by Intel) and the 6800 (designed by Motorola) come in 40 pin dual in-line packages that are (typically) 2 inches long and a half inch wide. **Dual in-line package (DIP)** just means that there are two rows of pins, with standard spacings.
A microprocessor, by itself, can't do much.

Q   Right.

A   First, you need a power supply. Different microprocessors have different power requirements. For instance, the 8080 needs three different voltages, namely, +5, -5, and +12 voltes. The 6800 needs just one (5 volts), as does the Z-80. The RCA COSMAC chip (CDP 1802) can run on a single power supply of anywhere from 3 to 12 volts. OK. A microprocessor and a power supply can't do much by themselves either.

Q 614 You need memory and i/o, of course.

A   Besides that, most microprocessors need an external source of their **clock signals.** For example, Intel offers a chip (the 8224) which generates the necessary clocking signals, and Motorola makes the 6871. The 8080 also need some external circuitry to interact with its busses. There's the Intel 8228 System Controller chip for that. And then, as you mentioned, you need memory and i/o interfaces. So the moral is, just because you see a micro-processor chip for sale for $20, don't be misled into thinking you can whip a microcomputer together for just $100 or so.

The newer microprocessor chips are coming with more and more circuitry packed in them, so you need less external circuitry to have a working system. Zilog's Z-80 goes the farthest along that route so far. It has built-in parallel and serial i/o interfaces, built-in dynamic memory refresh circuitry, and a number of other features that you have to provide externally with the older chips. Of course, it also costs more . . . but not that much when you consider everything.

Q 615 If I buy an assembled computer, or a kit, I don't have to worry about all that, right?

A   Right . . . although you do need to know something about what you've got — so you'll be able to read the circuit diagrams if you have to troubleshoot some problem.

I'm going to concentrate on the 8080 and the 6800. I think once you understand those two chips, you'll be able to figure out the manufacturer's descriptions of any other chip you might come across. Here's the basic organization of the 8080. (Figure 59)

You can see that there's one **accumulator,** and six **general purpose registers** called B,C,D,E,L, and H . . .

Q 616 Why on earth did they pick those letters?

A   I don't . . . well, H stands for High-order byte and L stands for Low-order byte — there are a number of instructions that use the contents of the H and L registers as a memory address. As for the others, they're just in alphabetical order. A stands for the Accumulator, and after that, it's just B,C,D,E. There are two other registers, both 16 bits long since they hold memory addresses, the **stack pointer register** and the **program counter.** I guess we haven't talked about stacks yet.

[Editor's note: The **program counter** is a 16-bit register which contains the memory address of the location in memory which stores the next instruction in the program.

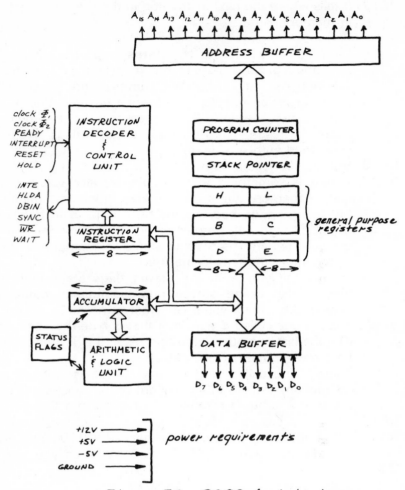

A_{15} A_{14} A_{13} A_{12} A_{11} A_{10} A_9 A_8 A_7 A_6 A_5 A_4 A_3 A_2 A_1 A_0

ADDRESS BUFFER

clock Φ_1,
clock Φ_2
READY
INTERRUPT
RESET
HOLD

INSTRUCTION
DECODER
&
CONTROL
UNIT

PROGRAM COUNTER

STACK POINTER

INTE
HLDA
DBIN
SYNC
WR
WAIT

INSTRUCTION
REGISTER

H   L

B   C

D   E

general purpose
registers

ACCUMULATOR

STATUS
FLAGS

ARITHMETIC
& LOGIC
UNIT

DATA BUFFER

D_7 D_6 D_5 D_4 D_3 D_2 D_1 D_0

+12V
+5V
−5V
GROUND

power requirements

Figure 59   8080 Architecture

Normally, the instructions in a program are carried out in order, so when a one, two, or three byte instruction is brought into the controller, the value in the program counter is increased by one, two, or three respectively. Branch and jump instructions are carried out by altering the value in the program counter, thus altering the order in which the instructions in the program are carried out.]
stacks Q656-Q666

Q 617 True.

A   **Stacks** are data structures — a technique for organizing memory. Having a **stack pointer** in hardware makes certain kinds of very commonly occurring programming problems easier. You remember what the **program counter** is, right?

Q617 It tells where the next instruction in the program is stored in memory, right?

A   Right.

Let's see . . . what else? The **status flags**. The **accumulator** is the register you use to manipulate data, do additions, subtractions, logic operations, complements, so on. After some operation has been performed on the value in the accumulator, the status flags are set to indicate something about the result. The 8080 has 5 status flags. We'll be concerned with 4 of them.

Q618 Hold it. What is a **flag**?

A   A **flag** is something that has a true/false value. It's a one-bit memory that's used to keep track of something. I'm being vague because the term is used in hardware (where it's usually implemented as a flip-flop) *and* in software (where it's a value stored in memory). I don't know where the term came from.

Let me tell you what the **status flags** are (sometimes they're also called **status bits,** sometimes **condition codes**) and I think you'll see what it means.

There's one called **Z** (for Zero) that is **true** (has the value **1**) if the last operation left a zero result (i.e. if the accumulator now contains 00000000).

There's one called **C** (for Carry) which is 1 if an add instruction resulted in a carry out of the most significant bit, or if a subtract resulted in a borrow into that bit.

Q619 Again?

A   OK. Suppose the accumulator has 00000101 in it, and we add the value 11111011 to it. What do you get?

Q620

$$\begin{array}{r} 00000101 \\ +\,11111011 \\ \hline 1\ 00000000 \end{array}$$

A   So, after that, the Carry flag would have the value **1,** and so would the Zero flag.

There are two other flags, the Sign flag (S), and the Parity flag. The sign flag has the same value as the most significant bit in the accumulator, and the parity flag is 1 if there is an even number of 1's in the accumulator. So the 8080 makes it really easy to test a value for even or odd parity.

[Editor's note: Checking parity is a method for detecting errors in the transmission of data. For example, when a terminal transmits an ASCII character (see Appendix — ASCII Character Set), it can send an additional bit (a **parity bit**) along with the 7 bits necessary to specify the character. The terminal chooses the 8th bit so that the total number of 1's in the value is even (if it is using **even parity**) or odd (**odd parity**). Once the controller has received the transmitted value, it can check to see if the parity is the same as when the character was transmitted. If not, an error occurred in the process of transmitting the value from the terminal to the controller.]

How do you use the flags, though?

Q621 There are instructions that have different results depending on the values of the status flags. But we'll get to that in a minute. First, I wanted to show you the 6800 innards.

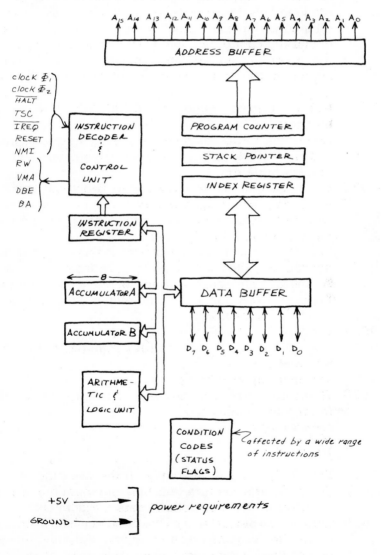

Figure 60 6800 Architecture

Q622 Oh. I forgot to ask you something from the last picture. What does **buffer** mean exactly?

A In this context, it means the same as **latch.** In general, it means a subsystem that serves as a go-between for two other sys . . .

Q623 No, that's what I don't get. What's the difference between a **buffer** and an **interface?**

A It's a strange language at times, isn't it? A **buffer** is a particular kind of interface. Usually, a buffer is an interface between two systems that have different speed or timing requirements. And (at least in all the cases I can think of) a buffer includes some form of memory. The idea here is that the control unit lets a 16 bit value flow from (say) the program counter into the address buffer, and the address buffer holds it while it's broadcast over the address bus.

Q624 I've got a question about the 6800. You show two accumulators . . .

A Right. The 6800 has three 16 bit registers, the **program counter, stack pointer,** and **index register,** and two 8 bit **accumulators.**

Q626 I can see that. What I wanted to know was this: if the status flags tell things about the status of the accumulator, why aren't there two sets of status flags? Or are there?

A Interesting you'd notice that.
OK. There's just one set of status flags. On the 6800, the flags are affected by a great many instructions, so here it makes more sense to think of them as being set by the most recent instruction, no matter which accumulator (if any) was involved.

Q627 Oh.
The 8080 didn't have an **index register,** did it? What's that for?

A For referring to memory.

Q628 That's not much of an answer — obviously the 8080 has to refer to memory too.

index register
Q 654
Table 7

A Yeh, it's just done differently on the two processors. Since the **architecture** (machine organization) of the two is different, the **instructions sets** are different.

Q629 **Instruction set** just means the basic machine instructions?

A Right. **Set** used to mean collection. Anyway, obviously, one of the ways the instruction sets must be different is in how the two processors can access memory, since they have different registers to use.

Q630 Does every computer have a different instruction set?

A Almost . . . it's fun to design instruction sets, and each designer thinks he or she can do a better job than the last, so it's fairly rare for two different models to have identical instruction sets. Of course that just adds to the (already bad) software compatibility problem.

There are a couple of microprocessors that have the instruction sets of older minicomputers (the Micro Nova comes to mind), and the advantage there is that you can use all the programs that were developed for the mini.

Also, there are a few examples of microprocessors whose instructions sets include all the instructions of some other machine (and more besides). The Z-80 includes all the instructions of the 8080 (with one small exception), and quite a few more. (Figure 61)

Q631 Well, what are they? The instructions, on the 8080, say.

A Let's think about it a bit.

Both the 6800 and the 8080 are byte oriented machines, and their instruction registers, therefore, are eight bits wide. So how many different types of instructions can there be?

Q632 You're asking how many different 8 bit patterns there are, I guess . . . 2^8, which is $2^6 \times 2^2 = 64 \times 4 = 256$.

But wait a minute. Why did you say different *types* of instructions? There must just be 256 different instructions, right?

A Don't forget that the instructions don't have to be just one byte long . . . Well, actually, I guess I'm being a little sloppy in my terminology here. Let me distinguish between a **command** and an **instruction**.

Q633 They don't mean the same thing?

A Not exactly.

Both the 8080 and the 6800 have a transfer of control command called JMP (for JuMP). To use it, you put the command in one byte in memory, and then in the next two bytes, you store the memory address you want the controller to JuMP to for its next instruction. Let's call the JMP by itself a **command**, and the JMP with the address (three bytes in all) an **instruction**. That way JMP to address 00000000 00000001 and JMP to address 00000000 00000010 are two *different* **instructions**, but both involve the *same* **command**. OK? So what I meant to say before was that both the 6800 and the 8080 allow for 256 different commands, and using those commands, you can write a huge number of different instructions.

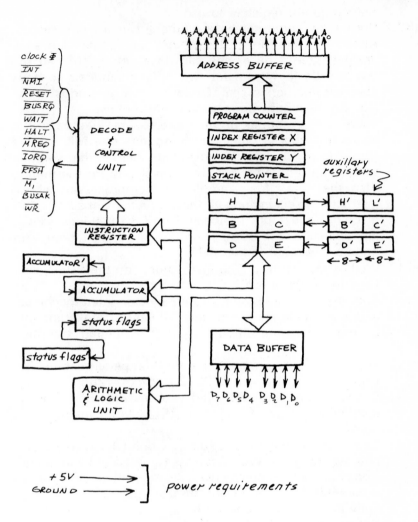

Figure 61   Z-80 Architecture

Now. Neither the 6800 nor the 8080 actually uses all the possible patterns for commands. Let's figure out what sorts of things they must have.

Remember the conceptual computer I drew a while back, I think it was the first day?

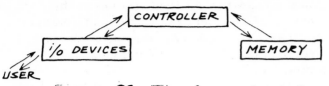

Figure 62   The Conceptual Computer

Q634   Yes.
A   If we think in terms of that, we'll be able to figure out
          what sorts of commands any computer needs.
          You need a number of commands that allow you to interact
          with memoy. Commands that bring values from memory
          into the controller, to store values into memory, and you
          need to be able to move values around in the registers
          in the controller. I'll call them **memory access commands.**
          Then you need some method of interacting with i/o
          devices. The 8080 includes **explicit i/o instructions,** the
          6800 doesn't.
Q635   You already mentioned something about that. You can
          treat i/o devices the same as memory locations, or some-
          thing like that.
A   Right. On the 6800, hardware outside the controller has
          to determine if a value on the address bus refers to memory
          or to an i/o device.
          OK. Then you need a range of **operate commands,** like
          add, subtract, shift, complement, **and, or, exclusive-or,**
          and so on. You need a range of **branching instructions,**
          kinds of jump commands that are conditional on the values
          of the status flags. And finally, you need some additional
          commands that don't fit in the other categories, like a
          halt command (which stops the controller), maybe some
          specialized commands for dealing with interrupts, com-
          mands for setting the status flags, and usually there's a
          NOP (for No OPeration) command which doesn't do any-
          thing.
Q636   Really? It doesn't do *anything?*
A   Well, it does do something — it takes up a byte in memory,
          and it takes time for the processor to do it . . .
Q637   It takes time to do nothing?
A   Just as with any other instruction, the processor has to
          fetch it from memory, **decode** it, update the **program
          counter** to get ready for the next instruction, so it takes
          time to do all that. It's just that that's *all* that happens
          for a NOP instruction. You can use it for a couple of things.

One is to take up space (on some computers, you have to make sure certain instructions start at the right place in memory, so you can use NOPs to pad unwanted space — but that doesn't apply to any microprocessors I know of). You can use them in a timing loop.

Q638 A **timing loop?**

A   Yeh. Suppose that you're using some kind of relatively slow i/o device and you want to do most of the timing in your program instead of buying a more costly i/o interface. Then you can repeat the NOP instruction some specific number of times to make the processor wait a given length of time before accessing the i/o device.

Q 663 Hmmm.

Instructions that access memory

A   I don't know how we managed to start with the NOP instruction — it's an oddball one. Let's really start with the **memory access instructions,** OK?

Q639 Sure. It seems like a simple thing, you just need to bring a byte from memory into the controller and vice versa, right?

A   It's a simple idea, all right, but it's one of the most confusing parts of microcomputers when you get down to the details. See, there are a number of different situations you can get into when you're writing a program, and different ways of accessing memory can be more or less convenient depending on the situation. So, the person who designed the instruction set gives you a number of options. To make things even more complicated, there's very little agreement on what to *call* the various schemes, so what one manufacturer calls, say, **direct addressing,** the next calls **extended addressing,** and a third may call something else again.

Fortunately, though, there is a fair amount of agreement on a notation we can use to figure out what's going on. Here it is.

(name)

means "the contents of the storage location identified by *name*". So, for example, if there's a memory location that we choose to call LOC1, then (LOC1) is the value stored there, that is, the **contents** of LOC1.

LOC 1 | 00001111 | (LOC1) = 00001111

Q640 That's *it*? That's the notation that's going to bring order out of chaos?

A   That's most of it. There's one other symbol we need, and then I can start explaining the memory access instructions. If I write   (LOC1) ← 00000000 it means "store the value to the right of the arrow in the place on the left." It says "make the contents of LOC1 be 00000000". $LOC\ 1$ [00000000] OK so far?

Q641 Sure, sure.

A   Then let me start with some of the instructions that move values around among the registers and the accumulators.

8080 command mnemonic	6800 command mnemonic	action performed
MOV B,A	TAB	(B)←(A)
MOV A,B	TBA	(A)←(B)

[Editor's note: A **mnemonic** word is a word intended to remind you of something. Thus, MOV is intended to remind you of MOVE, i.e. of the move instruction.]

See how the notation works?

Q642 I don't see why you're making such a big deal out of this. It's obvious. The first instruction takes the contents of A and sticks it in B.

A   Right.

Q643 I hope you're not going to go rushing on to something else, though, because the notation is about the only thing that makes sense there. For one thing, I think you've got the 8080 instructions backwards.

A   Just another example of how each manufacturer makes up its own notation . . . at least the notation I'm using is unambiguous. MOV B,A means, in Intel lingo, "MOVe the Accumulator to register B". They list the **destination** first.

The 6800 mnemonic TAB reads "Transfer the contents of accumulator A to accumulator B". They list the **source** first.

OK. The 6800 has just the two accumulators, and no other 8-bit registers you can use, but the 8080 has seven 8-bit registers A,B,C,D,E,H, and L. There's a MOVe command for each possible combination, like MOV D,C and MOV H,A and so on. So right there we've used up 49 of the 256 possible commands.

Now let's start in on some of the instructions that access memory.

The terminology starts to get really wild here. Let's look at commands which load a value from a specific place in memory into an accumulator. Virtually every computer ever built has a command that does that, and they're almost all called **LDA** (for LoaD Accumulator).

8080 command mnemonic	6800 command mnemonic	action performed
LDA *addr*	LDA A *addr* LDA B *addr*	$(A) \leftarrow (addr)$ $(B) \leftarrow (addr)$

addr stands for some specific memory address, and it's given in the second and third bytes of the instruction.

Q644   So these are three byte long instructions.

A   Right. I forgot to mention that the MOV and TAB instructions we saw before are one byte long. The LDA instruction has to be three bytes long because it includes a memory address. Let me call the second and third bytes of a three byte instruction $byte_2$ and $byte_3$. Both the 8080 and the 6800 LDA instructions require that the memory address of the value you want brought into the accumulator be stored in $byte_2$ and $byte_3$, but they require it to be stored in a different order. I can explain it easier if I use our notation.

On the 8080, the LDA instruction has this effect

$$(A) \leftarrow ((byte_3)(byte_2))$$

Q645   Wait. What have you got there? The contents of the contents of $byte_3$ . . .

A   Maybe an example will help. Let's suppose the memory location we want to access is 00000000 00111111. Then the instruction will look like this in memory (because the op code for LDA is 00111010 on the 8080).

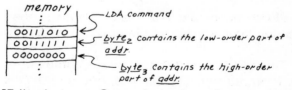

[Editor's note: **Op code** is short for **operation code**, i.e. the binary pattern corresponding to a specific machine command.]

So, by following through our notation, we can figure out what happens when this instruction is carried out.

$$(A) \leftarrow ((byte_3)(byte_2))$$

in this case is
(A)   (00000000 00111111)

so A is loaded with the contents of memory location
00000000 00111111, just as we wanted. OK?

Q646   All right. I guess that makes sense.

A   Now let me run through the same thing, but for the 6800.
I'll show an instruction that'll load accumulator A from
memory location 00000000 00111111. The op code
for LDA A is 10110110, and on the 6800, it does this
(A) $((byte_2)(byte_3))$

So, the whole instruction is

and interpreting our notation, we see that we get
(A)   (00000000 00111111)

I hope you can see that if you think in terms of what's
going on, and use the notation I'm suggesting, you won't
get hopelessly lost in all the quirky little details. A number
of the specific details *are* different from machine to machine, but the general ideas are remarkably similar.

Q647   But why do you put the two parts of the address in
differently on the 8080 and the 6800.

A   Don't ask me, I just work here.
Different designers make different decisions.
Incidentally, we're not quite done with the details yet. On
the 8080 the LDA instruction doesn't affect any of the
status flags, but on the 6800 it does. Specifically, carrying
out an LDA sets the V (oVerflow) flag to 0, and alters
the N (sign) flag and Z (Zero) flag appropriately
Everything OK?

Q 648   I guess so. I'm just amazed at all the little details . . .

A   There really aren't that many basic ideas . . . few enough
that you won't have any trouble remembering them. But
there are *scads* of little details . . . so many that you'll
have to keep the manual by your side.
Now let's go over another way to access memory.

Q 649   Before you go on, why don't you tell me what **effective
address** means? I came across it in an article I was reading,
and it seemed kind of complicated.

A   The **effective address** in a memory reference instruction
is just the address you finally wind up with . . . the place
in memory the instruction ultimately refers to. That isn't
a complicated idea in and of itself. What *can* get compli-

cated is the process the controller goes through to obtain the effective address from the information provided in the instruction.

In the case we've seen so far, it's pretty simple. The effective address in an 8080 LDA instruction is

$$(byte_3) (byte_2)$$

But we'll get to some that are more involved. Here's one that's slightly more complex.

In a number of situations, the address of the memory location your program needs to refer to next will have been stored in one of the registers in the controller by previous steps in your program. So it would be convenient to have instructions that use one of the registers (or a *pair* of registers if each register is only 8 bits long) to specify the memory address. I'm going to call that **register indirect addressing,** although it's sometimes called **implied addressing.**

8080
command mnemonic	action performed
LDAX B	(A)←((B)(C))
LDAX D	(A)←((D)(E))

Let me set up an example we can follow through.

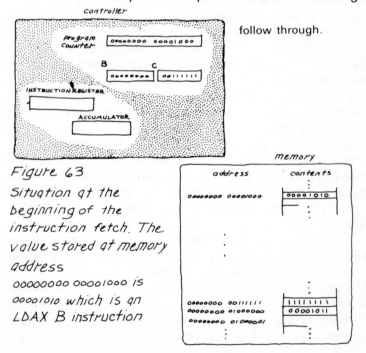

follow through.

Figure 63
Situation at the
beginning of the
instruction fetch. The
value stored at memory
address
00000000 00001000 is
00001010 which is an
LDAX B instruction

There's the situation. I'll tell you that the op code for LDAX B is 00001010, and that's all. What happens?

Q 650 I don't know quite where to start.

A   The **program counter** tells where to get the next instruction. Start there. With the **instruction fetch.**

Q 651 Right. Fetch the instruction. So 00001010 gets brought into the controller and put in the instruction register. And you said that was a LDAX B instruction. But there's no address after it.

A   Right. It's just one byte long, since it uses the B and C registers to form the effective address. That's another reason for using it. The program is shorter than if we had to use the LDA we saw before.

Q 652 I see what's going on, . . . the instruction does this

$$(A) \leftarrow ((B)(C))$$

so I have to take the contents of B and C. Register B has all zeros in it . . . so I've got

$$(A) \leftarrow (00000000 \ 00111111)$$

There.

A   What do you mean "there"? Now you've got the effective address, so go ahead and carry out the instruction.

Q 653 Oh. All right. Memory location 00000000 00111111 has all 1's in it, and I'm supposed to load that in the accumulator. There.

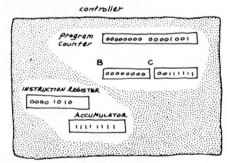

Figure 64

After the LDAX B has been carried out. No change has been made to memory.

A   One last thing. The program counter will have been incremented. Other than that, you've got everything.

Q 654   And I suppose the 6800 has something similar?

A   Similar, but a little more general. It's usually called **indexed addressing**. Here's how it works.

6800 command mnemonic	action performed
LDA A *offset*, X	$(A) \leftarrow$ ((index register) $+$ (*byte₂*))
LDA B *offset*, X	$(B) \leftarrow$ ((index register) $+$ (*byte₂*))

It's like the last scheme we saw in that a register which stores an address is involved, but now it's a two byte long instruction, and the second byte specifies an *offset* value which is added to the contents of the index register to get the effective address.

Q 655   I think I see what's going on . . . if the offset is 0, then it works pretty much like the last one, right?

A   Right.

There are quite a few more addressing schemes, but if you understand how to read the notation, you'll be able to figure them out. Also, of course, for each of the instructions we've seen there's a complementary one which goes the other way — **stores** a value in memory instead of bringing one from memory. Like, corresponding to the LDA instructions there are STA (STore Accumulator) instructions, and so on. (Table 7)

One of the other schemes, though, is so important that I think we should go over it. It's called **stacking**, and I think we should ease into it gradually so it'll make sense.

What are stacks?

Q 656   Seems to me you put off answering questions about stacks several times . . . is that the same thing? And what the **stack pointer register** is for?

A   Right.

Stacking is more than just a scheme for accessing memory, it's a way of *organizing* memory.

A 657   Of organizing memory? What do you mean? Obviously memory is already organized. Each location has an address, they come one after the other . . .

A   OK. Maybe I should have said that it's a way to organize a portion of memory that a program *uses.*

Q 658   For example.

A   When you're talking about simple programs that just use one memory location at a time to store isolated pieces

Table 7 Common addressing schemes (page 1 of 2)

common name	other names for something	effective address	comments (apply to byte oriented systems – 8080, 6800, Z-80, etc.)
direct	absolute, extended	$(byte_2)(byte_3)\leftarrow$6800 or $(byte_3)(byte_2)\leftarrow$8080	A *load direct* instruction requires 3 bytes. The last two bytes contain the address of the value which is to be brought into the controller.
register	inherent	register named in instruction	A *register move* instruction is 1 byte long. Typically, two registers (called the **source** and **destination**) are specified within that one byte. The contents of the **source** are copied into the destination.
immediate		(program counter) +1	A *load immediate* instruction occupies 2 bytes. The value to be loaded is stored as the second byte of the instruction. (Called *immediate* because no memory reference is required beyond that needed to fetch the instruction itself.)
register indirect	implied	(16-bit register) or (pair of 8-bit registers)	A *register indirect* load instruction is 1 byte long. It specifies a register (or pair of 8-bit registers) whose contents are used as the address of the value to be brought into the controller. (Other instructions must have previously placed that address into the register [or registers].)
indexed		(16-bit register) + $(byte_2)$	An *indexed* memory reference instruction is 2 bytes long. The effective address is obtained by adding the contents of the second byte of the instruction to the value stored in a register (usually – surprise – an index register). Some microprocessors treat the value stored in the second byte as a positive number (between 0 and 255_{10}), others treat it as a signed (twos-complement) number (-128 to $+127$).
indirect		$((byte_2)(byte_3))$	An *indirect* memory reference instruction occupies 3 bytes. The address of the value being referenced is taken from the two memory locations which begin at the address given in $byte_2$ and $byte_3$ of instruction. Sort of like a treasure hunt.

Table 7 Common addressing schemes (page 2 of 2)

common name	other names for same thing	effective address	comments (apply to byte oriented systems - 8080, 6800, Z-80, etc.)
paged	base paged, page/off-set	(8-bit register)(byte₂)	2 byte instruction. The value stored in the second byte of the instruction is appended to the value stored in a register (often a special register called the *base register* or *page register*). Thus, the register provides the high-order byte of the effective address and byte₂ provides the low-order byte (or *offset*).
base page	direct, page zero	00000000 (byte₂)	The contents of the second byte of the instruction are appended to 00000000 to form the effective address. Allows direct reference to the first 256₁₀ memory locations in a 2 byte instruction.
page relative	paged direct	(high order byte of program counter)(byte₂)	The contents of the second byte of the instruction are appended to the high-order byte of the program counter (i.e. to the current page) to form the effective address.
relative	program relative	(program counter) + (byte₂)	The contents of byte₂ are added to the current value of the program counter to form the effective address. The contents of byte₂ are treated as a signed number (-128 to +127) on most microprocessors.

of data or temporary results, then things happen fairly naturally. You can keep track of where particular values are fairly easily as you write the program. In larger programs, or in situations where you have a large number of data items, you need to come up with some way of organizing things so you don't get hopelessly confused as you try to write the program. One particular organization that's particularly useful is the **stack,** which is a **last-in, first-out** organization. It's used all the time to handle subroutine **calls** and **returns,** and it's virtually indispensable if you're writing a program (a Basic interpreter, for example) that carries out arithmetic expressions. And it's extremely useful in writing programs that have to consider a number of alternative possibilities (like a chess playing program, for example).

Q 659 That's all very nice, but what *is* it?

A   Well, it's not as if a stack is a *thing.* It's an organization. Here. Let me tell you how you set one up.

First you set aside a chunk of memory. Some number of successive memory locations.

Q 660 What do you mean, "set aside"?

A   I mean that you decide to use them for the purpose of implementing a stack, that you don't use the memory locations for anything else in the program you're writing. OK?

Q 661 I suppose.

A   In addition, you need two more memory locations (or 16-bits worth of registers) which you use to store an address. That address will be the address of one of the locations in the stack, and it's called a **stack pointer.** It **points** to, or indicates, one of the locations in the stack. The location the pointer specifies at a point in time is called the **top** of the stack. So far we've got something like this

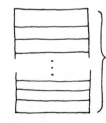

stack pointer

a contiguous block of memory locations

Figure 65

Q 662 And then?

A   OK. There are two operations (and only two) that you can
         perform on a stack. You can add a new item at the top
         of the stack, which is called **pushing** a value onto the
         stack. And you can remove the top value from the stack,
         which is called **popping** the stack. [Some prefer the term
         pulling.] So let's suppose that we have a stack set up,
         and have pushed a number of values on it. Then we'd
         have this sort of situation.

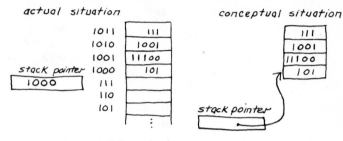

Figure 66

Then suppose I **push** the value 110 onto the stack. The
situation would be like this.

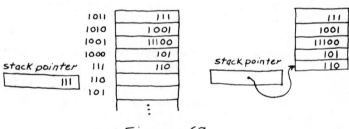

Figure 67

And now if I **pop** the stack twice, we'd have this.

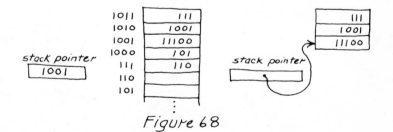

Figure 68

So what the stack organization does is to preserve the ordering of the items you put on and take off it. Last-in, first-out.

It's used so often in programs like Basic interpreters, assemblers, and compilers that virtually every microprocessor has a stack pointer register, and machine commands for pop and push. For instance,

6800

command mnemonic	action performed	
PSH A	((stack pointer)) ← (A) (stack pointer) ← 　　　(stack pointer) − 1	**push** accumulator onto the stack
PUL A	(stack pointer) ← (stack pointer) + 1 (A) ← ((stack pointer))	
		pop (pull) top of stack into accumulator

Now obviously, you can do all the things involved there using the instructions we already have available . . . we could set aside a particular pair of memory locations and call them the stack pointer, and do all the same things by loading the contents of the "stack pointer" into the index register, then storing the contents of the accumulator wherever the index register says to, then subtracting 1 from the index register, and storing the result back in memory, but that would take 8 bytes worth of program. Since pushing a stack is such a common operation, all those instructions are, in essense, hardwired in, and we can do it all with a one byte PSH A instruction.

Q 663　How do the designers know what you're going to want to do in a program, though?

A　　You mean how do they decide what to throw into the instruction set?

Q 664　Basically.

A　　Past experience, guesses, like that. Obviously if there was agreement on what types of things programmers do a lot, all the microprocessor instruction sets would be the same . . . It's a two way thing — the instruction set you get used to determines what types of programs you write, to some extent.

Q 665　The 8080 has a stack pointer register too, doesn't it? Why did you just show the instructions for the 6800?

A　　I didn't want things to get too confusing too fast — the 8080 stack instructions are a little different. That is, the details are a little different. The main idea is exactly the same.

8080 command mnemonic	action Performed
PUSH B	((stack pointer) − 1) ← (B)
POP B	((stack pointer) − 2) ← (C)
	(stack pointer) ← (stack pointer)-2
	(C) ← ((stack pointer))
	(B) ← ((stack pointer(+ 1)
	(stack pointer)←(stack pointer) + 2

Q 666 It does more.

A Right. The PUSH and POP instructions on the 8080 store two bytes at a time. That makes them more convenient to use if you're storing addresses in your stack (as you do to handle subroutines).

for another convenient use of the 8080 PUSH and POP commands, see the program listing in Figure 84, near Q 790

Q 667 Look. I'm sure this is vital and all that, but I don't see what it's really getting me . . . maybe if I knew more about programming, I could make more sense out of it . . . Why don't you tell me what it's like to program. What do you do?

A Let's get into that next time. I'm beat.

DAY 6:
WHAT'S IT REALLY LIKE TO PROGRAM IN MACHINE AND ASSEMBLY LANGUAGE

Languages

Q 668   What's it like to program?

A   What do you mean "what's it like?" It's like planning a task. It's like writing really detailed instructions to tell someone how to build something. It's like . . .

Q 669   No. I mean, how do you *do* it? How do you decide what goes into a program? I look at the program listings in these magazines and I don't have any idea how they were written, or what I'd do to write one.

A   Well, there are some general guidelines to follow in writing programs, some attitudes to guide you.

Q   I don't want generalities. Tell me what you *do.*

A   You're your old loveable self again today, aren't you . . . OK. There are three different classes of languages people use to program home computers. There's **raw machine language,** then a step up from that is **assembly language,** and above that are the **higher-level languages.**

A670   What do you mean "a step up"? Is assembly language *better* than machine language?

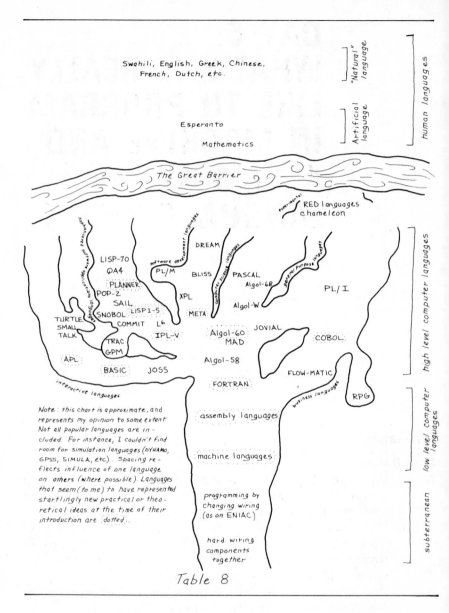

Table 8

A No, I don't mean that it's *better,* the progression is from a form that's very close to the machine but difficult for people to deal with, "up" to forms that are closer (but still not very close) to human languages. It's a human-centered point of view. It's like we say humans and apes are "higher" mammals. It's an ego . . .

Q 671 Come on. Start somewhere. What's it like to program in machine language?

Programming through front panel switches

A   OK. Suppose you have a machine like an Altair 8800 or an Imsai 8080 that has a front panel with switches and lights, but you don't have any other kind of i/o devices. Then the only way to program it is to enter values through the **panel switches,** storing them in memory one byte at a time, and then hitting the **run** switch when you're through. You'd be programming in **raw machine code.** You have to figure out the binary representation of each instruction in your program to know how to flip the switches as you store the program.

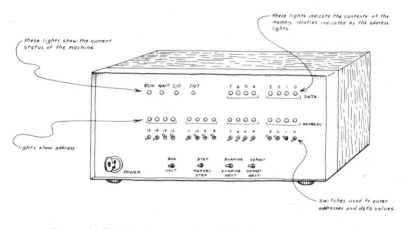

Figure 69 Typical microcomputer with front panel

Q 672 Let's do it.

A   OK. How about writing a little program that we can use to get a feeling for how fast the microprocessor is? Let's have it start with some number and then count down from that number to zero. Then . . .

Q 673 All right, but how's that tell us how fast it is?

A   After we write the program, enter it, and make sure it works OK, we'll enter a number and time how long it takes to stop after we hit the **run** switch.

Q 674 And we'll know when it stops . . .

A   . . . when the lights stop flashing.

Let's see. Our program will start by bringing the number we enter from memory into the accumulator. Then it'll keep subtracting 1 from it until it gets zero for the result. Then it'll stop. Here's two ways to describe that.

do by hand
```
┌ store program in memory.
│ store a number in memory.
└ run program.
```

the program

*a verbal
description*
```
┌   bring the number we stored into the
│   accumulator.
│ loop: subtract 1 from the number.
│     if the result wasn't zero, go back to "loop",
└     otherwise, halt.
```

*the program
a graphic description*

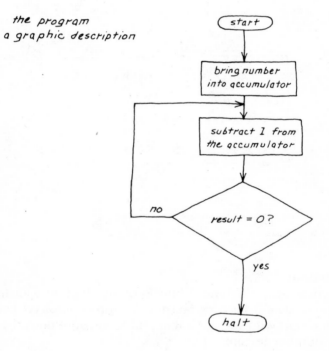

Figure 10   Two different ways to describe
the program

See how it's supposed to work?

Q 675 Yes. What now?

A   We have to translate the flowchart into machine language. Here. You take the manual [*Intel 8080 Microcomputer Systems User's Manual*] and find the instructions we need. I'll write them down as we go. I'll also draw out what our program will look like when we load it into memory. The first thing we have to do is load the accumulator. The LDA instruction we went over last time will do that. We have to specify what memory location to load, that is where our number will be. Let me call that location DATA for the time being. OK? Then we can go back and fill in the right address later. What's the op code for LDA?

Q 676 Uh . . . 00111010.

A   So far we have

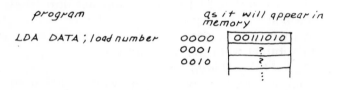

Q 677 Wait a minute. Why can't you fill in the address now?

A   I thought we'd put the number in the first free location after the program. And we don't know how long the program is going to be yet. OK. Next our flowchart tells us to do a subtract operation, but . . .

Q 678 There's a whole bunch of subtract instructions. Which one do we want?

A   We can write the program so it uses any one of them, but some will be less convenient than others in our particular situation. Maybe it would be good to go over them so you can see what the differences are, and so you can see how you go about choosing instructions for a program.

Q   All right. If it doesn't take too long.

A   I'll just outline them. Let me see the manual [or Appendix 8080 Instruction Set]. The first one we could use is SUB *r*, or **subtract register.** Its effect is $(A) \leftarrow (A) - (r)$, so for example, SUB B would subtract the contents of register B from the contents of the accumulator and, of course, store the result back in the accumulator. And it says it affects all the status flags.

Q 679 So you can tell if the result was Zero, or if it was negative, or . . .

A   . . . or if there was a borrow, so on.

To use that instruction, we'd have to put a 1 in register B before we do the subtract.

The next one they list is SUB M, or **subtract memory.** The action is $(A) \leftarrow (A) - ((H)(L))$. See what that does?

Q 680 That says . . . the contents of the accumulator become the old contents of the accumulator minus the contents of the contents of H and L . . .

A   Right. It accesses memory using the **register indirect** scheme we went over last time. To use it, we'd have to store a 1 somewhere in memory and bring the address of where we stored it into registers H and L. The high-order byte of the address in H, and the low-order byte in L.

For our particular situation, that would be a lot of extra work.

Don't believe we should use that one.

The next one is SUI *data,* or **subtract immediate.** Unlike the first two (which are one byte long), this is a two byte instruction. The second byte contains the value you want to subtract from the accumulator.

$(A) \leftarrow (A) - (byte_2)$

Q 681 That sounds like the one we want, right? It sounds like the easiest to use . . .

A   Could be, could be. But let's go through the rest so you can see what's available.

Corresponding to the three subtract instructions we've seen so far, there are three more that subtract with borrow. There's SBB *r* **(subtract register with borrow),** SBB M **(subtract memory with borrow),** and SBI *data* **(subtract immediate with borrow).** The . . .

Q 682 What's the difference?

A   I'm trying to tell you. Actually, instead of calling them **subtracts *with* borrow,** it would be informative to call them **subrracts *including* borrow** . . . What they do is include the C flag (C stands for Carry, but is used both for *carry* and *borrow*) in the subtraction, so if a previous subtraction left a borrow . . .

Q 683 Why would you want a previous operation to affect what you're doing now?

A   Suppose you're using more than one byte to store your numbers, and you want to subtract something from a given number. You start by subtracting from the low-order byte of the number (because only one byte fits in the accumulator at a time) and if there's a borrow left over, you have to take it from the next byte, right?

Q 684 Could you draw that out? It's hard to imagine.
A Sure

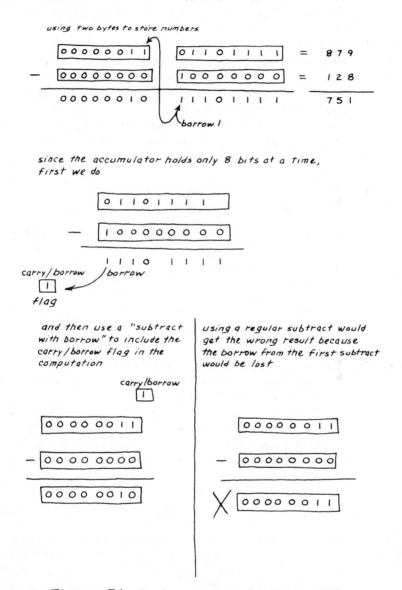

using two bytes to store numbers

```
 0 0 0 0 0 0 1 1      0 1 1 0 1 1 1 1   =   8 7 9
-0 0 0 0 0 0 0 0      1 0 0 0 0 0 0 0   =   1 2 8
 0 0 0 0 0 0 1 0      1 1 1 0 1 1 1 1       7 5 1
                      borrow 1
```

since the accumulator holds only 8 bits at a time,
first we do

```
  0 1 1 0 1 1 1 1
- 1 0 0 0 0 0 0 0
  1 1 1 0   1 1 1 1
```

carry/borrow   borrow
[1]
flag

and then use a "subtract with borrow" to include the carry/borrow flag in the computation

using a regular subtract would get the wrong result because the borrow from the first subtract would be lost

carry/borrow
[1]

```
  0 0 0 0 0 0 1 1
- 0 0 0 0 0 0 0 0
  0 0 0 0 0 0 1 0
```

```
  0 0 0 0 0 0 1 1
- 0 0 0 0 0 0 0 0
X 0 0 0 0 0 0 1 1
```

Figure 71 Doing a 16 bit subtraction, using the **subtract with borrow** instruction.

Q 685 But since we're using one byte to store our number we don't have to worry about that, right?

A   We'll see.

There's another **subtract operation**. A lot of times, you need to add or subtract 1 from a register, or the accumulator.

Q 686 A lot of times. Like when?

A   Oh, when you're counting something, or going through a sequence of memory locations one by one (like in the stack operation). Anyway, for that, there are **increment** (add 1) and **decrement** (subtract 1) commands. In fact, it looks to me like the DCR *r* **(decrement register)** is perfect for us. It takes up just one byte, and we don't have to store a 1 or any addresses to get started. What's the op code for DCR A?

Q 687 It's 00111101.

A   So far we have

program   *as it will appear in memory*

    LDA DATA ; load number   0000 | 00111010 |
    DCR A   ; count down by 1   0001 | ? |
                                      0010 | ? |
                                      0011 | 00111101 |
                                      0100 | |
                                      0101 | : |
                                             | : |

Q 688 Now we go back to the flowchart [Figure 70], I suppose. The next thing is to test whether the result was zero. That means testing the Zero flag, right?

A   Right. It also means that we'd better look in the manual again to make sure the DCR instruction sets the Z flag . . . and it does, so we're OK. According to the flowchart, if the result was zero, we're done; and if it wasn't, we should go back and subtract 1 again. OK.

There are quite a few Jump instructions in the 8080 instruction set. Let's use the one that Jumps if the Zero flag is 0 (i.e. if the result of the last decrement wasn't zero). And we want to jump back to the DCR instruction, which we stuck in memory location 3. All the 8080 Jump instructions are three bytes long . . . the first byte tells what conditions to jump on, the next two tell where to jump. The 6800, on the other hand, has a number of two byte long jumps . . . the first byte tells what conditions, the second tells how far *back* from or *ahead* of the *current value of the program counter* to go.

Anyway, now we have this.

program   as it will appear in memory

```
LDA  DATA  ; load number          0000   00111010
 DCR  A    ; count down by 1       0001      ?
 JNZ       ; if not done, go back  0010      ?
                                   0011   00111101
                                   0100   11000010
                                   0101   00000011
                                   0110   00000000
```

To make it easier to read, let me give a name to the DCR instruction so I can write the program out like this.

```
        LDA
SUBTR   DCR A
        JNZ SUBTR
```

It doesn't change what we'll actually put in memory, of course, just makes it easier for us to read.

Q 689 This isn't too bad! I see what's going on! Now you put in an instruction to stop, right?

A Right. We put in a HALT instruction. What's the op code?

Q 690 01110110

A OK. Now that we know what the first free memory location is after our program, I can go back and fill in the missing address, . . . and we have our finished program.

program   as it will appear in memory

```
        LDA  DATA  ; load number           0000   00111010
SUBTR   DCR  A     ; count down by 1        0001   00001000
        JNZ SUBTR  ; if not done, go back   0010   00000000
        HLT        ;                        0011   00111101
DATA               ; number goes here       0100   11000010
                                            0101   00000011
                                            0110   00000000
                                            0111   01110110
                                            1000      ?
```

I put the question mark in the last memory location, because that's where we'll store the value we want our program to start counting from.

Everything look O.K. so far?

Q 691 Far as I can tell. What now?

Actually entering the program

A   Let's fire up the machine and see how it works.
I'd better go over the switches . . . because we'll use them
to enter the program.
I'm sure you can figure out what the **power on / off** switch
is for. We'll use the **deposit / deposit next** switch to enter
our program, one byte at a time. The **examine / examine
next** switch will let us go to any location in memory, and
see what's stored there. But that's too much talking . . .
turn it on.

Q   Ta da!

A   Now. Pushing the **examine / examine next** switch to the
examine position (up) does two things. First it loads the
processor's program counter with the address represented
by the 16 switches that are in that row there . . . the second
row from the bottom. Then it displays the contents of that
memory word in the **data lights,** the top row of lights.
Oh, and of course, it displays the address you entered
in the row of 16 lights [Figure 69].
Since we want our program to start at location 00000000
00000000, I'll just flip all the 16 switches down, and
now I'll hit **examine.** OK. Now we're sitting looking at
the contents of memory location 0. We don't particularly
care what's there, because we're going to replace it with
the op code for our LDA instruction. To do that I'll enter
00111010 into the switches numbered 7,6,5,4,3,2,1,0
. . . (Figure 72)
OK. Now I flip the **deposit** switch up and, yes, now the
lights show that we're still at location 0, but now the
contents are 00111010. See how it works?

Q 692 Yes. Let me enter the next one. I set the switches for
location 1, right?

A   Well, you *could* do that, but there's an easier way to get
to the next higher memory address. If you hit **deposit
next,** it automatically adds one to the current address
before depositing the value on the switches. So all you
have to do is set switches 7 through 0 to the next byte
of our program . . . which is 00001000 . . . and then
hit **deposit next.** Let's just keep doing that and finish
loading the whole program.

[time passes]

Q 693 Now we run it?

A   Only if we were rank beginners.

A 694 Only if we were rank beginners?

Get ready to start
entering the program
by going to address
00000000 00000000.

1. set upper row of switches
   to the desired address
   (all zeros in this case)

2.
   examine

   examine next

3. result

all switches down
(in the 0 position)

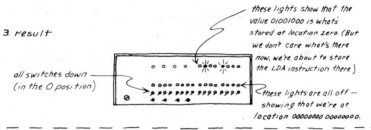

these lights show that the
value 01001000 is what's
stored at location zero. (But
we don't care what's there
now, we're about to store
the LDA instruction there)

these lights are all off —
showing that we're at
location 00000000 00000000.

- - - - - - - - - - - - - -

Now enter the op code for LDA, namely 0011 1010.

1. set the rightmost 8 switches to the desired value.

2. deposit

   deposit next

3. result

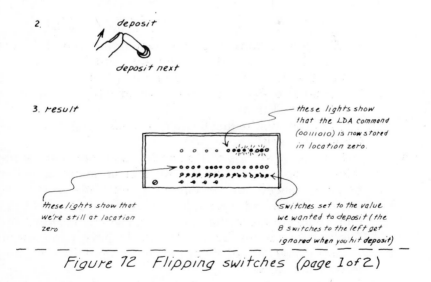

these lights show
that the LDA command
(0011 1010) is now stored
in location zero.

these lights show that
we're still at location
zero

switches set to the value
we wanted to deposit (the
8 switches to the left get
ignored when you hit deposit)

- - - - - - - - - - - - -

Figure 12 Flipping switches (page 1 of 2)

Now enter the lower order byte of the address the LDA instruction will use, namely 0000 1000 (see text).

1. set the rightmost 8 switches to 0000 1000.

2.

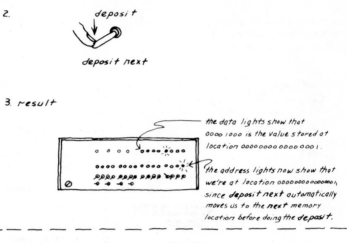

deposit

deposit next

3. result

the data lights show that 0000 1000 is the value stored at location 0000 0000 0000 0001.

the address lights now show that we're at location 0000 0000 0000 0001, since *deposit next* automatically moves us to the *next* memory location before doing the *deposit*.

— — — — — — — — — — — — — — — — — —

At this point, memory looks like this

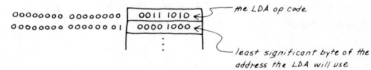

the LDA op code.

least significant byte of the address the LDA will use

A   Right. Only a rank beginner would assume that just because he or she had gone through and entered all the values that they had done everything right. Us old-line hardened veterans *know* there's bound to be some mistake in what we've done.

Q 695   Oh come on. You're just being pessimistic. Don't you have faith in yourself?

A   Heh. Entering strings of 1's and 0's isn't the most natural thing in the world. I have faith that at some point I've probably spaced out . . . flipped a switch the wrong way . . . misinterpreted the manual on some arcane point . . . didn't concentrate all the way through writing the program. There are so many things that could have gone wrong — and if any one of them *did,* the program isn't going to do what we want.

Another way to put it is that I have an ongoing contest with myself. I'll be so pleased if any program I write works the first time that I'm willing to take triple precautions to avoid being disappointed.

Q 696 I think you're being silly.

A   Indulge me. Call it superstition or whatever, but before we push the **run** switch let's check what we've entered.

Q 697 Oh all right.

A   First I'll look over our flowchart one last time . . . I'll especially concentrate on the tests — to make sure they work the right way. To be sure I didn't really mean, say, "less than or equal to" instead of just "less than", and so on. It looks OK. Now let's go through the program byte by byte.

Q   Go on.

A   The program starts at location 0, so I'll set the switches to all 0's and hit **examine.**

Q 698 And the **data lights** show 00111010.

A   And that's the op code for LDA. OK so far. Now hit **examine next.**

                      [time passes]

Q 699 The data lights show 11000100. Is that right? For the JNZ?

A   Ooops. No . . . it's supposed to be 11000010. You were watching, why'd you let me make that mistake?

Q 700 I don't know . . . after a while, all those 0's and 1's start to run together. I guess you were going too fast.

A   Well, at least you're getting a taste of what it's like to program in raw machine code.
       Let me set the data switches to the right op code, and hit **deposit.**
       I'll **examine next** through the rest . . . OK.

Q 701 All right. Now let's run it. I just hit **run,** right?

A   Wait. We have to enter the number it's going to count down from. Let's use the biggest one possible. That would be all 1's.

Q 702 Which is what?

A   In base ten? I'll show you a quick way to figure it out. We have eight ones. 11111111. That's one less than 100000000, right? And that's 2^8, so the number we're using must be $256-1=255$.

Q 703 All right. So I'll load that in location 00000000 00001000. There. *Now* do I hit **run?**

A   No, because that would start the thing running at location 8_{10}. Our program starts at 0. Set the address switches to all 0, hit **examine,** and now hit **run.**

Q 704 All right. Here goes.
       Phew! That was quick . . . or did anything happen?

A   No, it ran, I saw a little flurry of lights . . . But I guess our program isn't going to be much use to us. I don't think I could push the button on the stop watch anywhere near that fast. We should have had it count down from a lot bigger number.

Q 705 How fast do you think it was?

A   Well, why don't we figure it out? Grab the manual again, and read off how many machine cycles each of the instructions in our program takes.

program	clock cycles per instruction	number of times carried out		totals
LDA DATA	13	x 1	=	13
SUBTR DCR A	5	x 255	=	1275
JNZ SUBTR	10	x 255	=	2550
HLT	7	x 1	=	1
				3845

So our program took 3845 clock cycles. Each clock cycle is about a half a microsecond, so that's

$\frac{1}{2}$x10^{-6} x 3845 = 1922x10^{-6} seconds = 1.9 milliseconds=.0019 seconds

No wonder we couldn't time it!

We should have used two bytes to store the number . . . then we could have counted down from a much bigger number.

Why don't we re-program it to do that?

Q 706 All right. What do we do?

Using assembly language

A   Tell you what. You've had a taste of programming in raw machine language. Why don't we use **assembly language** to do it this time?

Q 707 All right. Is that a lot different?

A   I've already sneaked you into it. The things I wrote to the left here as we were figuring out our program [see in Q 690, for example] is the assembly language version of it.

You don't have to look up the op codes like we were doing — the assembler does it for you. And you don't have to worry about the exact memory addresses — the assembler figures those out for you too. Also, we'll be able to use the keyboard for quite a bit of what we have to do . . . we won't be flipping switches all day long. We still have to figure out all the details of moving things in and out of memory, shoving things into the accumulator, and so on, but a lot of the more gruesome and error-prone work will be done for us.

Since we just turned the machine on, we've got a bit of

work to go through before we can use the assembler. Grab the cassette tape there that says **monitor** . . . if you can find it in that pile!

Q 708 What all do we have to do?

[Editor's note: Q and A are here faced by the task of starting up the machine. Since the program required to read data and programs from cassette tape is not currently in the machine, they must initially enter a program (the **bootstrap loader**) by hand. Having done so, they can read a **monitor program** from tape. The monitor program includes routines which interpret inputs from the keyboard. Using the monitor, they can display (and alter) memory locations and read (and write) from (and to) tape by entering commands at the keyboard.

Some systems include a monitor program in read-only memory. In that case, the first two steps Q and A are taking here are accomplished by simply turning the power on to the machine.]

A   With this particular machine, we have to go through a number of steps. First of all, I'm going to enter the **bootstrap loader** through the switches, and then we'll use that to enter the monitor.

(time passes)

OK. Now that we've got the monitor in, we can use it to load the text editor. While the text editor tape is reading in, we can start working on our program . . .

Let's see. We have to figure out some way to use more than one byte to store the number. Suppose we use two bytes. Then what would be the largest number we could store?

Q 709 Let's see . . . that would be 16 1's . . . so using your trick, that would be $2^{16}-1$. But what's 2^{16}?

A   Uh . . . it's the same as $2^{10}\times2^6$, and 2^{10} is 1024, or one K. 2^6 is 64, so it's 64K bytes. Multiplied out, I get 65 536.

Q 710 Is this what you usually have to do? Use two bytes?

A   Depends. In some higher-level languages, two bytes are used to store **integer** values (whole numbers, but both positive and negative instead of just positive like we're doing), and four bytes are used to store numbers that can have decimal points (and so, fractional parts). And in some versions of Basic, for example, there's a kind of number called **double precision** that's stored in eight bytes. It depends on how much accuracy you want.

Q 711 What are we going to do? The accumulator holds only one byte at a time, so I suppose we've got to move things in and out of it.

A   Right. Basically we want to keep subtracting 1 from the rightmost byte of our number until the Carry flag gets set, indicating a borrow. Then we bring the leftmost part of the number into the accumulator, take 1 from it, and then go back and repeat on the rightmost part . . . until we've counted all the way down in both bytes.

Let me sketch out a flowchart.

How's this look?

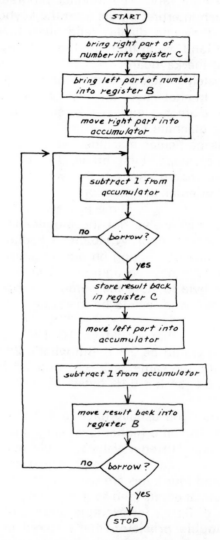

Figure 73 The initial bug-infested version

Q 712 Makes sense. You're using registers B and C to store the
partial results . . . and you store one then take the other
part of the number to work on . . . wait a minute. Is that
right? Didn't you forget to move the right part of the
number back into the accumulator?

A   What? Where?

Q   Down near the bottom . . . right above the test to see
if you stop or not. Shouldn't it say "move right part into
accumulator" like before?

A   Oosh. You're right. What did I . . . oh. I drew the arrow
to the wrong place. Here. I meant to do it like this.

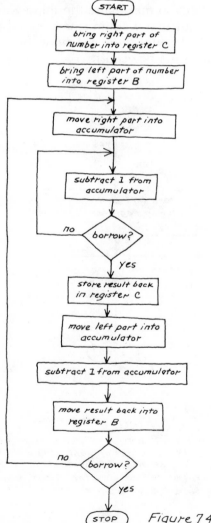

Figure 74   Revised Version

Good thing you caught that. Looks like that would have made the thing quit a lot sooner than it should have . . . It makes sense now?

Q 713 Yes. But what if we hadn't caught the mistake?

A   Oh that happens all the time. We might have gone ahead and written the program, assembled it, loaded it and run it . . .

Q 714 And then found the mistake?

A   Only if we checked carefully . . . if we had just flipped **run** and timed how long it took, we probably wouldn't have noticed that anything was wrong. In fact, we should probably add a few statements that store the final value so we can check to make sure the thing went all the way through . . . but that wouldn't have caught this mistake . . . But I'd feel better if we did store the final result. Let me add that to the flowchart.

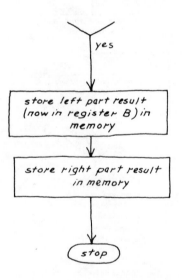

Figure 75

Revised version of the bottom of the revised flowchart
shown in Figure 74. Instead of just stopping as soon as
there's a borrow out of the left part of the number, now
we store the results before we stop. That way we can
check to make sure the program worked right.

Every major program has bugs in it (really)

Q 715 Wait a minute. Are you telling me that it's that easy to make mistakes, and if you don't go looking for them, you won't even know they're there?

A   Yes.

Q 716 But then why aren't programs that people use full of mistakes?

A   Who said they weren't? The mistakes that make things obviously wrong are discovered and corrected, but there's no way to guarantee that you've found every last bug in a program.

Q 717 But that's awful! Surely commercial computer manufacturers can't get away with selling software that has errors in it.

A   Well of *course* they can. They make real efforts to check everything, but the basic fact of life is that any sizable program will have bugs in it, and even after extensive use and repeated de-bugging, you can never be sure that some don't remain. In fact, with some monstrously large, poorly written programs, it's been found that fixing one bug introduces (on the average) more than one new bug! That's the sort of thing that led to the structured programming movement that's swept commercial computing. But, to put things in perspective, let's remember that there are bugs in everything. Have you ever seen a car that works perfectly in every detail? And well-done software that has seen steady use and has been maintained by devoted people *is* very reliable (such software is said to be **mature**). Anyway, the thing to remember is that bugs are going to happen, and as you write a program, you'd better do everything you can think of to make it easy to understand . . . take your time, think clearly, check over everything you do, check the results on a number of test cases.
Now let's go ahead and translate our flowchart into assembly language.

Q 718 Wait a minute. I have another question about this. In the magazines I've been reading, there are lots of listings of programs. Also, I hear that there are people who offer programs for sale at the local club meetings. Are you telling me that there are mistakes in those?

A   I'd be awfully surprised if there weren't. But so what?

Q 719 I want programs that *work*.

A   It's just a fact of life that if you want stuff that works perfectly, you're going to have to pay for it in one way or another. Either you'll have to pay enough to get really well-designed, well-tested software plus a guarantee that the supplier will fix any bugs that crop up, or you'll have to pay in time spent fixing things yourself. Software isn't magic . . .

Q 720 But where did all the stuff you read in the newspaper about computers being infallible come from? You're making it sound like nothing ever works.

A   Let's not get carried away here. All I'm saying is that its easy to write programs that have bugs in them, and it's hard to get them all out.
       As for computers being infallible, . . . you don't see many stories like that anymore, do you? Now the papers are full of stories about screw-ups. I suppose the original image of computers came from early demonostrations showing a computer multiplying big numbers time and time again without error. That's something most humans can't do . . . Look. You can figure out what you think about this for yourself.
       Why don't we get back to the program we're working on?

Q 721 All right. Now what do we do?

Coding the program in assembly language

A   Once we've checked our plan (as expressed in the flow-chart) thoroughly, we can translate it into assembly language statements.
       Most assembly languages have the features of the one we're using, although some of the specific details may vary.
       An assembly language program is a **sequence of statements.** Each **statement** (or **line**) has four different regions or **fields.** The **label field** is used to name specific lines in the program (and so, specific memory locations in the assembled version). The **operator** (or **mnemonic**) **field** specifies the operation to be performed (e.g. LDA). The **operand field** gives the values, names of values, addresses, or registers that the operation will use. The **comment field** is used to write notes explaining what the programmer thinks is going on at each point in the program.
       Here. Let me show you the four fields in the statements we wrote down before.

label field	operator field	operand field	comment field
	LDA	DATA	;load number into accumulator
SUBTR	DCR	A	;subtract 1 from the number
	JNZ	SUBTR	;if not zero, do it again
	HLT		;through counting down

You can use any of the machine command mnemonics in the operator field, as well as some operators that affect how the assembler interprets your program, but which don't get translated directly into machine language. For instance, we'd need to add two of the special operators (also called **assembler directives**) at the bottom to make a complete assembly language program.

DATA	DB	;leave space for number
	END	

The assembler directive DB (for Define Byte), simply sets aside a byte of memory. I listed a label on that line — now we can refer to the memory location the DB set aside by just using the label — DATA. In the machine language version of the program, the LDA instruction will include (as the second two bytes) the actual address of the location we've called DATA. Different assemblers have slightly different directives, so you might see DC (for Define Constant), which sets aside a byte and fills it with the value given in the operand field. Or you might have DS (for Define Space) which sets aside the number of bytes specified in the operand field. Still others have DA (for Define Address) which sets aside two bytes. Again, if you see what's going on, it should be easy to dig the details for your specific assembler out of the manual. . .

The last line I wrote includes the assembler directive END, which signals that . . . well you know what END means. Another assembler directive is ORG (for ORiGin). It takes one operand, an address, and it specifies the **starting address** of the program.

Q 722   All programs don't start at O?

A   No, of course not. You may have a large program made up of a number of individual routines which call one another. You can write them (and test them) separately, but since eventually you'll want them all in memory at the same time, each will have to have a different starting address. Also, since most microprocessors include instructions which do special things with the first few memory addresses, you'll probably want all your programs to start higher in memory.

Anyway, here's a translation of our flowchart into assembly language. Look it over for a while.

label field	operator field	operand field	comment field
	ORG	400H	;program starts at location $1024_{10}=400_{16}$
	LDA	RNUMB	;get the right part of the number
	MOV	C,A	;tuck it away in register C
	LDA	LNUMB	;get the left part of the number
	MOV	B,A	;store it in register B
START	MOV	A,C	;move right part into accumulator
SUBTR	SUI	1	;subtract 1 from the right part
	JNC	SUBTR	;if no borrow yet, keep subtracting
	MOV	C,A	;store result back in C
	MOV	A,B	;get left part of number
	SUI	1	;subtract 1 from current value of left part
	MOV	B,A	;save left part result
	JNC	START	;if no borrow yet, keep subtracting
DONE	STA	LRES	;store left part of final result (it's still in ; the accumulator)
	MOV	A,C	;store right part of final value
	STA	RRES	
	HLT		;finished.
LNUMB	DB		;space for left part of initial value
RNUMB	DB		;space for right part of initial value
LRES	DB		;space for left part of final value
RRES	DB		;space for right part of final value
	END		

Q 723 The H in the first line?

A   Oh. That signals that the value (400) is expressed in
hexadecimal. The exact notation for that varies from
assembler to assembler. If you keep in mind that all
assemblers do the same basic tasks, the variations aren't
confusing, though.

Every assembler has the problem of figuring out what a
sequence of digits means. If the sequence 400 appears
in a statement, does the programmer mean 400_{10}, 400_8,
or 400_{16}? The particular assembler we're using assumes
that numbers are expressed in octal unless told otherwise.
Other assume decimal, and still others (Data General
assemblers for the Nova series, for example), leave it up
to the programmer.

Q 724 Leave it up to the programmer. What?

A   What the **default** base is. You can give an assembler
directive that makes subsequent numbers be interpreted
as being in any specific base. But we're getting off the
subject.

Here are a couple of common notations — different ways
to write 1024_{10}.

notation for the assembler we're using	interpretation	another common notation
1024D	decimal	1024
400H	hexidecimal	$400
100 00000000B	binary	%100 00000000
2000	octal	@2000

Q 725 So learning assembly language on different systems is just a matter of looking up the little details.

A   Hold it a minute. That's not what I said. The basic things that an assembler does — accepting a sequence of statements and converting them into the equivalent machine language program by looking up the op code for each machine command mnemonic, converting labels into the appropriate memory address, etc. — are common to all assemblers on all computer systems. Some have more bells and whistles than others, but they do the same basic tasks. And the differences between two assemblers which are used for the same microprocessor, like two different manufacturers' versions of an assembler for the 8080, are small. A matter of details. But that doesn't mean if you know assembly language for an 8080 based system that you can walk right in and write assembly language programs on a 6800 based system. Remember: assembly language is just a convenient way to do machine language programming. The operators you write in an assembly language program are mnemonics for specific machine commands, and those are different from microprocessor to microprocessor.

Q 726 You don't have to get carried away. That's what I meant. What about the comments? Do you really need them for anything? The machine can't do anything with them, can it?

A   I don't . . . the comments? They're there for us to look at and use to help us (or anyone else who goes over the program) . . . to help us understand what the program does and how it does it. For when we go back over the program later.
        Are you *sure* you understand what I was trying to say about different assemblers?

Q 727 So you don't really *have* to put in the comments, right?

A   What are you thinking? That you won't have to go back over a program very often? Even if you plan to use the program only once, you have to get it de-bugged.
        Besides that, thinking up the comments is an integral part of writing the program. If you have trouble writing comments that describe what you're doing, it's a sign to yourself that you don't *know* what you're doing. And if you don't have a clear picture in your mind of what the program is supposed to do at each step, you can be sure that you'll make some kind of mistake sooner or later. Mostly sooner.

Q 728 I just noticed that you're not using the DCR command

for the subtraction. You've got SUI . . . was that **subtract immediate?** Why'd you change?

A   Sorry, I should have mentioned that . . . Now we're using the presence or absence of a borrow to tell if we're through subtracting.

Q 729   So what? That just means you have to use a JNC instead of a JNZ like before.

A   look in the manual again. The DCR *r* instruction doesn't affect the carry (borrow) flag at all. The SUI does. That's why I switched.

Q 730   What do we do now? The program looks all right to me.

A   Well then, we can start entering our program into the text editor. Where's the manual for the text editor? I have to look up the command symbols every time I use the thing.

Q 731   Let me make sure I remember. We use the text editor to make a tape of our program, and we'll run that into the assembler.

A   Right. We don't type directly into the assembler for two. . .uh, two and a half reasons. The first reason is that I for one can't type that many characters in a row without making a mistake, and if there are any mistakes, the assembler will give us back an error message and no translated program. The second reason is that if we do that, we won't have a copy of the assembly language program, and if we should ever want to make any slight alterations to it, we'd have to type the whole thing over (maybe even *write* the whole thing over again if we forget to keep our notes). And the half reason is that this assembler is set up to take its inputs from the cassette tape recorder, and I'm too lazy to alter that.
That text editor we'll be using is pretty typical of **line oriented text editors.**

Q 732   **Line oriented** as opposed to?

A   As opposed to **character oriented.** Ours lets us remove lines and add new lines. A character oriented text editor lets you add and remove individual characters, groups of characters, and whole lines. To change one little mistake in the middle of a line, we have to re-type the whole line. On a more elaborate, character. . .

Q 733   I get the idea. How do you use this one?

A   Well, it allows a dozen or so commands like **I**, which stands for Insert, and which inserts everything you type up to the next special symbol (on ours the special symbol is $$) immediately after the current line.

Q 734   The *current* line?

A   Right. There's an internal pointer or **cursor** that keeps track of what line you're on. And of course there are commands to move the cursor around.

Q 735 But there aren't any lines in it yet. Are there?

A   Oh. Well, it just starts at the beginning. So we can type the **I** command and follow it by our program, terminate it with a **$$,** and then use the other commands to go back and fix any mistakes I didn't catch as I was typing. **R** is one of the other commands. It stands for Replace, and, for example, **R2** says to Replace line 2 (with whatever I type after the **R2** up to the next **$$**). There's also a symbol to indicate the current line (i.e. the line the cursor is pointing to). It's a period. So, a command like **P.** says to Print the current line, and **P.-2** says to Print the line which is two lines above the current one.

Let's get going here. I'll type our program in, and you can help me spot typing mistakes.

[time passes]

OK. I think we've got everything right, so I'll transfer the text to tape with the **S** (for Save) command, and we can see if it assembles OK.

Now we need to load the assembler itself.

[time passes]

OK. The assembler is on the machine, so now we can feed our program in for the **first pass,** and watch the screen for error messages.

[Editor's note: The assembler Q and A are using here is a **two-pass assembler.** That is, the entire assembly language program must be read into the machine twice. While **one-pass assemblers** are more convenient to use, they are incapable of assembling large programs, and so are less common. A two-pass assembler is capable of handling programs which, after being translated into machine language, fill all available memory.

Figure E8 illustrates the steps required to write, assemble, and run an assembly language program. For further elaboration, see Q203-228 in Vol. 1.]

Q 736 I don't see any . . . and it says that's the end of the first pass. What that?

A   That's a listing of the **symbol table** — it shows the memory addresses that's been assigned to each of the labels we used in the program. OK. Now I'll read the tape in again for pass two, and we'll finally have our machine language version to try out.

Incidentally, we were pretty lucky here. Usually after the first pass, you have some error messages that point out things you have to fix in your program. If that had happened, we would have re-loaded the text editor, read our program tape into it, fixed the offending statements, saved the new version of our program, and tried pass one again. Fortunately, our program is so small, and we were careful enough, that we didn't have any errors.

Q 737 All right. That's the end of pass two, I guess, and all that stuff on the screen shows . . .

A   It shows our original program plus the machine language that was generated for each statement. Of course, just the machine language went onto the tape.

Q 738 Why don't you go over what all the numbers and things are?

```
ADDRESS code


ADDRESS CODE LABEL OP  OPERAND  COMMENT
                  ORG 400H       ;PROGRAM STARTS AT LOCATION 1024 (BASE 10)
004/000 072       LDA RNUMB      ;GET THE RIGHT PART OF THE NUMBER
004/001 037
004/002 004
004/003 117       MOV C,A        ;TUCK IT AWAY IN REGISTER C
004/004 072       LDA LNUMB      ;GET THE LEFT PART OF THE NUMBER
004/005 036
004/006 004
004/007 107       MOV B,A        ;STORE IT IN REGISTER B
004/010 171 START MOV A,C        ;MOVE RIGHT PART INTO ACCUMULATOR
004/011 326 SUBTR SUI 1          ;SUBTRACT 1 FROM RIGHT PART OF NUMBER
004/012 001
004/013 322       JNC SUBTR      ;IF NO BORROW YET, KEEP SUBTRACTING
004/014 011
004/015 004
004/016 117       MOV C,A        ;STORE RESULT BACK IN C
004/017 170       MOV A,B        ;GET LEFT PART OF NUMBER
004/020 326       SUI 1          ;SUBTRACT 1 FROM CURRENT VALUE OF LEFT PART
004/021 001
004/022 107       MOV B,A        ;SAVE LEFT PART RESULT
004/023 322       JNC START      ;IF NO BORROW YET, KEEP GOING
004/024 010
004/025 004
004/026 062 DONE  STA LRES       ;STORE LEFT PART OF FINAL RESULT
004/027 040                      ;   (IT'S STILL IN THE ACCUMULATOR)
004/030 004
004/031 171       MOV A,C        ;STORE RIGHT PART OF FINAL VALUE
004/032 062       STA RRES
004/033 041
004/034 004
004/035 166       HLT            ;FINISHED.
004/036 000 LNUMB DB             ;SPACE FOR LEFT PART OF INITIAL VALUE
004/037 000 RNUMB DB             ;SPACE FOR RIGHT PART OF INITIAL VALUE
004/040 000 LRES  DB             ;SPACE FOR LEFT PART OF FINAL VALUE
004/041 000 RRES  DB             ;SPACE FOR RIGHT PART OF FINAL VALUE
                  END
```

Figure 76. Assembly listing, version 1

A   OK. This is a fairly typical assembler listing, but each one is a little different. This one lists the memory address of each byte of the machine language program using the **split octal** scheme, and just to the right of each address is the value which will be stored there (in octal).
[Editor's note: In the split octal scheme, a 16 bit (two byte) value is specified by giving two three digit octal values, one for each byte. As explained in Q262-267 (Vol. 1), this has one odd consequence — since the byte of all I's is expressed as 377₈, the memory location immedi-

ately after 000/377 is 001/000 instead of 000/400 as would be expected.]

To the right of that is the assembly language statement that resulted in that part of the machine code.

Q 739 Why are there more spaces after some of the assembly language statements? Oh, never mind, I see. LDA RNUMB is a three byte instruction, so it takes three lines to list the machine language version.

A   Right. Another popular format gives the addresses and machine instructions in hexadecimal, with each instruction appearing on one line, no matter if it's one, two, or three bytes long. In fact, why don't we assemble our little program on another assembler (still an 8080 based machine though, of course). After you've seen two different formats, you'll be able to understand the listing of most any assembler you come across. A friend of mine has an assembler that lists things in hex.

[Editor's note: The conversation which follows actually occurred three days after the rest of this day's discussion. It has been spliced in here for the sake of continuity.]

OK. Let's compare the two.

```
TAG     ADDRESS B1 B2 B3 MNEMONIC OPERANDS  COMMENT
                         ORG      400H      ;PROGRAM STARTS AT LOCATION 1024 (BASE 10)
        0400    3A 1F 04 LDA      RNUMB     ;GET THE RIGHT PART OF THE NUMBER
        0403    4F       MOV      C,A       ;TUCK IT AWAY IN REGISTER C
        0404    3A 1E 04 LDA      LNUMB     ;GET THE LEFT PART OF THE NUMBER
        0407    47       MOV      B,A       ;STORE IT IN REGISTER B
START   0408    79       MOV      A,C       ;MOVE RIGHT PART INTO ACCUMULATOR
SUBTR   0409    D6 01    SUI      1         ;SUBTRACT 1 FROM RIGHT PART OF NUMBER
        040B    D2 09 04 JNC      SUBTR     ;IF NO BORROW YET, KEEP SUBTRACTING
        040E    4F       MOV      C,A       ;STORE RESULT BACK IN C
        040F    78       MOV      A,B       ;GET LEFT PART OF NUMBER
        0410    D6 01    SUI      1         ;SUBTRACT 1 FROM CURRENT VALUE OF LEFT PART
        0412    47       MOV      B,A       ;SAVE LEFT PART RESULT
        0413    D2 08 04 JNC      START     ;IF NO BORROW YET, KEEP GOING
DONE    0416    32 20 04 STA      LRES      ;STORE LEFT PART OF FINAL RESULT
                                           ;  (IT'S STILL IN THE ACCUMULATOR)
        0419    79       MOV      A,C       ;STORE RIGHT PART OF FINAL VALUE
        041A    32 21 04 STA      RRES
        041D    76       HLT                ;FINISHED.
LNUMB   041E    00       DS       1         ;SPACE FOR LEFT PART OF INITIAL VALUE
RNUMB   041F    00       DS       1         ;SPACE FOR RIGHT PART OF INITIAL VALUE
LRES    0420    00       DS       1         ;SPACE FOR LEFT PART OF FINAL VALUE
RRES    0421    00       DS       1         ;SPACE FOR RIGHT PART OF FINAL VALUE
                         END
```

Figure 77. Assembly listing, version 2

Q 740 Whoa. From what you've been saying, I thought they'd be almost the same . . . but almost everything is changed around.

A   But exactly the same information is there.

      What I've been calling a **label,** the second assembler calls a **tag,** and it lists them way out to the left. I suppose the person who wrote the assembler thought they'd be easier to spot that way. The two listings represent two

different opinions about what makes an assembler's printed output easy to read and use.

Q 741 Which one do you like better?

A   If I really had to choose, I suppose I'd say the second
one. . . It's more convenient to use with TV i/o because
you can have more of the listing on the screen at once.
Anyway, just to make sure you see that they're basically
the same, why don't we go over what each one lists for
the first instruction in our program, the LDA RNUMB
instruction.

The first version takes three lines to display the machine
language version:

```
004/000 072    LDA RNUMB    ;GET THE RIGHT
004/001 037                  PART OF THE
004/002 004                  NUMBER
```

Let's translate all those numbers into hexadecimal.

Q 742 Be my guest.

A   Don't you remember how? Convert them to binary first,
and then convert that to hex. Let's start with the addresses.
What's 004_8 in binary?

conversions from octal to binary to hexadecimal Q 259-260 or see
Editor's Introduction

Q 743 Well, 4 is 100_2.

A   OK. And recalling that each of the two parts of a split-octal
representation is equivalent to eight binary bits, you can
see that the first address is $100\ 00000000_2$. Divide that
up four bits at a time from the right, and convert each
group of four bits into a hex digit, and what do you get?

Q 744 Uh . . . 400_{16}, right?

A   Right. And $072_8 = 00111010_2$ Grouping that four bits at
a time gives $3A_{16}$
Continuing with the other two lines gives
0400 3A
0401 1F
0402 04

Now let's compare that to what the second version gives
for the LDA RNUMB statement.

0400 3A 1F 04

Look familiar?

Q 745 Yes . . .

A   And as a final check on what's going on, see if you can
        find what command the op code 3A corresponds to. In
        the 8080 manual.

Q 746   Load accumulator. LDA.

A   Right. And remembering that the 8080 makes you give
        the low order byte of the address first in the instruction,
        we can see that the memory location whose contents are
        to be loaded is 041F, which is the address listed beside
        the tag RNUMB.

Q 747   I suppose you get used to it all.

A   Let's load the translated version of our program and see
        how fast the 8080 is.
          [time passes]
        There. Now. Let's see. Where did I put the stop watch?
        And why don't you look on the listing and see where we're
        supposed to put the number we want it to count down
        from.
        Let's have it count from 2^{15}.

Q 748   All right. What's that in decimal?

A   Uh . . . 2^{10}x2^5= 1024x32 = 32 768.
        And that's 10000000 in LNUMB, and all zeros in
        RNUMB. Want to flip the switches?

Q 749   And now I'll hit **run**.
        Phew! It was longer than last time . . . but not much.

A   Yeh . . . seemed like about a half a second. Looks like
        the thing is too fast for our new program too. Oh well.

Q 750   Are you sure it's working right?

A   Let's check to make sure. First, we can examine the final
        result . . . we had it stored in RRES and LRES. If that
        looks OK, we can make absolutely sure that the thing is
        working by using the **single step** switch to take the
        computer through the program one instruction at a time,
        to make sure it's doing what we thought.
        [Editor's note: Q and A established that the program
        worked properly. Q then seems to have taken the position
        that "the whole thing was a waste of time" because they
        weren't able to time the program — it ran too fast. A
        seemed to want to change the subject.
        The discussion of the program and its development have
        been retained because it serves three purposes. First, it
        graphically illustrates the details of programming in ma-
        chine and assembly languages. Second, it presents a
        number of ideas about representing numbers and manipu-
        lating values. Third, it gives an impression of how fast
        microprocessors really are.
        After an extended, heated argument about the ''relevance''

of what they were covering, Q and A finally agreed to go over another example of assembly language programming. Specifically, they decided to write a program which performs multiplication in a more efficient manner than the method they had discussed on Day Two (Q306).]

Multiplication

A OK. Let's see if we can figure out how to multiply two one byte positive numbers. Once you know how to do that, it's not too hard to change the program so it can deal with two or more byte numbers, and it's not hard to make it work with both positive and negative numbers. Let's do an example to get the general idea of what's involved.

$$
\begin{array}{r}
00000110 \\
\times 00001001 \\
\hline
00000110 \\
00000110 \\
\hline
00110110
\end{array}
\qquad
\begin{array}{r}
(6_{10}) \\
\times (9_{10}) \\
\hline
\\
\\
(54)_{10}
\end{array}
\qquad
\begin{array}{l}
\textbf{multiplicand} \\
\times \textbf{ multiplier} \\
\hline
\\
\\
\textbf{product}
\end{array}
$$

For each 1 in the **multiplier,** you add in an appropriately shifted copy of the **multiplicand.** Since it's awkward for the results of arithmetic operations to be longer than the numbers your program started with, we'll just throw away everything but the rightmost eight bits of the **product.** So . . .

Q 751 The example you picked was easy though . . . for several reasons. I can see how you'd write a program to add the two intermediate terms, but how would you keep track of things if there had been more than two 1's in the multiplier? How about this?

$$
\begin{array}{r}
00000010 \\
\times 10101100 \\
\hline
\end{array}
$$

A Oh. That's no problem. We'll keep a **running sum.** Each time we come across a 1 in the multiplier, we'll add to the partial result. Incidentally, totalling a bunch of items by keeping a running sum (i.e. keeping the "sum so far" and adding in each new term as you come to it) is also called **accumulating a sum.** That's where **accumulators** got their name.

Although we can handle the first thing you were worried about, your example will cause us some worry.

The problem is that the product won't fit in one byte.

```
          00000010                    the running sum
        x 10101100                    (in accumulator)
        ──────────                  ──────────────────
                 0                    00000000
                 0                    00000000
          00000010                    00001000
          00000010                    00011000
                 0                    00011000
          00000010                    01011000
                 0                    01011000
        00000010                    ➔①01011000
        ──────────                  no room for this bit
         101011000
```

The problem is obvious — it's possible to multiply two one byte numbers and wind up with an answer that's too big to fit in one byte.

Q 758 What do you do about that?

A   You call it an **overflow,** and maybe give an error message.

Q 753 Come on. Seriously.

A   I *am* serious. What else can you do?

Q 754 You could use two bytes to store the answer.

A   And then what if you want to use that in another computation — use three bytes for the result of that? No, the solution has to be to stop somewhere; you might as well keep all your numbers the same length. If you need to use larger numbers in your program, use two bytes for all the numbers. Of course, you can still have an overflow since multiplying two 16 bit numbers can yield a product that requires 32 bits to store, but you'll be able to deal with much bigger values before it happens.

      [Editor's note: A is talking about the usual way this problem is handled. It is certainly *possible* to represent numbers using a variable number of bits, and this *is* done in some cases. For instance, the programs which compute pi to 1000 decimal places obviously must make use of such techniques. In most cases, however, numbers are represented in a fixed number of bits.

      Even if the programming language you are using implements numbers in a fixed length, you are not necessarily limited by that — see the program in Appendix Powers. Even though it is written in a version of Basic which uses four bytes per number, the program is capable of dealing with products which include hundreds of decimal digits.]

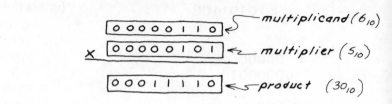

$$\begin{array}{r} \boxed{0\ 0\ 0\ 0\ 0\ 1\ 1\ 0} \quad \text{multiplicand}(6_{10}) \\ \times\ \boxed{0\ 0\ 0\ 0\ 0\ 1\ 0\ 1} \quad \text{multiplier}\ (5_{10}) \\ \hline \boxed{0\ 0\ 0\ 1\ 1\ 1\ 1\ 0} \quad \text{product}\quad(30_{10}) \end{array}$$

First method (like we learned in grade school):
Add in shifted versions of the multiplicand

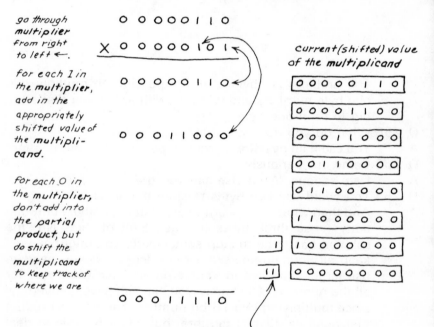

go through multiplier from right to left ←.

for each 1 in the multiplier, add in the appropriately shifted value of the multiplicand.

for each 0 in the multiplier, don't add into the partial product, but do shift the multiplicand to keep track of where we are

current (shifted) value of the multiplicand

here's why we'll do it the second way. Even though there's no overflow, some of the 1's in the multiplicand have been shifted out of the byte storing it. We'd have to keep track of that fact to jump to the OVERFLOW exit if we come across another 1 in the multiplier

Figure 78 Two ways of Multiplying
(page 1 of 2)

Q 755 Somehow this seems a little strange.

A   Yeh . . . computer numbers aren't as general as the ones we deal with when we're using pencil and paper . . .
The way binary multiplication algorithms are usually written, they work a little backwards from the way I've been talking so far. You'll agree that we'll get the same (correct) answer if instead of shifting the multiplicand to the left and adding it to the accumulating sum, we shift the accumulating sum to the right and add in the multiplicand as it is?

Q 756 No, I won't agree to that.

A   Let me do an example both ways, and I think you'll see what I mean.

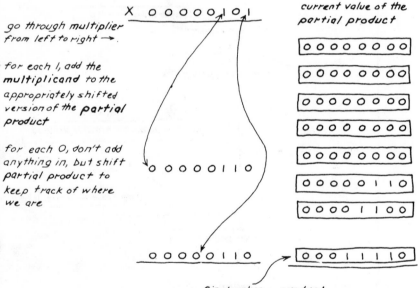

Second method: leave the multiplicand alone, shift the partial product.

go through multiplier from left to right →.

for each 1, add the multiplicand to the appropriately shifted version of the partial product

for each 0, don't add anything in, but shift partial product to keep track of where we are

current value of the partial product

final value = product

Figure 78

This way, if a 1 ever comes out of the partial product, there's been an overflow.

Q 757 All right. I suppose you get the same thing. But why do you want to do it that way?

A   It's easier to write the program. Specifically, it's much easier to check for overflow that way. If you shift the accumulating sum and a 1 pops out the left, you've had an overflow. You'll see. Here's the flowchart I came up with this morning before you came over.

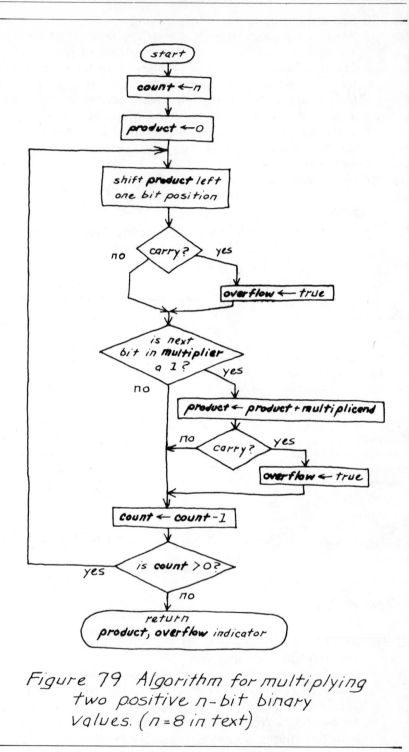

Figure 79 Algorithm for multiplying
two positive n-bit binary
values. (n = 8 in text)

See how it works?

Q 758 What is **count** doing?

A We have to go through the loop once for each bit position in the **multiplier**. So **count** keeps track of how many times we've gone through the loop. See? At the bottom of the loop? Each time through we subtract 1 from **count**, and we keep going as long as **count** is still greater than zero.

Q 759 I see why you have to tell if the next bit in the **multiplier** is a 1, but how do you do that?

A Yeh. That's not spelled out in the flowchart. Let me expand **(refine)** that part.

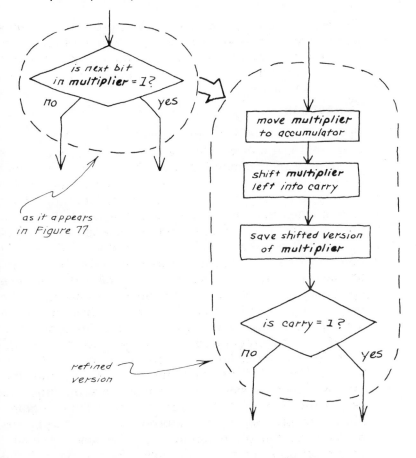

is next bit
in multiplier = 1?

no   yes

as it appears
in Figure 77

move multiplier
to accumulator

shift multiplier
left into carry

save shifted version
of multiplier

is carry = 1?

no   yes

refined
version

Figure 80 Refinement of the test
on the next bit of the
multiplier.

Q 760 Why didn't you put that in the flowchart to begin with? You need to do all that in the program, right?

A   When I worked out the flowchart, I wasn't thinking in complete detail. When you're developing a program, you start with the general idea, get an overall plan. The first flowchart shows the way I was thinking about the problem. I went over a number of examples, then, once I saw roughly what the program has to do, I expressed that as the flowchart. Then, before translating the flowchart into the language we're using, we expand or refine the original plan until all the details are resolved. Ready?

Q 761 All right.

A   The first thing we have to do is figure out what things we need to store, how we're going to set things up. Since we'll probably want to be able to use our multiply program in a number of different situations, I think we should write it as a subroutine.

Subroutines

Q 762 Have you ever defined **subroutine?**

A   Don't recall. A **subroutine** is a subpart of a program. It's a sequence of statements that can be referenced by other parts of the program. Particular operations that are frequently used in a program are often made into subroutines so that when the operation is needed, instead of copying the instructions for doing it, you can just **call** the subroutine. A **call** to a subroutine is a special kind of jump or transfer of control. You might think of it as a temporary transfer of control, because the subroutine performs some operation that's part of the ongoing flow of events in the program that calls it. After the subroutine has done what it's supposed to, it **returns** control to the program that called it, so that program can continue with what it's doing. In the process of calling a subroutine, a **return address,** i.e. the location of the instruction immediately after the call instruction, is saved so that after the subroutine has been carried out, control can return to the calling program. Most microprocessors have **subroutine call instructions** which push the return address on the stack. Usually, people set up some sort of discipline for dealing with the registers . . .

Q 763 Slow down! I think I followed everything but the last part. Each microprocessor has basic machine commands for calling subroutines.

A   Right. And basic machine commands for returning from a subroutine. The **call command** automatically stores the

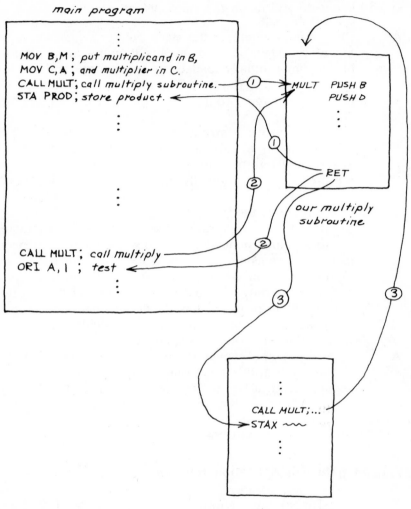

Figure 81 Typical uses of the multiply sub-
    routine. Each occurrence of CALL MULT
    transfers control to the subroutine,
    and the RETurn statement in MULT re-
    turns control to the routine that made
    the CALL.

current value of the program counter on the stack, that is, it pushes the return address onto the stack.

Q 764 What do you mean *the* stack. What stack?
        stacks Q 656-666

A   Oh. I meant wherever the stack pointer register says the top of the stack is. That means that the main program has to have initially loaded an appropriate address into the stack pointer register. The address of some region of memory that your program isn't going to use for anything else.

        Then the **return instruction,** which, of course, will be the last thing a subroutine executes, pops the stack, loading the return address into the program counter, so the program that originally made the subroutine call can continue.

Q 765 And what was the bit about a "discipline"?

A   Suppose the main program is using some of the registers to store values it needs. Probably the subroutine needs to use the registers to do its work. If you're not careful in the way you write your program, when you call a subroutine it may wipe out a value in one of the registers that the main program was depending on.

Q 766 Oh. I see. It's something you have to consider when you're writing the subroutine. What do you do?

A   Typically, some convention is adopted. A common one is this: if a subroutine uses a register (other than the accumulator), it has to store whatever was in it to begin with, and restore that value when it's through. Why don't we adopt that rule?

Q 767 All right, go ahead. See if I care.

Finishing the Multiplication Routine

A   OK. The multiply subroutine. Let's assume that it gets the two values it's supposed to multiply . . . in registers B and C. We'll have it return the **product** in the accumulator, and I suppose that we should return the value that tells whether or not there's been an overflow in some memory location . . . let's call it OVRFL.

Q 768 Wait . . . why not just return it in one of the registers? Or does it matter?

A   Matter?
        What is matter? Never mind. What is mind? No matter. [??] Ah. Don't forget our convention — we're to return all the registers (except the accumulator) with their original values, so we can't return it in one of the registers.

We *could* return the overflow indicator in the carry flag, I suppose.

Q 769 Return it in the *carry flag*? What would that mean?

A OK. The overflow indicator is either **true** or **false,** 1 or 0, right? Either at some point in the multiplication process an overflow occurred, or else it didn't. So we really need only one bit to store it. When we get around to returning from the multiply subroutine we could set the carry flag appropriately. That might be convenient because the program that calls our subroutine can easily discover if an overflow has occurred by testing the carry bit immediately after the subroutine has completed its job. In fact, let's do it that way. OK. We know where the input values will be, and where we'll leave the result. Now let's look over our flowchart and see what registers the subroutine will need to use. [Figures 79 and 80.]

Q 770 You have to store **count** somewhere, right?

A Right. Let's throw that in register D.

And . . . look. In the section where we determine if the next bit of the **multiplier** is a 1, we need to have the **multiplier** in the accumulator, so we can't just leave the **product** in the accumulator all the time, we'll need a place to store it occasionally. Let's use register E for that.

And let's use register H to store the **overflow indicator.** OK. Now that we've got a general idea of what registers we'll be using, we can start translating our flowcharts into assembly language. Let's start by writing some comments that tell what the subroutine does.

```
;multiply subroutine — MULT.
;forms the (8 bit) product of the
;values in registers B and C.
;returns the product in the accumulator,
;and sets the carry flag to indicate
;that an overflow occurred at some point
;in the process. (1 = overflow, 0 = none)
```

OK. Now we've got to store copies of the contents of the register we'll be using — to satisfy our convention. We can just PUSH the registers onto the stack, and then at the very end of the subroutine, we'll POP them back into place. We can use the PUSH instruction which pushes two registers at a time, so . . .

8080 PUSH and POP move two bytes at a time Q 665

Q 771 Wait. Wait. Now you've got me confused. I thought you said that the return address was on the stack. Put there by the subroutine call. And that we had to leave it alone, or something like that . . . so the return knows where . . .

A   Maybe you've forgotten how stacks work. Pushing a new
         value on a stack doesn't disturb anything that's already
         on it. As long as we POP as many items off at the end
         (before the **return** statement) as we PUSHed on at the
         beginning, everything will be fine. That's the beauty of
         using stacks.
         OK?
         Here goes. After the comments, we'll have
         MULT PUSH B   ;save registers B and C.
              PUSH D   ;save registers D and E.
              PUSH H   gsave registers H and L.

         Now. The first thing our flowchart says to do is to start
         count off at 8. And then make **product** start at 0, and
         ooops! We forgot to say anything about the overflow
         indicator. Obviously we have to start it off at 0 too, since
         there can't have been an overflow before we've started
         doing the multiplication.
              MVI D,8D   ;**count** starts off at 8 (decimal).
              MVI H,0   ;overflow indicator starts at 0 (false).
              MVI E,   ;**product** starts off at 0.

         OK. Now, the flowchart says to shift **product** left one bit.
         To do that, we've got to have the **product** in the accumula-
         tor, since the shift instructions work on the contents of
         the accumulator.
Q 772 So you need to MOVe the contents of E into the accumula-
         tor.
A   We could do that. In fact, it would be a lot clearer than
         the way I was going to do it.
Q 773 How else *could* you do it?
A   Well, since we know the **product** is zero at this point,
         I was going to use a one byte long instruction to zero
         the accumulator . . . and zero the carry flag in one swell
         foop.
         I was thinking of using the XRA A instruction.
Q 774 *The XRA A instruction?* What in the world is the XRA
         A instruction?
A   XRA A stands for **eXclusive-oR the Accumulator with
         the Accumulator.** Remember what the **exclusive-or** is?
Q 775 I think. The exclusive-or of two values is 1 if one and
         only one of them is 1. Right?
A   Right. The XRA command performs the **bit-wise exclu-
         sive-or.** That is, it takes two bytes, and produces a one
         byte result in which each bit is the **exclusive-or** of the
         corresponding bits in the original two bytes. And on the

8080, at the same time, it resets the carry flag. So if you **exclusive-or** a value with itself, the result is always zero.

bit-wise exclusive-or of two different values	bit-wise exclusive-or of two identical values

```
    00101101              00101101
  +10000111            +00101101
    10101010              00000000
```

See why that works?

Q   Yes.

A   But the way you suggested is definitely clearer.

   MOV A,E   ;bring **product** into the accumulator.

Let's see. Now we'll have to do something to make sure the carry flag is zero, because . . .

Q 776 Wait a minute. The way you suggested does all that in one byte . . . right? You said the XRA A just takes up one byte? And my way takes a number of bytes . . . so our subroutine is going to be longer if we do it my way. Isn't it important to make your programs as short as possible?

A   Well, using the XRA A does take a little less memory . . . and it would be a few microseconds faster. But you've got to remember whose time, effort, and mental health you're working to save. Yours, not the machine's. Think it through. What if a year from now you (or someone else) want to take our little subroutine and re-do it so it multiplies 16-bit values? The first thing you'd do is go over the subroutine to figure out how it works. If you come to the XRA A instruction, and you don't quite remember all the details of what it does, you'll have to look it up in the manual, and puzzle out why we used it, what it does to the carry flag, etc. Think how many microseconds of your time *that* takes.

Q 777 I guess what you're saying makes sense, but I've come across things in the magazines that give tips for doing things faster . . . in less memory . . .

A   OK. I'm not saying that it's *never* worth it to try to produce the shortest, fastest program you can. For instance, some companies sell microcomputers that come with little operating systems on ROM chips. If they can squeeze the same amount of program on one less chip by pulling every trick they can think of, they're going to save a lot of money, because they're going to be making thousands of systems. Or back in the old days, when computers had teeny amounts of incredibly expensive memory, "tight coding" may have made some sense . . .

Q 778 All right, all right. Let's not get hung up on this. I don't care how you do it, let's get on with the program.

A Your wish is my . . .

Let's see. We've got everything initialized, I guess. Let me do the next few boxes in the flowchart.

```
                    ;main loop starts here:
LOOP    STC         ;make sure carry=0 so upcoming shift
        CMC         ;doesn't introduce an extraneous 1 into product
        RAL         ;shift product left one bit.
        JNC   NVFL  ;no carry means no overflow.
        MVI   H,1   ;have overflow, set indicator.
NVFL    MOV   E,A   ;save current version of product.
```

Q 779 Wait, slow down! I don't know what the first three instructions you used are . . .

A Keep the manual by your side. [Or see Appendix 8080 Instruction Set.]

The STC stands for **SeT Carry.** It makes the carry flag have the value 1, no matter what it was before.

Then the CMC, which stands for **CoMplement Carry,** flips it to 0 . . .

Q 780 Why didn't you just set it to 0 to begin with?

A I don't think the 8080 has an instruction to do that. At least I couldn't find one in the manual. Can you?

The next thing we have to do is shift the *product* left one bit. There's two instructions that shift left, RAL and RLC. I guess the easiest way to explain them is to draw a picture.

RLC (*rotate left*)

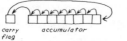

RAL (*rotate left through carry*)

Figure 82 Comparison of the 8080's two different rotate left instructions. Note different effect on rightmost bit (bit Ø).

Q 781 And the difference is . . . oh. It's whether the leftmost bit goes just into the carry, or into both the carry and the rightmost bit. Why did you decide to use the RAL instead of the RLC?

A Because if the leftmost bit of the **product** is a 1 before the shift, we don't want it to come around into the **product** again.

Q 782 Let me see . . . but the only time that would happen is if there's an overflow, right? Because . . .

A That's right.

Q 783 So what difference would it make? If there's an overflow, the answer is going to be wrong anyway. So what if an extra 1 gets put in the **product?** I mean, that's something I haven't quite understood all along. If there's an overflow, why don't you just have the subroutine give up? Why do you have it always stay in the loop until **count** gets down to zero?

A Well, I thought it would be more polite to let the program that calls our subroutine decide what to do if there's an overflow. In some cases, it may not matter, the calling program may just want the rightmost eight bits of the product. [Editor's note: for example, some random number generator programs would want this.]

Q 784 All right, I guess . . .
So now you're on the part that checks the next bit of the **multiplier,** Right?

A Right.

```
MOV    A,C      ;get multiplier to check next bit.
RAL             ;shift multiplier left into carry.
MOV    C,A
```

Q 785 Hold it. What are you doing? Aren't you supposed to check to see whether the carry is 1 or not? To tell if we're supposed to add in the **multiplicand?**

A Well, yes, but we have to store the **multiplier** and bring the **product** back into the accumulator no matter what, so we might as well do it now . . . let me draw out the two different ways.

```
MOV    C,A      ;save shifted multiplier.
MOV    A,E      ;get product.
JNC    NO       ;if leftmost bit of multiplier was 0, don't
                ; add in the multiplicand this time around.
```

OK. Now we're up to the part where we add in the **multiplicand.** The ADD *r* instruction adds the contents of register *r* to the accumulator, and since we've got the **multiplicand** in register B, all we have to do is

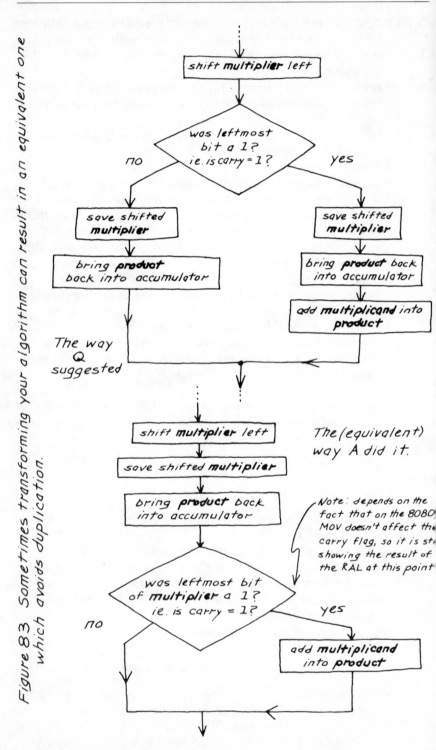

Figure 83 Sometimes transforming your algorithm can result in an equivalent one which avoids duplication.

ADD B   ;add **multiplicand** into accumulating **product.**

Let's see. Now the flowchart says to check for overflow here too, and then decrement *count* . . .

```
         JNC    NO      ;no carry means no overflow.
         MVI    H,1     ;store overflow indicator.
NO       DCR    D       ;count ← count - 1
         JNZ    LOOP    ;if count >0, keep going.
```

Q 786 Hold it. You can have more than one overflow condition, right?

A   Sure. Everytime a bit pops out the left end of **product,** our program detects it. So?

Q 787 Shouldn't you test to see if there's already been an overflow?

A   What for? If there's already been an overflow, then register H will have a 1 in it, and storing a 1 on top of it isn't going to hurt anything. Or am I missing what you're saying?

Q 788 I don't know. Go on.

A   Well, that's the end of the main loop. Now we have to set the carry flag to indicate whether there's been an overflow or not . . and then restore the registers, and then we're done.

```
                     ;done with main loop — clean things up and quit.
         MOV    E,A   ;save product temporarily.
         MOV    A,H   ;get overflow indicator.
         RAR          ;move rightmost bit (0 or 1 depending on
                      ;whether there's been an overflow) into carry.
         MOV    A,E   ;leave product in accumulator.
         POP    H     ;restore H (and L) to their original values.
         POP    D     ;restore D and E.
         POP    B     ;restore B and C.
         RET          ;return
         END
```

Q 789 And we're done?

A   Well, we should go back over everything, add some more comments at places that are tricky . . . test it out . . . so on, but I'm getting pretty tired.

```
LABEL OPERATOR OPERANDS  COMMENTS
      ORG      200H      ;MULTIPLY SUBROUTINE--MULT.
                         ;FORMS THE (8 BIT) PRODUCT OF THE
                         ;VALUES IN REGISTERS B AND C.
                         ;RETURNS THE PRODUCT IN THE ACCUMULATOR,
                         ;AND SETS THE CARRY FLAG TO INDICATE
                         ;THAT AN OVERFLOW OCCURRED AT SOME POINT
                         ;IN THE PROCESS.  (1=OVERFLOW, 0=NONE)
                         ;MULTICAND IS IN REGISTER B.
                         ;MULTIPLIER IS IN C.
                         ;COUNT IS IN D.
                         ;PARTIAL PRODUCT IS KEPT IN E.
                         ;H HOLDS THE OVERFLOW INDICATOR.
MULT  PUSH     B         ;SAVE REGISTERS B AND C.
      PUSH     D         ;SAVE REGISTERS D AND E.
      PUSH     H         ;SAVE REGISTERS H AND L.
      MVI      D,8D      ;COUNT STARTS OFF AT 8 (DECIMAL).
      MVI      H,0       ;OVERFLOW INDICATOR STARTS AT 0 (FALSE).
```

```
            MVI     E,Ø        ;PRODUCT STARTS OFF AT Ø.
            MOV     A,E        ;BRING PRODUCT INTO THE ACCUMULATOR.
                               ;MAIN LOOP STARTS HERE:
    LOOP    STC                ;MAKE SURE CARRY=Ø SO UPCOMING SHIFT
            CMC                ;DOESN'T INTRODUCE AN EXTRANEOUS 1 INTO PRODUCT.
            RAL                ;SHIFT PRODUCT LEFT ONE BIT.
            JNC     NVFL       ;NO CARRY MEANS NO OVERFLOW.
            MVI     H,1        ;HAVE OVERFLOW, SET INDICATOR.
    NVFL    MOV     E,A        ;SAVE CURRENT VERSION OF PRODUCT.
            MOV     A,C        ;GET MULTIPLIER TO CHECK NEXT BIT.
            RAL                ;SHIFT MULTIPLIER LEFT INTO CARRY.
            MOV     C,A        ;SAVE SHIFTED MULTIPLIER.
            MOV     A,E        ;GET PRODUCT.
            JNC     NO         ;IF LEFTMOST BIT OF MULTIPLIER WAS Ø, DON'T
                               ;ADD IN THE MULTIPLICAND THIS TIME AROUND.
            ADD     B          ;ADD MULTIPLICAND INTO ACCUMULATING PRODUCT.
            JNC     NO         ;NO CARRY MEANS NO OVERFLOW.
            MVI     H,1        ;SET OVERFLOW INDICATOR.
    NO      DCR     D          ;COUNT ← COUNT - 1
            JNZ     LOOP       ;IF COUNT > Ø, KEEP GOING.

                               ;DONE WITH MAIN LOOP--CLEAN THINGS UP AND QUIT.
            MOV     E,A        ;SAVE PRODUCT TEMPORARILY.
            MOV     A,H        ;GET OVERFLOW INDICATOR.
            RAR                ;MOVE RIGHTMOST BIT (Ø OR 1 DEPENDING ON
                               ;WHETHER THERE'S BEEN AN OVERFLOW) INTO CARRY.
            MOV     A,E        ;LEAVE PRODUCT IN ACCUMULATOR.
            POP     H          ;RESTORE H (AND L) TO THEIR ORIGINAL VALUES.
            POP     D          ;RESTORE D AND E.
            POP     B          ;RESTORE B AND C.
            RET                ;RETURN
            END     Figure 84.  The multiply subroutine all in one place
```

Feel like you got a taste of what it's like to program in assembly language? I trust you see that to do machine or assembly language programming, you have to have a fairly intimate understanding of the workings of the processor you're using?

Q 790 Yes. It isn't quite as easy as I was hoping . . .

A As with anything, I guess, there are both advantages and disadvantages . . . Here's some of the advantages:

A good programmer, with a deep understanding of the machine he or she is working on, can write programs that use less memory and run faster in assembly or machine language than in any other language. In addition, both are made to order for extremely small systems with limited i/o capabilities. A third advantage is that by learning to program in machine or assembly language, you'll gain a real understanding of the hardware you're working with, and many of the techniques you'll pick up will be useful even when you start using a new machine.

Oh yes. I just thought of a fourth advantage, one that applies to some home computers. For a number of the newer chips, nothing else may be available.

Q 791 Those sound pretty convincing.

A OK. Why don't we stop for today? I'm pretty much worn out.

Q 792 All right. So next time you'll go over the disadvantages. Or are they completely outweighed by the advantages?

A OK. Actually, the disadvantages outweigh the advantages, at least in the long run.

DAY 8:
WHAT'S IT LIKE
TO PROGRAM
IN BASIC?

And still counting

Q 793 Well, are you rested up?
If I remember correctly, you were going to go over some of the *dis*advantages of programming in assembly language.
Are you up to it? You still look pretty tired.

A I'll be OK. I was thinking over what we were going to cover, and I came to the conclusion that we shouldn't go into that today — until you've seen an alternative to assembly language, what I have to say about the disadvantages won't make any sense. Why don't we do a couple of programs in Basic?

Q 794 All right by me. What's it like to program in Basic?

A Glad you asked. Let's start by re-doing the little program that counts down from a number we give it. The one that gives us a feeling for how fast the system is. I guarantee you that this time we won't have any trouble getting the stop watch started in time. Let's begin by drawing out a flowchart.(Figure 85)

Q 795 You drew it a lot simpler than last time [Figure 74].

A Right. Now we won't have to worry about which register things are in, we don't even have to know about carry bits, it'll be much easier for us to do. Trivial, in fact.
OK.
A Basic **program** is a sequence of lines. Each **line** is given a **line number,** and when the program is run, the lines are carried out in order of their line numbers, unless the program directs otherwise.

Q 796 No big deal so far. That's the same as in machine language

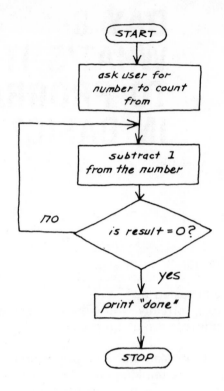

Figure 85

except you're calling the memory addresses **line numbers**
for some reason.

A   Don't go overgeneralizing. There are a number of differences . . . well, just hold on a minute. I'll just translate
the flowchart into Basic before your very eyes. In fact,
since I loaded the Basic interpreter (the program that
converts Basic statements into machine language and
carries them out in the process) before you came, I'll just
sit down at the terminal and enter the program as I write
it.

First I'll type in a comment (called REMarks in Basic) that
says what the program does, then I'll type two statements
that do what the first box in the flowchart says.

```
10  REM : PROGRAM TO HELP US ESTIMATE EXECUTION SPEED.
20  PRINT "WHAT NUMBER DO YOU WANT TO START WITH";
30  INPUT N
```

You can probably tell what the statements do by just looking at them. Line 20 will print out the message I put in quotes, and line 30 will accept the number from us (we'll type it on the keyboard) and store it in memory cell N.

Q 797 By **memory cell** do you mean memory location? A byte in memory?

A   It's similar. Each Basic numerical value is stored in four bytes on most microcomputers, but you don't need to know those kinds of details to program in Basic. You can think of memory cells as containers for values. You can use them by just listing their name in the appropriate place. Legal names are the letters, A,B,C, . . . ,Z, and the letters followed by a single decimal digit, as in A0,A1,A2 . . . ,Z9.

      Any more questions before I go ahead?

Q 798 Did you make a typing mistake in line 20? And do you have to number the lines by tens for some reason?

A   No and no.

      The semicolon at the end of line 20 has to do with spacing of the output. The best way to learn about it is to try a bunch of things on a terminal . . . but I'll give you some of the details. The semicolon means "don't skip any spaces before the next thing that's output". The other options would be to have put a comma there, which would skip over a ways before the next output value, and to put nothing there which would make the next output come on a new line.

Q 799 What I meant was, don't you want a question mark there since you're asking a question?

A   Oh. Well, the INPUT statement prints a question mark to indicate to the person at the terminal that it's time to enter a value. So if I run what we've got so far . . . well, let's do it. All I have to do is type RUN

WHAT NUMBER DO YOU WANT TO START WITH?

See, it's waiting for our response. Whatever number we type now will be stored in memory cell N.

Q 800 And then?

A   And then the program will stop, because I haven't entered any more statements.

Q 801 Let me see.

A   OK. I'll type in a number, say 5, hit the **return** key, and READY *the Basic system types this to inform you that it's READY to accept commands from you, i.e. that it's currently inactive*

READY ⟵

Let's finish the little program.

The next thing we want to do is to subtract 1 from the value in memory cell N. For that we can use a LET-statement, or **assignment statement** as it's also called.

40   LET N = N - 1

The general form of the **LET-statement** is a **line number** followed by the word **LET** followed by a **memory cell name,** an **equals sign,** and an **expression.** The meaning is "LET the value of this memory cell become whatever value the expression has". It's just like the arrow I've been using in flowchart boxes all along.

OK. Next our flowchart says to test if we're through counting, and I can write that in Basic as

50   IF N.0 THEN 40

[Editor's note: It is common practice to write the number zero as Ø in cases where it might otherwise be confused with the letter O.]

This type of statement is called an **IF-THEN.** This particular IF-THEN means "IF the value stored in N is greater than zero, THEN go to statement 40 next. Otherwise, go on to the next statement as usual."

Q. 802 If you wanted to see if N was greater than or equal to zero would . . .

A   You'd write it

50   IF N > = 0 THEN 40

simply because there's no $\geq$ sign available on the keyboard (or in the ASCII character set).

Let me go ahead and finish the program, because we're almost done.

The next statement is the one that gets carried out when the IF test fails, that is, when the program is through counting.

60   PRINT "DONE"

I guess that one should be obvious, and then at the very end of the whole program I'll throw in

70 END

OK, that's it. The whole program is written and in the machine. To run it, all we have to do is type RUN. But first, I'll type the command LIST, so I can check over what I entered.

LIST

```
10   REM : PROGRAM TO HELP US ESTIMATE EXECUTION SPEED.
20   PRINT "WHAT NUMBER DO YOU WANT TO START WITH";
30   INPUT N
40   LET N=N - 1
50   IF N> =0 THEN 40
60   PRINT "DONE"
70   END
```

Notice that statement 50 is the way I typed it last?

Q 803 You mean when you type a line over again it replaces what was there before . . . makes sense. Is that the way you want it, or did you mean to have N > 0?

A   I think I'll re-do it . . . and while I'm at it, I'm going to indent the IF to make it stand out. It's a good idea to indent statements that make up a loop so you can spot them easily . . . All I have to do is type the line the way I want it.

50   IF N > 0 THEN 40

Q 804 Now type LIST again.
A   Here. You take over.
Q 805 All right.

LIST
```
10   REM : PROGRAM TO ESTIMATE EXECUTION SPEED.
20   PRINT "WHAT NUMBER DO YOU WANT TO START WITH";
30   INPUT N
40   LET N=N-1
50      IF N >0 THEN 40
60   PRINT "DONE"
70   END
```

Now I just type RUN?

RUN
WHAT NUMBER DO YOU WANT TO START WITH?
What should I put?

A   I don't know . . . how about the number we used in ou
           assembly language version. I think that was 32 768
           wasn't it?

Q 806 Ready with the stop watch?

A   Sure. Go ahead.

Q 807 32 768
           Nothing seems to be happening.

A   You have to hit the RETURN key there. The program i
           still at statement 30, waiting for you to finish entering
           the number.

Q 808 Oh. All right . . . it's running . . . and it's still running
           . . . and it's still running . . . is something wrong? Ah
           there it goes.

           DONE
           READY

A   OK. The READY means that Basic is ready for the nex
           command . . . Let's see. That took just about 64 seconds
           So running the program in Basic took about what? A
           hundred times as long as in assembly language.

Q 809 Whoa . . . Basic is really slow!

A   Don't forget, though, it took *us* much less time overall
           It took us about 5 minutes to write and run the Basi
           version, versus, what would you say — two hours for the
           assembly language version? Also, if we want to make a
           minor change to our Basic program, we can do it in a
           matter of seconds. With our assembly language program
           we would have had to have thrashed around, loading the
           text editor, changing the program, loading the assembler
           making the two passes, loading the machine language
           version, and finally running the new version.
           Just as an example, let me toss in a different ending
           message . . .

           65 PRINT "THANK YOU FOR YOUR MUCH APPRECIATED PATRONAGE."

           Or, we could alter the program so it asks us if we wan
           to run again with another number . . .

           61   PRINT "IF YOU WANT TO RUN AGAIN, TYPE 1.";
           62   INPUT A
           63   IF A=1 THEN 20

           See what that does?

Q 810 Think so, Let me RUN it.

RUN
WHAT NUMBER DO YOU WANT TO START WITH? 100
DONE
IF YOU WANT TO RUN AGAIN, TYPE 1. ? 1
WHAT NUMBER DO YOU WANT TO START WITH? 200
DONE

IF YOU WANT TO RUN AGAIN, TYPE 1. ?0
THANK YOU FOR YOUR MUCH APPRECIATED PATRONAGE.
READY

And I can just type LIST to see what the whole program looks like, right?

```
LIST
10  REM : PROGRAM TO HELP US ESTIMATE EXECUTION SPEED.
20  PRINT "WHAT NUMBER DO YOU WANT TO START WITH";
30  INPUT N
40  LET N=N - 1
50  IF N > 0 THEN 40
60  PRINT "DONE"
61  PRINT "IF YOU WANT TO RUN AGAIN, TYPE 1.";
62  INPUT A
63  IF A=1 THEN 20
65  PRINT "THANK YOU FOR YOUR MUCH APPRECIATED PATRONAGE."
70  END
```

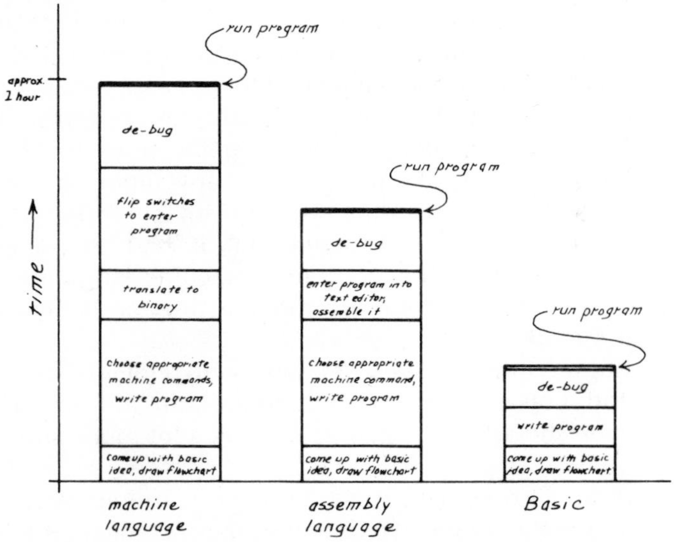

Figure 86 Rough estimate of the time spent designing, coding, running a typical small to medium
sized program.
The more debugging that's necessary, the more
time we save using Basic.
Note, however, that if we were going to run the
program thousands of times, the time spent in
preparation would become insignificant, and
assembly language would gives us the smallest
time overall.

That's neat.

. . . but why does the program run so much slower in Basic? It seems to me that most of the statements in the program are just . . . well, sort of disguised machine language instructions . . . except for the PRINT statements.

A   What do you mean?

Q 811 Well, look. The statement LET N = N - 1 is just about the same thing we did in the machine language version — right?

A   In essence. It involves bringing a value from memory into the controller, subtracting 1 from it, and storing the result back in memory.

Q 812 And the IF N > 0 THEN 40 is just some kind of Jump command, right?

A   True.

But you're missing two things. First of all (this is a minor factor), Basic interpreters usually use four bytes to store numbers, so subtracting 1 from the value of N is a little more complicated than what we did before. That might make Basic three or four times slower at arithmetic . . .

The main reason Basic programs run slower than assembly language or machine language programs is that Basic is doing all the work of a text editor, an assembler, a monitor, and running the translated program besides. Actually, Basic keeps a copy of our original program (that's why you can LIST your program at any time), and to run it, it translates each statement into machine language as it comes to it. That means that it had to translate the statement LET N = N - 1 into machine language 32 768 times (the first time we ran the program). That's where it spends the extra time.

But remember — *you* get away with a lot less work overall, and it takes much less time to prepare and run a program, even though the machine spends a lot more time running it.

[Editor's note: Of course, there is no requirement inherent in the language itself that forces a statement like LET N = N-1 to be translated into machine language more than once. It's just easier to write the interpreter that way.

Another option would be to use an **incremental compiler** in which statements are translated as they are called for, but a copy of the machine language is saved, so that a statement like LET N = N-1 would be translated only once. After that the machine language version would be used directly whenever the statement is called for. This would make Basic programs run much faster, but of course there is a penalty. An **incremental compiler** must carry out a more complex task than an **interpreter,** and so will occupy a larger portion of memory.]

Does using Basic limit what you can do?

Q 813 But isn't it true that you have a lot more control over things if you use assembly language? I came across an article showing how to conserve memory space, and it told about something called **packing** . . .

A   That's two questions, I guess. First, let's run through the idea of **packing** and **unpacking.**

Usually, we think of a single memory location as holding a single value, or part of a value. We've already seen that to store anything but small numbers, we need to use more than one byte. Packing goes the other way. What if you need to store a large number of values, but each value is one of a very small number of possibilities?

Q 814 An example . . .

A   For example, in a data file, you might want to record whether or not each person is male or female, whether they want on the mailing list or not, and which of 4 membership plans they choose. Of course, you could use three bytes for each record, one for each value, but most of the bits would be wasted, since you need just 1 bit for sex, 1 bit for the mailing list question, and two bits for the membership plan. If you need to save memory overall, you could pack all three answers into one byte, like this:

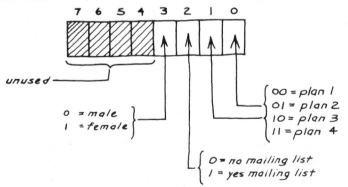

Figure 87 Packing a number of different sorts of information into a single memory location.

[Editor's note: This is another instance of a **time / memory tradeoff**. As in the interpreter vs. incremental compiler case mentioned above, here we see a technique **(packing)** which represents a savings in **memory usage** at the expense of **time**.]

Q 815 I see . . . I think. Let me work out an example to check. This pattern would mean that the person is a female,

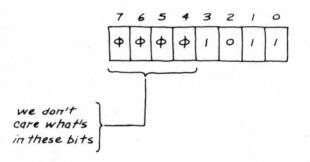

Figure 88   A sample byte of packed data. According to our conventions, this byte represents a female who doesn't want on the mailing list and who has elected membership plan 4.

doesn't want on the mailing list, and chose plan 4, right? But how would you write a program to put all that together?

A   By using combinations of **and** , **or** , and **shift (rotate)** instructions. Exactly what you'd do depends on what language you choose to do it in. Let's do it in assembly language for my 6800 based system. Here.

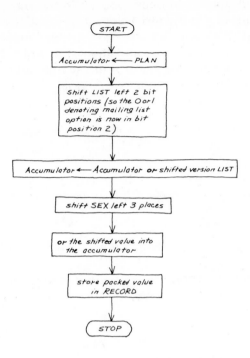

START

Accumulator ←——— PLAN

Shift LIST left 2 bit positions (so the 0 or 1 denoting mailing list option is now in bit position 2)

Accumulator ←—— Accumulator or shifted version LIST

shift SEX left 3 places

or the shifted value into the accumulator

store packed value in RECORD

STOP

Figure 89 (page 1 of 2) Routine for packing the values stored in memory locations PLAN, SEX, and LIST, according to the packing scheme in Figure 83.

in 6800 assembly language.
⋮

| A | | | |
| 0 0 0 0 0 0 1 1 | | | |

PLAN
| 0 0 0 0 0 0 1 1 | LDA A PLAN ; start with member-ship plan datum.

LIST
| 0 0 0 0 0 0 0 0 | ASL LIST ; shift LIST value left 1 bit.

LIST
| 0 0 0 0 0 0 0 0 | ASL LIST ; do it again

A
| 0 0 0 0 0 0 1 1 | OR A LIST ; or shifted value into accumulator

SEX
| 0 0 0 0 0 0 1 0 | ASL SEX ; shift SEX value left 1 bit.

SEX
| 0 0 0 0 0 1 0 0 | ASL SEX ; shift it 3 places

SEX
| 0 0 0 0 1 0 0 0 | ASL SEX ; in all.

A
| 0 0 0 0 1 0 1 1 | ORA SEX ; or shifted value into accumulator
                        STA A RECORD ; store packed value.

the effect of each instruction when packing the value corresponding to a female member who doesn't want on the mailing list and who elects plan 4. (see Figure 87)

And then to **unpack,** you undo the process. Suppose we want to get the **sex** field out of RECORD. First we'd copy RECORD into accumulator A, then **mask** out everything but bit position 3, and then shift right three times. That would leave the value of the **sex** bit sitting in the accumulator for us to use as we please.

```
LDA A RECORD        ;bring packed value into A
AND A
#00001000B          ;AND immediate to wipe out (mask) everything but
                    ;bit 3.
ASR A               ;shift right one bit
ASR A
ASR A
```

Suppose the packed record looks like this

```
| 1 1 0 1 0 0 0 0 |
```

Then after the AND, the accumulator looks like this

```
| 0 0 0 1 0 0 0 0 |
```

because everything but the **sex** bit gets set to zero by the AND. Then, after the three shifts, we'd have

```
| 0 0 0 0 0 0 0 1 |
```

And then . . .

Q 816 Now, but see, that was my original question. You're using machine language because it gives you control over the individual bits.

A   I was just trying to show you what **packing** and **unpacking** mean. There's no reason you can't do the same thing in Basic even though Basic doesn't have **ands** and **shifts** . . . you can do it using normal, everyday arithmetic.
Here. Follow through this program. I've drawn the value stored in memory cell P to the right so you can follow along.

```
10   REM :PACK THREE VALUES INTO MEMORY CELL "P".
20   REM :ASSUME "S" IS 0 IF MALE, 1 IF FEMALE.
30   REM :      "M" IS 0 IF NOT ON MAILING LIST, 1 IF ON IT.
40   REM :      "L" IS 0,1,2, OR 3 DEPENDING ON PLAN.
50   REM :GIVE "S","M", AND "L" VALUES FOR EXAMPLE.
60   LET S = 1
70   LET M = 0
80   LET L = 3
90   LET P = L
100  LET P = P + 4*M
110  LET P = P + 8*S
```

And there you are. Just like before.
Oh. The * stands for "multiply" . . . you couldn't use an X, because that would get confused with memory cell X. I don't think I told you that yet.

Q 817 Hmmm. And to get the values back out?

A   OK. To get, say, the **sex** bit back out, we just undo the process. Divide by 8, and throw away the fractional part of the answer.

Q 818 The fractional part?

A   Aargh. Rats. I'm getting ahead of myself. I should have told you that the numeric values that Basic deals with can have fractional parts, just like the numbers we're used to using in everyday life. Maybe the easiest way to show you is to write the number 1 in a bunch of different ways. These are all the same number in Basic — you can write it any way you want.

If you have a number with a fractional part, say 3.56, and you just want the whole part, there's a built-in function in Basic called INT that does it for you. The value of INT(3.56) is 3.

So to get the **sex** bit out of the value packed in P, we'd just do INT(P/8). Similar things will unpack the other values. [To get the mailing list option, take INT((P-INT(P/8)*8)/4), i.e. remove the sex bit by taking (P-INT(P/8)*8), and then shift by dividing by 4.]

But I don't think we should go running through all the details of Basic. The best way to learn Basic is to sit down at a terminal and play around with it. It's fun to use, and it's really forgiving as computer languages go.

built-in functions in Basic Appendix — Minimal Basic

Computer games

Q 819 I came across a book [*What To Do After You Hit Return,* see Bibliography] that's filled with games written in Basic. And some of the magazines have games in them. Is Basic best for games for some reason?

A   It's really good for a certain kind of games . . . It's easy to write programs that ask the user questions . . . like we did in the program we wrote. It's certainly not limited to that . . . it's a general programming language.

Q 820 That's good. I think games are silly. I want to use the computer for something more meaningful . . .
applications — things you can reasonably expect to do with a home computer Day 10

A   Well, if all you could do with a home computer was play games . . . that would get old pretty fast. On the other hand, sitting someone down at a terminal and letting them play a game is a good way to get them over the basic fear of computers that a lot of people seem to have. And, perhaps more relevant to your situation, writing game programs is a really good way to learn to program, of learning to write programs that are easy for people to use.

Q 821 Tell me about Star Trek. The magazines all seem to mention it somewhere.

A Star Trek, huh? It's probably the most famous of all the computer games . . . It's loosely patterned after the TV series. There's a number of versions of it floating around. Typically, you pretend that you're Captain Kirk of the USS Enterprise, and your mission is to flit around the galaxy destroying Klingon warships. It's a little blood thirsty . . . you just try to destroy Klingons, never to make peace with them . . .

Q 822 Make peace with a back-stabbing, power-mad Klingon? You must be mad!

A OK. You'd probably like Star Trek.
You get to move the Enterprise through space, fire your phasers, photon torpedoes, shift energy into your shields . . . a lot of people really like it. In fact . . .

Q 823 Would you want your sister to marry a Klingon?

A I've got to tell you this story. It really happened.
I was working on the local college's time sharing system one Sunday afternoon. I finished what I wanted to do on the video terminal, and walked down to the computer center to get a listing to take home. I was the only person on campus . . . I thought. As I walked into the computer center through the back door, I saw a police officer walking briskly away from a Teletype, crinkling up a piece of output paper. I said "Hi", and he looked sort of funny, and immediately began telling me that he'd heard the Teletype running, and came in to check. There was no one there, so he logged it off.
I said "Oh," and he kept on. He said that when he logged it off, it said that the elapsed time was 23 hours and 17 minutes, and that it looked like someone had been playing Star Trek on it, and had just walked away and left it the day before. I smiled inside when I saw how worried he looked, and tried to convince him that he'd done the right thing.

Q 824 So what? What kind of story is this, anyway?

A No, see, the school's terminals are logged off automatically if there hasn't been any activity for ten minutes. It was obvious that *he* had been in there playing Star Trek because there wasn't anybody around to see him, and he felt really guilty because he was on duty!

That's the problem with Star Trek.

Q 825 What's that?

A   It's addictive.

Q 826 What are some other games that a lot of people play?

A   Tell you what. Why don't we write a game program ourselves? That'll give you a chance to see some more features of Basic, and it'll give you an idea of how you go about planning, designing, and writing programs. Once you get the general idea, you can make up your own games. And if you stick to things that are allowed on most versions of Basic (that's all I'll show you), you can share your programs with your friends.

I've got a game in mind, and I worked out some of the details last night, because I didn't want us to get all hung up figuring out what the game should do.

Drag race

It's a drag race game. You're to imagine that you're driving a hopped-up 1966 Datsun pickup truck and . . .

Q 827 A 1966 Datsun pick-up truck?

A   Heh . . . I just happened to have a shop manual for 1966 Datsuns, and since it has all the information we need (like gear ratios, torque curve, etc.) I went ahead and worked it out for a, uh, 1966 Datsun pick-up truck.

Q 828 It's not going to set any world records for the quarter mile.

A   Well, the idea of the game is to see how well you can do with what you've got. If you can find the necessary data for a supercharged, unlimited class fuel dragster, we can change it to that easy enough.

Q 829 All right. What do you do to play the game? Do you need pedals and stuff for your computer?

A   No, I thought we should do a game that would run on any home computer that has Basic . . . so we won't do steering or pushing pedals . . . the program will handle that.

Q 830 What's left, then?

A   The part where brains come in when you're driving a dragster. Choosing the proper shift points to get the most out of the car. Racing engines usually put out a lot of power in a fairly narrow rpm range. If you shift too soon, you'll lose time as the engine slowly revs up to its power

peak. If you shift too late, you'll lose time . . . or blow
up the engine.

Our program will figure out the car's speed, engine rpm,
and so on for each second of the race, and you'll tell it
which gear to be in. After it's gone a quarter of a mile,
the program will tell you how you did, and you can try
again, try to make it down the strip in as little time as
possible.

Q 831   But how is it going to do all that?

A   Yeh. I'm getting a little ahead of myself.

Here's a flowchart that shows what's involved in creating
a game program.

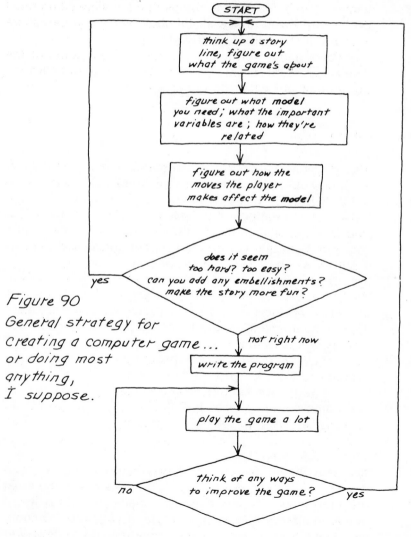

Figure 90
General strategy for
creating a computer game...
or doing most
anything,
I suppose.

Q 832 What does **model** mean there in the flowchart?

A It means some sequence of computer instructions which capture the essence of the physical structure you're trying to describe or deal with.

Hmmm. Let me try it this way. Whenever you're writing a program that purports to describe the behavior of a system, you need to include information (in the form of program statements and data) about how the system works, how its parts interact. Suppose you were writing a program that plays some kind of board game, oh, say, checkers. Obviously you'd have to have some way of storing the position of each man on the board, you'd need a **model** of the board and the men . . . And in the case of a program that simulates a 1966 Datsun pickup truck going down a quarter mile track, obviously you have to include information about how the engine speed affects the speed of the truck, how the gears affect things, like that.

Q 833 That's what you're calling a **model**?

A Right. It's a **model** because it shares some of the characteristics of the real system.

Another way you could look at it is from the idea of **state**. [Editor's note: **State** means condition or status. Formally, the **state of a system** is the set of values necessary to derive the system's behavior from the rules of operation. For elaboration, see Q103-110 in Vol. 1.] We need to store the **state of the system.** In the case of the pickup truck, we need to know its position, speed, what gear it's in, so on. And we need to incorporate the rules which tell how various inputs cause one state to change to another. In our case, the particular gear the user chooses affects what the truck's next position and speed will be.

Q 834 I'd like to see an example.

A Only one way to do that . . . stay right where you are. Here's a general flowchart for any kind of game program. (Figure 91)

Q 835 Do you really use these things when you program?

A You mean flowcharts like this? Yes, or if you prefer, **verbal descriptions** that express the same thing.

Q 836 But it seems so obvious . . . why would you bother to write it down?

A It may seem obvious now, when you're thinking about it, but as you get farther and farther into the details of the program, it's incredibly easy to lose track of how things are supposed to fit together. If you have a question, you can just refer to the flowchart without having to think it

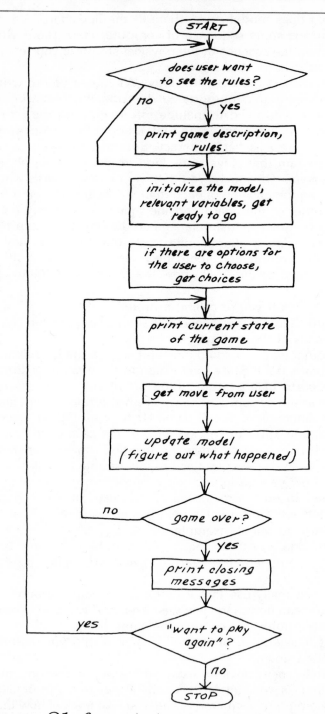

Figure 91 General structure of any game program.

all through again.
It lets you concentrate on what you're doing.

Q 837 All right. What do you do now? Start from the top and fill in the details?

A No, I usually start in the middle. You can't write a really good description of the game until you know exactly what's in it, you can't initialize things until you know what values you're going to use in the program . . .

I think we should start with the innermost loop. The one that makes the moves.

Let's start by figuring out what I called the **model**. We need to store the truck's position and speed. We need to know what gear it's in. We need to know the relationships between speed, engine rpm, the engine's torque output, and acceleration. Let's start with the engine's output.

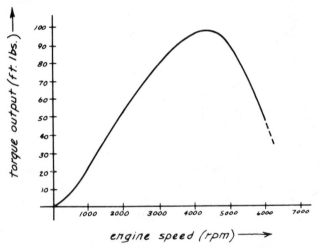

Figure 92 The modified engine's torque curve.

Q 838 You got that out of the shop manual?

A Basically. I altered the stock torque curve to correspond to the changes that would occur if you stuck a hot cam in the engine . . . Anyway, the graph gives us a way to relate engine rpm and torque output.

Q 839 But how are you going to store a graph in the computer?

A There are two ways to store data like this. Either you store a number of individual points on the graph (using an **array**), or else you come up with a mathematical expression to represent it.

What's an array?

Q 840 An **array** . . . how would you use that to store it? What is it?

A An **array** is a **data structure** — that is, it's a collection of memory cells that you access in a special way. (The other data structure we've seen is the **stack** [Q656].)

In Basic, if you want to use an array, you can **declare** that fact by mentioning the array name and telling how many memory cells are to be in the array. For instance, I was planning to store the gear ratios in an array, an array I'll call G.

```
...REM : STORE GEAR RATIOS. 0.0 FOR NEUTRAL, 3.95 FOR FIRST, ETC.

   DIM  G(4)  ◄————— this statement declares the array G
                     (DIM stands for DIMension, we've given the array
   LET  G(0) = 0.0 ◄  5 memory cells, G(0), G(1), G(2), G(3), G(4) )
   LET  G(1) = 3.95◄
   LET  G(2) = 2.40  ⎫——— neutral
   LET  G(3) = 1.49  ⎬
 ↖ LET  G(4) = 1.00  •——— 1ˢᵗ gear


       ——— in a real program, each statement
       would have a line number
```

See how that works? There are 5 memory cells in the array G, and they have the names G(0), G(1), G(2), G(3), and G(4). From 0 up to the number that appears in the DIM statement.

Q 841 Wait a minute. How is that different from having memory cells names G0, G1, G2, G3, and G4?

A So far I haven't told you. You're right . . . so far the array notation just gives a different name to memory cells. But you can do a lot more with arrays.

The number you write in the parentheses after the array name is called a **subscript** or **index**.

*Figure 93 An array consists of a specific number of contiguous memory cells. A specific element in the array is specified by giving the array name followed by a **subscript** expression in parentheses.*

The thing that makes arrays so useful is that the index or subscript doesn't have to be constant — it can be an **expression,** even an expression involving values stored in other memory cells.

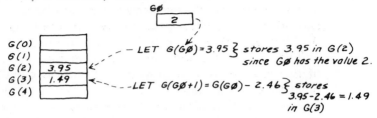

$G(0)$
$G(1)$
$G(2)$ 3.95
$G(3)$ 1.49
$G(4)$

$G\emptyset$
2

— LET $G(G\emptyset)=3.95$ ⎰ stores 3.95 in $G(2)$
since $G\emptyset$ has the value 2.

—LET $G(G\emptyset+1)=G(G\emptyset)-2.46$ ⎰ stores
3.95-2.46 = 1.49
in $G(3)$

Figure 94 Using arrays. G is an array,
consisting of the 5 memory cells G(0),
G(1),...G(4). G∅ is a simple memory
cell, that is, it's not part of an array.

Q 842 I'm still not sure how you would use an array to store a continuous shape like the torque curve you drew.

A   Oh. Well, no, you can't store a *continuous* curve. You'd store the values at a number of points and then interpolate . . . but actually, I was planning to store the torque curve by fitting an equation to it, and then writing a Basic statement that represents that equation.

The easiest way to store the torque (Figure 92) curve
seems to be to find an equation which approximates it.
Obviously the curve isn't a straight line, nor is it a parabola, so
we need an equation involving at least the third power of
the engine speed. Choosing the three points

torque (2000) = 52
torque (4400) = 96
torque (6000) = 48   and solving for the

coefficients a, b, and c in

torque (rpm) = $a*rpm^3 + b*rpm^2 + c*rpm$

gives the expression used in the program, namely

torque (rpm) = $-1.723 \times 10^{-9} \times rpm^3 + 9.287 \times 10^{-6} \times rpm^2$
$+ 1.432 \times 10^{-2} \times rpm$

Figure 95 Representing the engine's torque
output as a function of engine speed.

I don't want to bore you with all the details of figuring out the truck's speed and position once we know the torque supplied by the engine. The idea is that knowing the current engine rpm we can figure out the acceleration, and knowing the current speed and the acceleration, we can figure out the speed at the end of the next second. And knowing that, we can figure out the truck's position and so on. There's one complicating factor — at the start of the race (or whenever you're starting a car up), you have to slip the clutch (and wheels too in some cases) to get started because no engine puts out much power at real low rpm. Here's the scheme for updating the model.

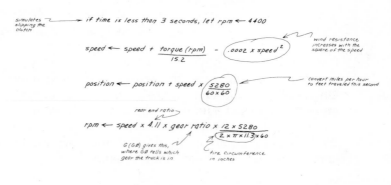

These serve as our model of the truck's behavior each second:

simulates slipping the clutch ⟶ if time is less than 3 seconds, let rpm ← 4400

$$speed \leftarrow speed + \frac{torque\ (rpm)}{15.2} - (.0002 \times speed^2)$$ wind resistance increases with the square of the speed

$$position \leftarrow position + speed \times \frac{5280}{60 \times 60}$$ convert miles per hour to feet traveled this second

rear end ratio
$$rpm \leftarrow speed \times 4.11 \times gear\ ratio \times \frac{12 \times 5280}{(2 \times \pi \times 11.3) \times 60}$$
G (GØ) gives this, where GØ tells which gear the truck is in   tire circumference in inches

Figure 96 The model

Q 843 You want me to just take that on faith?

A   Yeh. Mainly because I think we should be concentrating on the programming aspects of the problem . . . and partly because I had to make up the wind resistance term — I couldn't find any numbers for it. But we're making a game, not a perfectly accurate simulation, so the real test is whether the thing is fun to play.

OK. Let's get back to the program. After we update the model, we need to have our program check a number of things.

Q 844 Like whether the truck has gone a quarter of a mile?

A   Right. That . . . and I suppose we should check to see if the engine is being over-revved. We can make the engine blow up if you rev it over 7000 rpm, or whatever you want to do.

Q 845 How would you do that?

A   Just put in a test, and if the new value of the engine rpm is over 7000, print out a message, and jump out of the loop.

Q 846 But what statements would you use exactly?

A Tell you what. Why don't we start writing the whole program. Let's write out a preliminary version, check it over, and then go back and add in some frills.

Let's put our flowchart here where we can see it easily . . .

First we need to decide what to call the various values we need to store. It would be nice if we could call the *speed* variable SPEED, but Basic doesn't allow memory cell names to have that many letters.

[Editor's note: The results of the ensuing discussion are shown in Figure 97.]

memory cell name	variable
T	*time* -- the current elapsed time in seconds. One second goes by per move.
S	*speed* -- the current speed of the truck.
R	*rpm* -- current engine speed in revolutions per minute.
GØ	*gear* -- gear the truck's in (supplied by user.)
G( )	*gear ratios* -- the ratios of the four gears (and neutral).

Figure 97 The memory cells used in the program.

OK. Let's keep this list nearby so we can refer to it . . . and if we have to add any more variables.

The next thing we can do is write some REMark statements that describe the program . . .

```
10  REM :DRAG RACE GAME.
20  REM :SIMULATE A HOPPED UP 1966 DATSUN PICKUP RUNNING THE
30  REM :    QUARTER MILE.
40  REM :ASK IF USER WANTS INSTRUCTIONS.
```

OK. Now we ask if the user wants instructions. The version of Basic we're using lets you use string values. That is, we can have the user answer YES or NO, and test their answer . . . if the version of Basic you find yourself using doesn't allow that, you can ask the user to answer 1 for YES and 0 for NO . . .

Another thing . . . since we're just making a first pass at the program, I think I'll leave lots of room between line numbers so we can add things in later as the need arises.

Q 847 What if you don't leave enough room?

A We'd have to re-type some of the lines, giving them different line numbers.

```
60  PRINT "WANT INSTRUCTIONS FOR HOW TO PLAY";
70  INPUT A$
80  IF A$   "YES" THEN x
```

We'll have to go back and fill in the line number there later, when we figure out what statement we want to go to . . . I'll put an *x* there for now . . . That's why I'm writing this first pass out by hand instead of entering it into the machine.

Let's see . . . we have to do something if the user *does* want a description.

```
90   REM :CALL SUBROUTINE TO PRINT OUT INSTRUCTIONS
91   REM : AND STORY LINE.
100  GOSUB 5000
```

Q 848 So Basic lets you have subroutines too . . . Are they pretty much like the ones you talked about in assembly language?

A Same general idea, yes. The subroutine appears somewhere else (here I've assumed it'll start at line 5000), and when the subroutine is through, it returns control to the statement after the one that called it. You use a RETURN statement in Basic.

```
110  REM :DECLARE ARRAY FOR GEAR RATIOS,
111  REM : INITIALIZE RELEVANT VARIABLES.
120  DIM G(4)
130  LET G(0)=0.0
140  LET G(1)=3.95
150  LET G(2)=2.40
160  LET G(3)=1.49
170  LET G(4)=1.00
180  LET T=0
190  LET R=4400
200  LET P=0
210  LET S=0
220  REM :PRINT HEADING SO USER CAN
221  REM : WHAT THE NUMBERS MEAN.
230  PRINT "ELAPSED TIME  DISTANCE  SPEED  ENGINE  GEAR"
240  PRINT " (SECONDS)     (FEET)    (MPH)   (RPM)  (1,2,3, OR 4)"
```

That looks OK for the time being . . . I guess we're ready to start in on the main loop. Any questions so far?

Q 849 Why did you start the *rpm*s off at 4400?

A That's part of simulating slipping the clutch. We'll have the program hold the engine at 4400 rpm for the first few seconds, so the truck can get started.

Q 850 No, I know *that,* I mean why 4400 as opposed to some other number?

A   Oh. I think that's what drag racers do — hold the engine
        right at the torque peak for the start.
        I don't know . . . maybe we should let the user select
        what rpm to start with. We can go back and do that later
        if you want.

Q 851   I guess I'll ask this . . . Why did you use the subroutine
        call? Why didn't you just leave enough space so you could
        fill in the instructions and stuff later?

A   I think it makes the program easier to read. If you're looking
        at our program to see how it works, just knowing that
        at that point the subroutine will print out instructions for
        playing the game is enough to see what's going on.
        OK?
        I'll start in on the main loop.

```
1000   REM :MAIN LOOP. DONE ONCE FOR EACH SECOND OF
1001   REM :ELAPSED TIME.
1010   REM :PRINT OUT THE CURRENT SITUATION, GET GEAR SELECTION
1011   REM :FROM USER.
1020   PRINT T,P,S,R,
1030   INPUT GO
1040   REM : SIMULATE SLIPPING THE CLUTCH FOR THE
1041   REM :FIRST 2 SECONDS.
1050   IF T>2 THEN 1070
1060      LET R=4400
1070   REM :FIGURE OUT TORQUE OUTPUT (TO) AND USE IT TO
1080   REM : COMPUTE NEW SPEED.
1090   LET TO= -1.723E-9*R^3 + 9.287E-6*R^2 + 1.432E-2*R
```

Q 852   Hold it. What's that funny symbol there? The ∧.

A   R∧3 means "R raised to the power 3", or "R cubed".
        The ∧ symbol means exponentiation. They wanted to use
        a ↑ I guess, but there's no ↑ in the ASCII character set, . . .
        OK. Now I'll use the equations we worked out before
        [Figure 96.]

```
1100   LET S=S + TO/13.9 - 2*(1 + 0.0001*S  2)
1110   REM :USE SPEED TO COMPUTE CURRENT POSITION.
1120   LET P=P + S*5280/(60*60)
1130   REM :SPEED AND GEAR SELECTED DETERMINE CURRENT
1131   REM : ENGINE SPEED.
1140   LET R=S*4.11*G(G0)*12*5280/(2*3.14159*11.5*60)
```

OK so far?

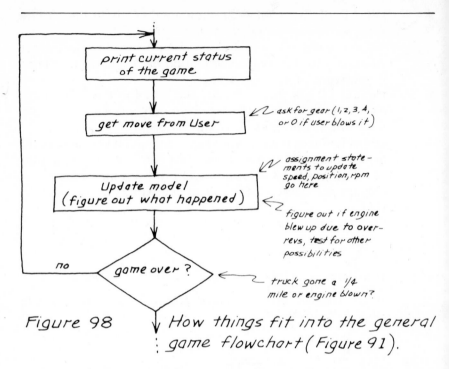

print current status of the game

get move from User ↙ ask for gear (1, 2, 3, 4, or 0 if user blows it)

Update model (figure out what happened) ↙ assignment state-ments to update speed, position, rpm go here

↙ figure out if engine blew up due to over-revs, test for other possibilities

no   *game over ?* ← truck gone a 1/4 mile or engine blown?

Figure 98   ↓ How things fit into the general game flowchart (Figure 91).

Q 853 I think so. Now you have to do what? See if the truck has gone a quarter mile?

A   Let's see. Or do we want to check to see if the engine blew up? I suppose it would be OK if the engine blows up after you've crossed the finish line . . . I know. Since there's two different ways the race can be over, and both might happen during the same second, let's do it like this That way, either condition or both will mean the race is over . . . and we'll be able to tell the user everything that happened. So, plunging ahead, we have

```
1200  REM :CHECK FOR OVER-REVVED ENGINE.
1210  IF R / 7000 THEN 1250
1220     PRINT "AAARGH! THE ENGINE BLEW UP. IT COULDN'T STAND":
1230     PRINT R;" RPM. BETTER LUCK NEXT TIME.
1240     LET F=1
1250  REM :SEE IF THE TRUCK HAS GONE OVER A QUARTER OF A
1251  REM :MILE YET.
1260  IF P <1320 THEN 1290
1270     REM :RACE IS OVER, SET "F" TO SIGNAL THAT FACT.
1280     LET F=1
1290  REM :OTHER CONDITIONS AND TESTS GO HERE (IF WE
1291  REM :THINK OF ANY).
2000  REM :END OF MAIN LOOP. IF RACE IS OVER FOR
2001  REM :ANY REASON, F=1.
2010  LET T=T + 1
2020  IF F <>1 THEN 1000
```

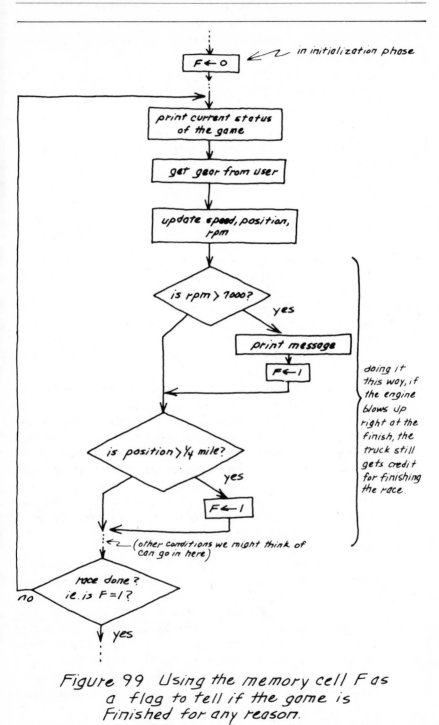

Figure 99 Using the memory cell F as a flag to tell if the game is finished for any reason.

So that finishes the main loop . . . now all we have to do is print out some kind of message telling the user how he or she did . . .

```
3000   REM :THE RACE IS OVER. IF BECAUSE OF A BLOWN ENGINE BEFORE
3010   REM :THE FINISH, TOUGH LUCK. OTHERWISE PRINT
3011   REM :CONGRATS, ETC.
3020   IF P< 1320 THEN 4000
3030   PRINT "END OF THE QUARTER MILE."
3040   PRINT "ELAPSED  TIME=";T;"
3050   PRINT "FINAL SPEED=";S; "MILES PER HOUR."
4000   PRINT "WANT TO MAKE ANOTHER RUN";
4010   INPUT A$
4020   IF A$="YES" THEN 60
30000  END
```

OK. Now let's go over it, check it, and see what improvements we can make to it.

As I was writing statement 3040, I thought of one thing we can improve. It's very unlikely that the truck will finish the race in an even number of seconds . . .

Q 854 What do you mean? You add 1 to T each time through the main loop, so of course the truck is going to . . . You mean that the truck will cross the finish line sometime in the middle of the last second, not right at the end of the last second, is that it?

A   Right. We have a problem because the time steps in our simulation are so big . . . If our goal was to make an extremely accurate simulation, we should update the truck's position and speed every fraction of a second instead of averaging over one second intervals. But I think that for our purposes, we can get the effect we want with less effort . . . if we keep track of the truck's position at the beginning and the end of the last second, we can make a good approximation to the time it crossed the finish line. Let me put a mark by statement 3040, and I'll figure out what to do later.

[Editor's note: Solutions to this and several other problems appear in the final version of the drag race program (immediately after Q861). If you take the time to compare the preliminary and final versions of the program, point by point, you will learn quite a bit about the process of refining a program. No one can sit down and write a finished program on the first try. Writing a program is a process of repeated refinement and re-organization.]

Q 855 How about adding some kind of penalty if the engine speed gets too low? If the person shifts too soon?

A   I see. Because you'd be fouling the plugs by lugging the engine? Sure, we can do that . . . we can simulate the plugs getting fouled by decreasing the torque output. [The changes corresponding to this consideration appear in lines 200,290,1160, and 6200-6230 of the finished program.]

I thought of another thing. If the user types in any value other than 1,2,3, or 4 for the gear, let's put the truck in neutral for the next second . . . as if the driver missed the shift.

We'll have to add the statements to do that right after we get the gear from the user . . .

```
1031   IF GO >0 AND GO <5 THEN 1050
1032     REM :NOT A LEGAL GEAR. PUT THE TRUCK IN NEUTRAL.
1033     PRINT "YOU SHIFTED INTO NEUTRAL. TOO BAD."
1034     PRINT "(GEARS=1,2,3,4)"
1035     LET GØ=Ø
```

Q 856 Maybe you should make the engine blow up if it goes over 6000 rpm . . . 7000 seems pretty high.

A I know! Why don't we have it get more likely to blow up the faster it turns?

Q 857 How would you do that?

Random numbers

A By using the **random number generator.** Basic has a built in function called RND (for RaNDom) which gives you a randomly chosen number between 0.0 and 1.0. That is, each time you use the function, you get a different number. For instance, . . . well, what am I talking for? We've got Basic right at our fingertips. Type in PRINT RND, and then hit the RETURN key.

Q 858 All right.

```
PRINT RND
.021752
```

A Now do the same thing a few more times.

```
Q      PRINT RND
.784
PRINT RND
.090021
PRINT RND
.3374
```

Will it keep that up all day? Putting out different numbers?

A   Actually, after a while (maybe after a few tens of thousands of numbers) it'll start repeating, but it's good enough for our purposes. The numbers it puts out satisfy a number of tests for randomness, so we can just think of them as random numbers. We can use it to throw a little bit of chance into our game — for people who like to take risks.
      What do you think this statement does?

      1225 IF RND < .5 THEN 1250

Q 859 If the random number is less than a half, it goes to statement 1250. So what?

A   That's right. The point is that since all the numbers that RND can put out are equally likely to occur, the branch to statement 1250 happens half the time in the long run. That means we have a way to make something happen with 50/50 odds. And by using a more complicated test, we can make things happen with whatever odds we want. Let's make the rule be that if the engine speed is below 6000, there's no chance the engine blows up. If it's over 7000, the engine always breaks, and in between the odds increase, so that at 6500 rpm, the odds are 50/50. [See Figure 100 and lines 6120-6180 in the finished program.] That make sense?

Q 860 Believe so, but I'd like to see it in action.

A   Well, let's start typing in our program then.
      After that, we can de-bug it, and start playing the game. I'm sure we'll find some things that need improvement . . . we can figure them out, enter them, de-bug *that,* play the game some more, etc. Finally we'll have a finished program.

Q 861 How long do you think it'll all take?

A   I don't really know. It depends on how much trouble we run into, and how many more embellishments we think up. I'll take a wild guess and say five hours, spread over a few days. You start to burn out if you try to do everything at one sitting.

The finished program

[Editor's note: The finished program and some sample runs appear below. If you are interested in learning to program, it would be quite beneficial to compare the new version of the program with the old, determining the purpose and effect of each change.]

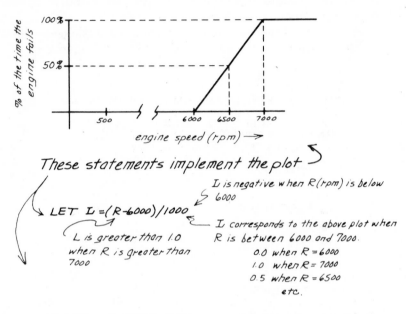

These statements implement the plot ⟩

L is negative when R(rpm) is below 6000

LET L =(R-6000)/1000

L is greater than 1.0 when R is greater than 7000

L corresponds to the above plot when R is between 6000 and 7000.

0.0 when R = 6000
1.0 when R = 7000
0.5 when R = 6500
etc.

IF RND >L THEN 1250 ← this determines whether the engine blows up or not

if R is below 6000, then L is negative. Since RND returns a random number between 0.0 and 1.0, RND will always be larger than L and the engine won't blow up.

if R is above 7000, the engine will always blow up since L will be greater than 1.0 and RND will never return a value > 1.0

if R is between 6000 and 7000, the test succeeds or fails depending on the exact value RND returns. In the long run, the closer L is to 1.0, i.e. the closer R is to 7000, the more often the engine will blow up.

Figure 100 Deciding whether the engine blows up or not becomes a more elaborate process, involving luck.

Although A intended to use only ANSI Basic statements in the program (so it can run as is on any system having ANSI standard Minimal Basic), he has erred in at least one instance.
Statement 1040 is not legal in Minimal Basic (see Appendix — Minimal Basic), and should be replaced by

```
1040  IF G0< 1 THEN 1050
1041  IF G0 < = 4 THEN 1100]
```

```
10    REM :DRAG RACE GAME.
20    REM :SIMULATE A HOPPED UP 1966 DATSUN PICKUP RUNNING THE
30    REM :QUARTER MILE.
40    REM :ASK IF USER WANTS INSTRUCTIONS (IF YOUR VERSION OF BASIC
50    REM :DOESN'T ALLOW STRINGS TO BE INPUT, USE "YES"=1, "NO"=0
70    PRINT "WANT INSTRUCTIONS FOR HOW TO PLAY";
80    INPUT A$
90    IF A$ < >"YES" THEN 120
100      REM :CALL SUBROUTINE TO GIVE STORY LINE & INSTRUCTIONS.
110      GOSUB 5000
120   REM :DECLARE ARRAY FOR GEAR RATIOS, INITIALIZE RELEVANT VARIABLES.
130   DIM G(4)
140   LET G(0)=0.0
150   LET G(1)=3.95
160   LET G(2)=2.40
170   LET G(3)=1.49
180   LET G(4)=1.00
190   REM :"T" IS THE ELAPSED TIME IN SECONDS.
200   REM :"E" IS THE TORQUE ADJUSTMENT CONSTANT (USED TO SIMULATE
210   REM :    FOULED SPARK PLUGS).
220   REM :"R" IS ENGINE RPM.
230   REM :"PO" AND "P1" ARE THE POSITIONS OF THE TRUCK AT THE START
240   REM :    AND END OF THE CURRENT SECOND.
250   REM :"S0" AND "S1" ARE THE SPEEDS OF THE TRUCK AT THE START
260   REM :    AND END OF THE CURRENT SECOND.
270   REM :"F" TELLS WHETHER THE RACE IS FINISHED (FOR ANY REASON).
280   LET T=0
290   LET E=1
300   LET P1=0
310   LET S1=0
320   LET R=4400
330   LET F=0
340   REM :LET USER CHOOSE REAR END RATIO "R1"
350   LET R1=4.11
360   PRINT "DO YOU WANT TO USE THE STOCK REAR END RATIO (4.11)";
370   INPUT A$
380   IF A$="YES" THEN 470
390      PRINT "WHAT RATIO DO YOU WANT THEN";
400      INPUT R1
410      IF R1< 3 THEN 430
420      IF R1< 6 THEN 470
430         PRINT R1; "ISN'T REASONABLE. TRY SOMETHING NEAR 4."
440         PRINT "REAR END RATIO";
450         GO TO 400
470      PRINT "OK — YOU'RE READY TO GO. FASTEN YOUR SEAT BELT, AND"
480      PRINT "GOOD LUCK"
500   REM :PRINT HEADINGS SO USER CAN TELL WHAT THE NUMBERS MEAN.
510   PRINT "ELAPSED TIME DISTANCE   SPEED    ENGINE       GEAR"
520   PRINT "(SECONDS)    (FEET)    (MPH)    (RPM)    (1,2,3, OR 4)"
1000  REM :MAIN LOOP. DONE ONCE EACH SECOND OF ELAPSED TIME.
1010  REM :PRINT CURRENT SITUATION, GET GEAR FROM USER.
```

```
1020   PRINT ''   ''; T,INT(P1),INT(S1),INT(R),
1030   INPUT G0
1040   IF G0 > = 1 AND G0 < = 4 THEN 1100
1050     REM :NOT A LEGAL GEAR. PUT TRUCK IN NEUTRAL.
1060     PRINT ''YOU SHIFTED INTO NEUTRAL. TOO BAD. (GEARS = 1,2,3, OR 4)''
1070     LET G0 = 0
1100   REM :UPDATE FOR THIS SECOND.
1110   REM :COMPUTE RPM AT BEGINNING OF THIS SECOND.
1120   GOSUB 6000
1125   REM :IF ENGINE IS BLOWN, UPDATE IS POINTLESS.
1126   IF F = 1 THEN 2040
1130   LET S0 = S1
1140   LET P0 = P1
1150   REM :GET NEW TORQUE OUTPUT (T0), USE IT TO COMPUTE SPEED, POS.
1160   LET T0 = E*(-1.723E-9*R^3 + 9.287E-6*R^2 + 1.432E-2*R)
1170   LET T1 = 17.0
1200   LET S1 = S0 + T0/T1 - (.15 + .0003*S0^2)
1210   LET P1 = P0 + S1*5280/(60*60)
1220   REM :DID ENGINE OVER-REV OR LUG BY END OF SECOND?
1230   GOSUB 6000
1300   REM :HAS THE TRUCK GONE A QUARTER OF A MILE YET?
1310   IF P1 < 1320 THEN 1400
1320     REM :YES — THE RACE IS OVER! SET ''F'' TO SIGNAL THAT FACT.
1330     LET F = 1
1400   REM :MORE TESTS AND FEATURES GO IN HERE . . .
2000   REM :THROUGH UPDATING FOR THIS SECOND.
2010   LET T = T + 1
2020   REM :END OF MAIN LOOP. IF RACE IS OVER FOR ANY REASON,
2030   REM :''F'' WILL EQUAL 1.
2040   IF F <> 1 THEN 1000
3000   REM :THE RACE IS OVER. IF DUE TO BLOWN ENGINE BEFORE THE END,
3010   REM :TOUGH BANANAS. OTHERWISE, PRINT CONGRATS.
3020   IF P1 < 1320 THEN 3100
3030     PRINT ''END OF THE QUARTER MILE.''
3040     LET T = T + (1320-P0)/(P1-P0)-1
3050     LET S1 = S0 + (S1-S0)*(1320-P0)/(P1-P0)
3060     PRINT ''ELAPSED TIME = '';T;'' SECONDS.''
3070     PRINT ''FINAL SPEED = '';S1;'' MPH.''
3080     IF T > 18.85 THEN 3100
3090     PRINT ''CONGRATULATIONS ON A FINE RUN.''
3100   PRINT
3110   PRINT ''WANT TO MAKE ANOTHER RUN'';
3120   INPUT A$
3130   PRINT
3140   IF A$ = ''YES'' THEN 10
3150   IF A$ = ''Y'' THEN 10
3160   GO TO 30000
5000   REM :SUBROUTINE THAT GIVES STORY, GAME DESCRIPTION.
5010   PRINT
5020   PRINT ''***************************************************''
5030   PRINT
5040   PRINT ''YES FRIENDS — YOU TOO CAN EXPERIENCE THE THRILLS,''
5050   PRINT ''THE CHILLS, THE SUSPENSE, THE EXCITEMENT, THE''
5060   PRINT ''G L O R Y AND F A M E''
5070   PRINT ''OF ***DRAG RACING ***''
5080   PRINT
5090   PRINT ''DRIVE THE MILLER BROS. MODIFIED 1966 DATSUN PICKUP''
5100   PRINT ''IN THE QUARTER MILE.''
5110   PRINT
5120   PRINT ''SO YOU DON'T GET HURT, I'LL STEER AND WORK THE''
5130   PRINT ''PEDALS FOR YOU. I'LL EVEN SLIP THE CLUTCH FOR THE''
```

```
5135  PRINT "FIRST FEW SECONDS TO MAKE SURE YOU GET OFF THE LINE"
5138  PRINT "CLEANLY. YOU GET TO DO ALL THE BRAINWORK —"
5140  PRINT "DECIDING WHEN TO SHIFT."
5150  PRINT
5160  PRINT "THE MILLER BROS. DATSUN HAS FOUR FORWARD GEARS (1,2,"
5170  PRINT "3, AND 4). EACH SECOND OF ELAPSED TIME, I'LL SHOW"
5180  PRINT "YOUR CURRENT POSITION, CURRENT SPEED, AND ENGINE"
5190  PRINT "RPM, AND THEN TYPE A QUESTION MARK. YOU TYPE THE"
5200  PRINT "GEAR YOU WANT TO BE IN FOR THE NEXT SECOND, AND THEN"
5210  PRINT "HIT THE 'RETURN' KEY."
5200  PRINT "A HINT: THE ENGINE (DATSUN 1300CC 'J' TYPE) IS PRETTY"
5230  PRINT "MUCH STOCK EXCEPT FOR HEAVY DUTY VALVE SPRINGS AND A
NEW"
5240  PRINT "CAM. THE ENGINE CAN GO UP TO 6000 RPM AND HIGHER IF YOU'RE"
5250  PRINT "LUCKY. THE CAM GIVES THE ENGINE A TORQUE PEAK AT"
5260  PRINT "ABOUT 4400 RPM, AND A HORSEPOWER PEAK AT ABOUT 5100
RPM."
5270  PRINT "IT ALSO HAS A QUICK-CHANGE DIFFERENTIAL, SO YOU CAN"
5280  PRINT "CHOOSE THE REAR END RATIO YOU WANT TO USE."
5290  PRINT
5300  RETURN
6000  REM :SUBROUTINE TO COMPUTE CURRENT RPM, AND TEST FOR
6010  REM :OVER-REV AND UNDER REV CONDITIONS.
6020  REM :CLUTCH GETS SLIPPED FOR THE FIRST 2 SECONDS—
6030  IF T > =2 THEN 6100
6040    REM :SLIP THE CLUTCH TO KEEP RPMS UP.
6050    LET R=4400*G(G0)/G(1)
6060    RETURN
6100  REM :NORMAL SITUATION — RPM DETERMINED BY SPEED AND GEAR.
6110  LET R=S1*R1*G(G0)*12*5280/(2*3.14159*11.5*60)
6120  REM :PROBABILITY OF ENGINE BLOWING UP INCREASES BETWEEN
6130  REM :6000 AND 7000 RPM.
6140  IF RND > (R-6000)/1000 THEN 6200
6150    PRINT "AAAARGH! THE ENGINE BLEW UP. IT COULDN'T"
6160    PRINT "HANDLE ";R;" RPM. BETTER LUCK NEXT TIME."
6170    LET F=1
6180    RETURN
6200  IF R>2500 THEN 6300
6210  IF G0=0 THEN 6300
6220  PRINT "YOU'RE LUGGING THE ENGINE — DOWN SHIFT IMMEDIATELY."
6230    LET E=E*1.1
6300  RETURN
30000  END
```

Figure 101   Getting Ready for Another Run

Sample runs

RUN
WANT INSTRUCTIONS FOR HOW TO PLAY? YES

YES FRIENDS — YOU TOO CAN EXPERIENCE THE THRILLS,
THE CHILLS, THE SUSPENSE, THE EXCITEMENT, THE
      G L O R Y AND F A M E
OF   *** DRAG RACING ***

DRIVE THE MILLER BROS. MODIFIED 1966 DATSUN PICKUP
IN THE QUARTER MILE.

SO YOU DON'T GET HURT, I'LL STEER AND WORK THE
PEDALS FOR YOU. I'LL EVEN SLIP THE CLUTCH FOR THE
FIRST FEW SECONDS TO MAKE SURE YOU GET OFF THE LINE
CLEANLY.   YOU GET TO DO ALL THE BRAINWORK—
DECIDING WHEN TO SHIFT.

THE MILLER BROS. DATSUN HAS FOUR FORWARD GEARS (1,2,
3, AND 4). EACH SECOND OF ELAPSED TIME, I'LL SHOW
YOUR CURRENT POSITION, CURRENT SPEED, AND ENGINE
RPM, AND THEN TYPE A QUESTION MARK. YOU TYPE THE
GEAR YOU WANT TO BE IN FOR THE NEXT SECOND, AND THEN
HIT THE 'RETURN' KEY
A HINT: THE ENGINE (DATSUN 1300CC 'J' TYPE) IS PRETTY
MUCH STOCK EXCEPT FOR HEAVY DUTY VALVE SPRINGS AND A NEW
CAM. THE ENGINE CAN GO UP TO 6000 RPM AND HIGHER IF YOU'RE
LUCKY. THE CAM GIVES THE ENGINE A TORQUE PEAK AT
ABOUT 4400 RPM, AND A HORSEPOWER PEAK AT ABOUT 5100 RPM.
IT ALSO HAS A QUICK-CHANGE DIFFERENTIAL, SO YOU CAN
CHOOSE THE REAR END RATIO YOU WANT TO USE.

DO YOU WANT TO USE THE STOCK REAR END RATIO (4.11)? YES
OK — YOU'RE READY TO GO. FASTEN YOUR SEAT BELT, AND
        GOOD LUCK

ELAPSED TIME (SECONDS)	DISTANCE (FEET)	SPEED (MPH)	ENGINE (RPM)	GEAR (1,2,3, OR 4)
0	0	0	4400	?1
1	8	5	4400	?1
2	24	10	4400	?1
3	46	14	3538	?11

clutch is being slipped

sometimes my terminal (an old TermiNet) screws up

YOU SHIFTED INTO NEUTRAL. TOO BAD. (GEARS = 1,2,3, OR 4)

4	67	14	0	?1
5	96	19	4690	?1
6	133	25	5934	?2
7	177	30	4333	?2
8	229	35	5089	?2
9	287	39	5745	?2
10	350	42	6181	?3
11	420	47	4271	?3
12	497	52	4704	?3
13	581	57	5108	?3
14	670	61	5459	?3
15	764	64	5739	?3
16	862	66	5943	?4
17	965	70	4238	?4
18	1075	74	4479	?4
19	1190	78	4708	?4
20	1310	81	4918	?4

risking danger trying to make up lost time. . .

END OF THE QUARTER MILE.
ELAPSED TIME = 20.0788 SECONDS.
FINAL SPEED = 82.138 MPH.

WANT TO MAKE ANOTHER RUN? YES

WANT INSTRUCTIONS FOR HOW TO PLAY? NO
DO YOU WANT TO USE THE STOCK REAR END RATIO (4.11)? NO
WHAT RATIO DO YOU WANT THEN? 4.5
OK — YOU'RE READY TO GO. FASTEN YOUR SEAT BELT, AND
                          GOOD LUCK

ELAPSED TIME (SECONDS)	DISTANCE (FEET)	SPEED (MPH)	ENGINE (RPM)	GEAR (1,2,3, OR 4)
0	0	0	4400	?1
1	8	5	4400	?1
2	24	10	4400	?1
3	46	15	3974	?1
4	76	20	5376	?2
5	114	25	4019	?2
6	159	30	4853	?2
7	211	35	5632	?3
8	271	40	3963	?3
9	337	45	4450	?3
10	411	50	4927	?3
11	491	54	5356	?3
12	577	58	5705	?4
13	668	62	4117	?4
14	766	66	4401	?4
15	871	71	4675	?4
16	981	74	4928	?4
17	1096	78	5155	?4
18	1215	81	5351	?4

END OF THE QUARTER MILE.
ELAPSED TIME = 18.8496 SECONDS.
FINAL SPEED = 83.4851 MPH.
CONGRATULATIONS ON A FINE RUN.

WANT TO MAKE ANOTHER RUN? YES

WANT INSTRUCTIONS FOR HOW TO PLAY? NO
DO YOU WANT TO USE THE STOCK REAR END RATIO (4.11)? YES
OK — YOU'RE READY TO GO. FASTEN YOUR SEAT BELT, AND GOOD LUCK

ELAPSED TIME (SECONDS)	DISTANCE (FEET)	SPEED (MPH)	ENGINE (RPM)	GEAR (1,2,3, OR 4)
0	0	0	4400	?1
1	8	5	4400	?1
2	24	10	4400	?1 grrr...
3	46	14	3538	?11 ←

YOU SHIFTED INTO NEUTRAL. TOO BAD. (GEARS = 1,2,3, OR 4)

4	67	14	0	?1
5	96	19	4690	?1
6	133	25	5934	?1
7	173	27	6579	?2
8	222	32	4753	?2
9	277	37	5471	?2
10	339	41	6016	?2
11	403	43	6318	?3
12	474	48	4358	?3
13	553	53	4787	?3
14	638	57	5183	?3
15	728	61	5521	?3
16	823	64	5785	?3
17	921	66	5976	?3 tempting fate
18	1021	68	6103	?3 once too often!
19	1122	69	6184	?3 ←

AAAARGH! THE ENGINE BLEW UP. IT COULDN'T
   HANDLE 6233.35 RPM. BETTER LUCK NEXT TIME.
WANT TO MAKE ANOTHER RUN? NO
READY

DAY 9: GENERALITIES ABOUT PROGRAMMING

What's the best language?

Q 862 You seem to like Basic quite a bit.

A   True.

        I think it's a really good compromise for normal use on home computers.

Q 863 But here [*Dr. Dobb's Journal,* see Bibliography] it says that Basic isn't a very good language, and they're asking people for PASCAL compilers . . . and here's a story on a new language called Tiny High . . . and in this other magazine, they say APL is a great language . . . There's so many possibilities, I don't know which way to go. It would help if you'd tell me: overall, what's the best language?

A   Fortunately, that's easy to answer. There isn't one.

Q 864 But that's no help . . .

        You mean you're just not willing to commit yourself, right?

A   Look. Each computer language was designed for a different purpose by people working on different classes of problems in different machine environments.

Q 865 All right. What's the best language for *me,* to run on a typical home computer?

A   It depends on what you want to *do,* whether you care about sharing programs with other people, whether you plan to do highly mathematical problems or elaborate word processing, whether you want to learn about language design, whether you're a beginner or already have some experience with some specific language, whether you're willing to write your own interpreter or compiler, whether you're trying to create a large programming system or

just trying to learn about using computers, on and on.
How much self-discipline you have, whether you want to
get status by using an exotic language . . . A key thing
to remember is that a competent programmer can do
anything that's computable in *any* popular general-purpose
language.

Q 866 You can't help me at all?

A   Here's what I *can* do. I can suggest some properties that
apply to most personal computer systems, and then I can
give you a list of some popular languages along with some
of their properties. After that you're pretty much on your
own. I would suggest, though, that one of the best ways
to choose a language is to talk with your friends and see
if you can't agree among yourselves to start out using
the same language. That way you'll be able to share
experiences (and programs), and make discoveries that
help each other . . .

For grid's sake, though, don't spend weeks sitting around
arguing with each other about what the ''best'' language
is. That's just a waste of time. If someone tries to turn
you on to their favorite language, to push it on you, try
to find out what it is about it that makes it advantageous
for their particular application. Often you'll find out that
the real reason they're so excited about it is that it's the
only one they know very well.

Q 867 You seem pretty cynical.

A   It's really more of the old ''reformed sinner'' syndrome.
Maybe I've gone to the other extreme, but now I really
could care less what language I'm using. I try to concentrate on what I'm trying to do, and choose a language
that won't get in the way too much. Often that comes
down to making do with whatever is available. It's not
as if you're faced with a tremendous range of languages
when you sit down at a home computer. Today, at least,
you *hear* about a lot more languages than are actually
available on home systems.

Q 868 Hummph. I still bet you have a favorite language.

A   As of right now, probably the most common property of
home computer systems is that they are small — they
don't have great gobs of high-speed memory. That would
tend to bias things away from large general purpose
languages that have a large number of features and options
. . . PL/I comes to mind.

Second, most home computer users can't afford elaborate
i/o devices. That would tend to bias things against languages that require large and unusual character sets on

our keyboards — APL comes to mind here.

Also, we tend to want to be able to write programs that we can interact with easily. We want to sit at the terminal and have our programs ask us questions, tell us things as it runs, draw pictures that we can play around with . . . On the other hand, if we have an occasional program that does a tremendous amount of processing, we don't mind waiting a while . . . there's no reason we can't let a program run over night, or all weekend . . . Those considerations tend to bias things toward interpreted languages (Basic and APL come to mind).

Fourth, we probably want to be able to trade programs with other people quite a bit. We may even use programs as a communications medium — we might send a program to a friend that asks him or her a series of strange questions in order to print out an appropriate, very personal "happy birthday". That tends to bias things toward languages that are standardized, that can run on a number of different systems (See Table 9, page 124)

Have any questions about the table?

Q 869 I've heard of some languages you didn't include . . . like TRAC, and . . .

A   Obviously I couldn't include all computer languages that have ever seen the light of day. Jean Sammet's book [*Programming Languages,* see Bibliography] shows a Tower of Babel on the cover with over a hundred names of computer languages on it . . . and that was in 1969 or so. By now there must have been over a thousand computer languages that have run on some system or another. I tried to include a few of the more popular languages . . . ones that have been around for a while and have received heavy use.

Q 870 What does the heading about **interactive use** mean?

A   Languages that have a "yes" in that column are designed so that the user can sit at a terminal, enter parts of programs, run them, alter them, interact with them, and soon without going through any additional steps.

Q 871 No, I know that's what interactive means — I wanted to know what the "well suited" part of the heading was about.

A   Oh. Well, some languages (like Basic) were designed from the very beginning to be used in an interactive setting. Others weren't, but turned out to be suited to interactive use anyway. I was thinking mainly of LISP.

We've used the interactive feature in all the Basic programs

	available on (some) micro-computers now	likely to be available on microcomputers in forseeable future	standards exist or are in advanced stage of adoption	typical memory requirements	for interactive use or, well suited to it.	particularly good for complex mathematical problems	particularly good for text-handling non-numerical applications	"structured" language (helps produce clean, understandable programs)	used mainly in
raw machine language	yes		no	minimal	yes	no	no	no	emergencies
assembly language	yes		no	minimal	yes	no	no	no	situations where memory and execution time are at a premium and mainly when nothing else is available.
Tiny Basic	yes		no	minimal	yes	no	no	no	situations where memory space is tight, home computing.
Minimal Basic (ANSI)	yes		yes	small	yes	yes	no	no	interactive situations, home computing. great to learn as a first language. Very widespread.
Extended Basic	yes		yes	medium	yes	yes	yes	no	interactive situations, home computing. Very widespread.
Algol	no	no	no	large	no	yes	no	yes	academic and research institutions. The first "structured" language.
APL	no	yes	no	medium to large (also requires special character set)	yes	yes!	ok	ok	interactive, math oriented problem solving.
COBOL	no	no	yes	large	no	no	yes	ok	business applications. Very widespread on commercial machines.
FORTRAN	yes		yes	large	no	yes	no	no	"scientific" applications. Math oriented problems. Very widespread.
LISP 1.5 and successors	no	yes	no	medium to large	yes	no!	yes!	no	Artificial Intelligence research labs. Also good for blowing people's minds who've only seen Basic, Fortran, ...
PASCAL	no	yes	no	large	no	yes	ok	yes	academic and research settings. An influential experimental language.
PL/I	no	no	?	immense	no	yes	yes	yes	IBMish settings.
PL/M, PL/6800, etc.	yes		no	large	no	no	no	yes	Commercial development of microprocessor based systems
SNOBOL4	no	?	no	large	yes	no!	yes!	no	text processing, linguistic analysis

so far. We PRINT things for the user to see, INPUT values from the user . . .

Q 872 I can see that Basic made that easier than assembly language . . . but most of the languages you have listed are higher-level languages, right? Why isn't it easy to do that on all of them?

Interpreters vs. compilers

A   Maybe it would help if I went over the difference between an **interpreter** and a **compiler**.

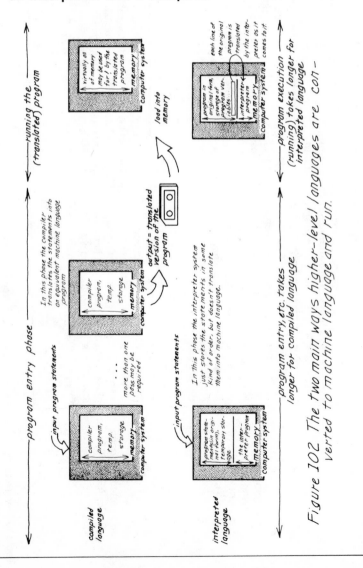

Figure 102 The two main ways higher-level languages are converted to machine language and run.

	memory available for program	length of time to prepare and de-bug a program	execution speed	making a small change to an existing program	dealing with terminal i/o, having program interact with user
compiled language (e.g. Fortran, COBOL, PL/I, etc.)	virtually all of (RAM) memory, plus program is in translated (machine language) form which is much more compact than the original. Allows large programs	longer, each series of changes means another compilation; harder to experiment to see what works	fast — the program is expressed in machine language, requires no further translation	hard — you have to go through the entire compilation process all over again	must be done explicitly, may require a user-written machine language subroutine to get characters from keyboard, etc.
interpreted language (e.g. Basic, APL, LISP, etc.)	limited — interpreter takes up a substantial amount of memory, plus program is stored in its original form.	shorter, you can easily change errors as you find them; easy to experiment to see what works, what the statements do	slow — each statement is translated each time the program calls for it to be carried out	easy, fast — old lines can be removed, new ones inserted as fast as you can type	a natural part of the language

Table 10 Using a compiled language vs. an interpreted language

Interactive, interpreter based languages tend to be more convenient to use, especially for beginners. Compiler based languages are the choice if you have a very large program, or are especially concerned about execution speed.

Q 873   All right. That seems to make sense, but then what's the difference between assembly language and a language that uses a compiler?

A   Simple. Assembly language isn't a higher-level language. Assembly language statements have a one-to-one correspondence to machine language instructions. [Editor's note: except, of course, for **assembler directives** (Q 721).] Not only does that make it more tedious to program in assembly language, and harder to learn, it means you can't trade finished programs with someone who has a system based on a different microprocessor.

Q 874   In the Table you have a column about **standards**. You seem to be making a big deal out of that.

A   Yeh . . . maybe too big a deal. I don't know. It sure seems to me that it would make things a lot easier and more fun if you could trade programs with most anybody. Also, I think there'd be a lot of really interesting, useful programs for sale if you didn't have to make a different version for each brand of machine.

Basic — variations on a theme

Q 875   You list three different kinds of Basic in the Table, Tiny Basic, Minimal Basic, and Extended Basic. In the ads for Altair computers, they talk about 4K Basic, 8K Basic, and Extended Basic. Are those the same thing?

A   Not really. They . . .

Q 876   I remember now . . . I've seen Tiny Basic in Dr. Dobb's Journal. They have listings of interpreters for Tiny Basic, and they're free. If I wanted to get the other kinds of Basic you list, I'd have to pay for them, right?

A   The . . . uh, the versions of Tiny Basic that they've had in Dr. Dobb's Journal don't have all the features of commercially available Basics, but putting that aside, there are a couple of other disadvantages to consider.

First of all, you have almost no idea what you're getting. An assembly language program that was written by a skilled programmer who has tested it for months to get most of the bugs out can look pretty much the same as a program that was hacked together and hardly tested at all when you glance at them on the printed page. Even if the program you're copying is the carefully done, thoroughly de-bugged product of an expert programmer, you're bound to make typing mistakes as you enter in the thousand lines or so of assembly language required to implement a Tiny Basic interpreter. That means that you're going to have a substantial job of de-bugging on your hands. And *that* means that, just as you need some knowledge of digital electronics to put a kit together and get it working, you need a familiarity with assembly language programming to get a version of Tiny Basic up and running. Keep that in mind when you're considering costs.

Q   And the second?

A   What?

Q 877 The second disadvantage. I'm not scared off by the first reason . . . I want to learn assembly language programming anyway.

A   It's the standards thing again. If you want to share programs with other people, you've got to be able to send them things that will run on their system. The versions of Tiny Basic I've seen (and this may change — hope I'm wrong on this) aren't just subsets of other versions of Basic. That is, not only don't they include all the capabilities of commercially available Basics, they do some things differently. We'll see what the future brings. The American National Standards Institute has been working on a standardized version of Basic, called ANSI Minimal Basic. [See Appendix] That's what I was referring to in [Table 9]. Once that's adopted and accepted by the computing community, I think a lot of the problems will go away.

In addition to Minimal Basic, ANSI is also working on standards for a number of extensions to Basic. Right now, if you buy "Extended Basic" from one manufacturer, it can include radically different things from another person's "Extended Basic".

Q 878 Well, Extended Basic must mean *something*.

A   I can give you an idea of what it might mean. To know for sure, you have to look at the manual that comes with whatever version you're interested in.

There are four main classes of enhancements that get added to Basic. **String manipulation, matrix operations, file manipulation,** and . . . uhm, **others.**

Q 879 What does **file manipulation** mean?

A   Let me see . . . how should I explain that . . .

Imagine that you were a doctor's office and you decided to get a microcomputer to keep the doctor's records, because you were tired of the ever increasing number of file cabinets the doctor kept putting in you, they were making marks in your rug, and . . .

Ω   Imagine you were a doctor's office . . . you're warped. Warped!

A   So the question is, how would you go about storing the data you used to keep on paper? Suppose you need to keep each patient's name, address, and social security number, their insurance company's name and plan number, a record of your estimate of their income, and a summary of each of their office visits during the year. On the average, that would be something like 200 characters of data per person.

If you have 8K of memory to use for storing patients' records, you can fit records for 40 patients in memory at one time. What do you do with the rest? Doctors have more on the order of thousands of patients . . . certainly a lot more than 40.

Q 880 Keep them on tapes or something?

A   Right. Obviously you have to keep most of the data on some kind of **mass storage device**. High-speed tape equipment, or a disc, or (someday soon) magnetic bubble memory . . . at any rate, not in the main memory of the machine. But you can't just keep the records in one big clump — since only 40 will fit in memory at one time you need some plan of organization, some way of knowing which block of records to load into memory to get to a specific person's data. Blocks of records like that are called **files,** in analogy to the drawers of the file cabinets the computer is replacing. And the process of organizing, updating and using the files is called **file manipulation**. The file manipulation extensions to Basic give you a number of higher-level statements that make it much more convenient to cope with large amounts of data.
basic idea behind files Q 950-953

Q 881 I'm right, though, that you *could* do it all using assembly language programs? You don't *have* to use a higher-level language.

A   That's right. But it might take you quite a bit of time and effort to figure out how to do all the necessary things and de-bug your programs — it just depends on where you want to put your time and money.

Q 882 You said **matrix operations** was another kind of extension. Is that like matrices in math?

A   Exactly. Matrices come in handy in a lot of engineering problems, but if you don't already know what they are, and have a use for them, it's probably not worth it to go out of your way to get an Extended Basic with matrix operations.

The one extension that *I* find really useful is the **character string** extension.

Q 883 And what, exactly, are **character strings?**

A   Things in quotes in a Basic program. Look back at the Basic programs we've written. Almost all the PRINT statements have character strings in them. For example, the statement

3070 PRINT "ELAPSED TIME =";T;" SECONDS."

contains two character strings, namely "ELAPSED TIME=" and "SECONDS.".

Q 884 Wait a minute. You said the drag race program could run on any system that has Minimal Basic. Now you're saying that it uses the character string extension.

A   No I'm not. In Minimal Basic you can't *manipulate* them, but you can use character strings in certain, restricted ways.

drag race game program End of Day 8.

Q 885 You seemed to be able to do everything you wanted in the drag race program — when would you want to manipulate character strings, whatever that means?

A   Let me give you a little example.

Suppose you're writing a program that stores membership records for your computer club. You'd like to store the members' names in the time honored *last name, first name, middle initial* form to make it easier to put them in alphabetical order, and . . .

Q 886 I'm starting to get lost already. How would you write a program that puts people's names in alphabetical order?

A   By manipulating strings, of course.

To put a bunch of names in order, at the very least, you've got to be able to tell which of two given names comes first alphabetically, right?

Q   I'll grant you that.

A   Extended Basic with strings makes that very easy. The statement

1000 LET A$ = "ORVEDAHL, WALTER"

stores the string "ORVEDAHL, WALTER" in memory cell A$, and the statement

1010 LET B$ = "PEIRCE, CHARLES"

fills memory cell B$ with the string "PEIRCE, CHARLES". The statement

2000 IF A$ ‹ B$ THEN 6000

succeeds, i.e. transfers control to statement 6000, only if the string stored in A$ comes earlier alphabetically than the string stored in B$. So in this case, the test succeeds. By repeatedly swapping names that aren't in order, you can put a list of names into alphabetical order.

for **sorting algorithms,** see most any introductory programming textbook. (Bibliography)

Q. 887 That's interesting . . .
What was the **other** extension?
A   The committee that's coming up with the proposed standards is considering a number of "little" extensions. Things that give you more control over the output format, give you a range of ways of storing numeric values, letting you use a more advanced form of subroutine . . . Time will tell what they come up with.
Q. 888 You sure have a lot of faith in standards . . .
I was just thinking. I heard a talk in which the speaker said "we want *one* language", and jabbed his finger in the air. I almost expected the crowd to leap up and start chanting en masse "ONE tongue, ONE tongue, ONE tongue".
A   Heh. I'll bet that was Ted Nelson. That might be nice in some ways, but it would also tend to make things stagnate . . . I'm sure it's not going to happen, anyway.
Q. 889 Why not? Isn't what you're saying that there are so many different computer languages and so many dialects, that it, uh, splinters people apart, makes it hard for people to share programs?
A   See, the real problem is that no one has come up with a computer language that's good enough to be all things to all people. Every language that's become at all popular so far is good at some things and terrible for others. It would be nice if everyone could agree on a few standardized languages that you could use to share programs — so everybody didn't have to keep starting from ground zero. But there has to be room for people to play around with new and exotic languages, because there's still a lot of room for improvement.

Q 890 That sounds reasonable . . . but in a way you seem to keep contradicting yourself. You *did* say that a good programmer can do anything in any language, didn't you?

A Basically. The question is, how easy is it to do? How convenient are computer languages for humans to use? And the answer is, not very. Assembly language is a lot more convenient than raw machine language, and the higher-level languages are a lot more convenient and easier to learn than assembly language, but the whole batch of them still aren't very close to the way humans think about problems.

Q 891 Is it also true that there's always more than one way to write a program to do a specific problem?

A More than one way to do a specific problem in the same computer language?

Q Right.

A Sure. That's one of the really interesting things about programming — there are always many, many ways to solve a particular problem. When you're first learning to program, you might go through a phase where you struggle to find a way, any way, to solve a problem, but after you've programmed a while, you'll find that lots of possible solutions present themselves.

Q 892 I'm not sure I can imagine that. I'd think there would be some way to rule most of the different ways out. Like, some might make the program longer . . .

A Oh. You're right there. You can rule most of them out based on considerations like program length, clarity, ease of use by the person who will be running the program, execution time, things like that. The ideas in **structured programming** give you a rationale for throwing out a lot of the possibilities before you even begin.

What is structured programming?

Q 893 What is **structured programming?** Is it just a buzz word? I see it mentioned in all the magazines.

A **Structured programming** is a disciplined way of programming. The main ideas are: start with a natural language description of your proposed solution (i.e. don't try to *think* in a computer language); solve your problem by successive refinement of the statement of your problem; after you've solved the problem, translate your solution into whatever computer language you happen to be using; use comments (REMarks) that illustrate the details of your solution (i.e. don't dwell on minute details of the *program* — explain *how it works* so someone looking at your program has a chance of really understanding it). Also, there are suggested ways of writing the control structure of your program — a small set of "legal" standard branching possibilities.

Q 894 What do you mean by **branching possibilities?**

A   The ways your program uses IF-THENs and GO TO statements in Basic, and the various JuMP and Branch statements in assembly language. Here. Let me show you the suggested forms.

pretest or do while

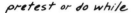

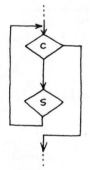

As *long as (while) condition C holds, do the statements (S) in the loop and repeat. If C doesn't hold, proceed from the next statement after the end of the loop.*

Example *in Basic*

```
210  REM : DO WHILE X IS LESS THAN 100.
220   IF X >= 100 THEN 260
230     LET K = K + X
240     LET X = X + 2
250     GO TO 220
260  REM : NOW GO ON AND DO SOMETHING
            ELSE.
                .
                .
```

Example *in 6800 assembly language.*

```
              .
              .
         CLC            ; clear carry
WHILE    BCS    DONE ; do loop as long as carry isn't set.
         ABA            ; add in next term
         BRA    WHILE ; last statement in loop.
DONE          .
              .
```

Figure 103 Part 1 Loop control structures

post-test or repeat until

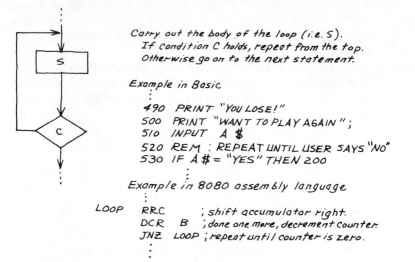

Carry out the body of the loop (i.e. S).
If condition C holds, repeat from the top.
Otherwise go on to the next statement.

Example in Basic

```
490  PRINT "YOU LOSE!"
500  PRINT "WANT TO PLAY AGAIN ";
510  INPUT  A $
520  REM : REPEAT UNTIL USER SAYS "NO"
530  IF A $ = "YES" THEN 200
```

Example in 8080 assembly language

```
LOOP  RRC        ; shift accumulator right.
      DCR   B    ; done one more, decrement counter.
      JNZ  LOOP  ; repeat until counter is zero.
```

multiple branch or case statement

C specifies a value which is used to select
one of the n different sequences of
statements $S_1, S_2, ..., S_n$

Example in Basic

```
900      REM : AT THIS POINT, "C" = 1, 2, 3, or 4
910      REM : DEPENDING ON USER'S ANSWER.
920      ON C  GOTO 1000, 1200, 1400, 1600

1000         REM : ANSWER WAS 1, SET UP FOR KLING-
                ONS.
1010         LET S $ = "KLINGON"
1020         LET D = A + 2
1030         GO TO 2000
1200         REM : CASE 2, SET UP FOR ROMULANS
1210         LET S $ = "ROMULAN"
1220         LET D = B
1230         GO TO 2000
1400         REM : CASE 3, VULCANS
1410         LET S $ = "VULCAN"
1420         LET D = 1000
1430         GO TO 2000
1600         REM : CASE 4, EARTH
1610         LET S $ = "EARTHLINGS"
1620         LET D = -1
2000         REM : END OF CASE STATEMENT
```

Figure 103 — continued —

two-way branch or if-then

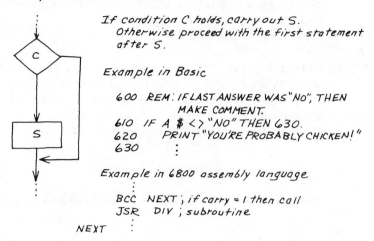

If condition C holds, carry out S.
Otherwise proceed with the first statement after S.

Example in Basic

```
600  REM: IF LAST ANSWER WAS "NO", THEN
           MAKE COMMENT.
610  IF A $ <> "NO" THEN 630.
620     PRINT "YOU'RE PROBABLY CHICKEN!"
630     :
```

Example in 6800 assembly language

```
        :
BCC  NEXT ; if carry = 1 then call
JSR   DIV ; subroutine
NEXT    :
```

if-then-else

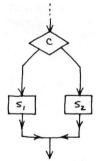

If condition C holds, do statements S_1.
Otherwise carry out S_2.

Example in Basic

```
800  REM : IF TIME IS LESS THAN 25,
810  IF TØ >= 25 THEN 850
820     REM : THEN YOU WON.
830     PRINT "YOU WON!!"
840     GO TO 870
850     REM : ELSE YOU LOST
860     PRINT "YOU LOST."
870     REM : END OF IF-THEN-ELSE.
        :
```

Figure 103 Part 2   Selection control
structures

The idea is that by using only a few, standard control structures, you'll produce programs that are more reliable, and easier to read, de-bug, and use.

Q   Wait. Wait a minute.

A   Yeh?

A 895   Hold it. I'm not making sense out of this yet. You flashed so many flowcharts past me I'm not sure what I was seeing. Why don't you show me a control structure that *isn't* structured.

A   That isn't one of the 5 holy forms? OK. Here.

A non-structured loop

mid-test *(do for a while, test, go on some more, repeat)*

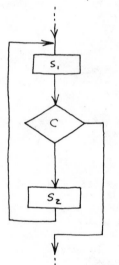

This form of control structure makes the loop harder to perceive as a whole because it changes some values (S_1), then tests to see if the loop should continue, and if so, changes some more things (S_2).

It can be transformed into a do-while by copying the statements in S_1 (or putting them in a subroutine and calling it twice), like this

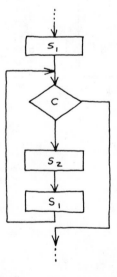

Figure 104

Q 896 Come on now. What's so awful about that? It looks like all the other ones.

A   What's wrong with it is it makes it harder to think of the loop as a unit. If you use a loop like the **mid-test,** you have to follow the details very closely to see what's going on

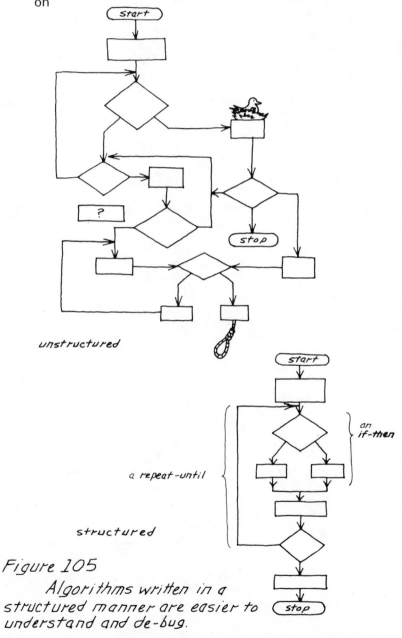

Figure 105

     Algorithms written in a structured manner are easier to understand and de-bug.

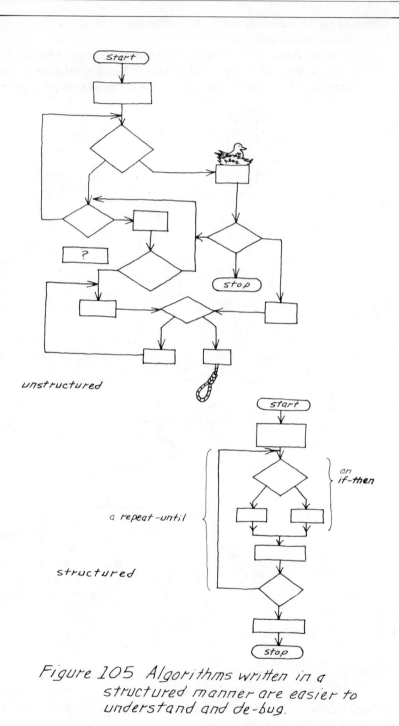

unstructured

structured

a *repeat-until*

an *if-then*

Figure 105 Algorithms written in a
structured manner are easier to
understand and de-bug.

Q 897 That seems like a pretty fine distinction.
A   May be. But the real reason that structured programming
         has caught on in industry is a pragmatic one. When
         programmers use only the structured control structures,
         they actually do produce working programs in a shorter
         time. You really do find that programs written that way
         are easier to de-bug.
Q 898 Do *you* actually use them?
A   I was afraid you were going to ask that.
Q   Well?
A   I try to. I'd say I use them 95% of the time.
         [Editor's note: It appears that all the programs and flow-
         charts that A has presented do follow the conventions he
         has presented here. Flowcharts you may wish to check
         appear in Figures 70, 74, 79, 80, 91 and 99.]
Q 899 Are there some things you can't do using those particular
         structures?
A   No, they're general enough to do anything you can do
         . . . it's just that in some cases I seem to wind up with
         tests at both the top *and* bottom of a loop. It's a minor
         heresy, because the overall idea is to write your program
         as clearly as possible. Doing something in an awkward
         way just so it conforms to the suggested control structures
         is self-defeating.
         There's a tremendous difference in reliability and reada-
         bility between a well-written program and one that's just
         hacked together with a control structure like a plate of
         spaghetti . . .
Q 900 I think I get the idea.
         Why don't you tell me what **hack** means. Is that where
         the word **hacker** came from?
A   Let's see. **Hack** is used in a number of ways. A **program
         hack** is . . . like a fix instead of a solution. If you have
         a bug, and you do something that makes the immediate
         problem go away, you've made a **fix.** If, on the other hand,
         if you make an alteration that's consistent with the overall
         purposes of the program, one that solves things by making
         the situation causing the bug no longer arise, you've found
         a **solution.**
         Hack is also used to describe a part of a program that
         uses a dirty trick.
         I know . . . what's a **dirty trick?**
         A **dirty trick** is something that depends on some obscure
         property of the particular machine the program is written
         for. Something that might not work on another machine
         even though the program is written in a higher-level

language that you have available on both machines.

Q 901 But don't computer hobbyists call themselves **hackers?**
Does that mean somebody who uses dirty tricks?!?

A   OK. The word **hacker** has gone through a number of
meanings. Now it usually means someone who is intensely
interested in computers.
[Editor's note: If you're interested in this etymological fine
point, you will enjoy comparing the different views of
hackers in the two books *II Cybernetic Frontiers* by Stewart
Brand and *Computer Power and Human Reason* by Joseph
P. Weizenbaum (see Bibliography).]
Phew! We've really covered a lot of different things today.
I hope at least you're getting a feeling for some of the
things that go into programming . . .

Q 902 I think I've gotten a feeling for what it's like to program
. . . and some ideas about the differences between programming languages, but I feel a little bit lost. It seems
like there's so many possibilities.

A   That's what I find irresistible about programming (and
what may scare some people off) — all the possibilities.
You can write programs that solve mathematical equations,
keep elaborate records, help with manuscript preparation,
simulate ecosystems, on and on and on. You can create
whatever sort of fantasy world you can imagine. If you
want to pretend you're hitting golf balls on the moon,
you can write a program that'll figure out the trajectories.
We could change our drag race program so it simulates
a Vespa motor scooter, a San Francisco cable car, or a
full-blown nitro-powered slingshot dragster. You can be
Capt. Kirk at the helm of the Enterprise or Bluebeard at
the helm of a pirate ship . . .

Q 903 You mean *you* can imagine that *you* could write programs
that would let you play at all those things. I'm not so
sure I can imagine myself doing all that.

A   It does take a while to learn to program, but I firmly believe
that anyone can learn to program. You start by writing
little programs of your own, and by making small alterations to programs you've gotten from someone else. Take
the drag race program and add some more options to it.
You'll learn a lot by trying to understand how programs
you see in the magazines work. Gradually, you'll come
to the point where you can program well enough to be
able to write a program to do anything you really understand in detail. It's true.

DAY 10: WHAT CAN YOU REALLY DO WITH IT, AND WHAT CAN'T YOU DO WITH IT?

Well?

A   Our last day! It's been fun. Really has.

Q   Yes. We've gone over quite a lot. I just have one major question left.

A   What's that?

Q 904   What Can You Really Do With It?

A   The big question, huh? I just happen to have an answer to that. What can you do with it? Anything that's **computable.**

Q   Very funny.

A   No, actually that does mean something. But I know what you're asking. After the fun of having a new gadget in the house wears off, will you feel like hiding your home computer in a dark corner of the garage, or will you be able to find enough practical uses for it to make it worthwhile.

There are two sides to the question of what you can do with a computer. There's the practical question of "what can I reasonably expect to do with a home computer?" Then there's the more theoretical question of "is there anything that a general purpose digital computer can't do?"

Q 905   A computer can't do something if you don't have a program that tells it what to do . . .

Why don't you go over the practical question first. I want to know what I can do with a home computer. Whether it would be reasonable for me to assume that I'll be able to make it help me with my income tax, figure out problems around the house . . .

A   A computer is an information processing device. Obviously

I can't list every specific sort of information you can process. Instead, I'll outline some general categories of applications, and then mention some specific examples within each category. It seems to me that these six (inter-related) categories span the range of computer applications:

1 **control**
2 **communication**
3 **computation**
4 **simulation**
5 **organization**
6 **recreation.**

And then . . .

Q 906 What about education? Can't you . . .

A   And then there are three different approaches you can take to each of those categories,

1 **personal use**
2 **education**
3 **profit making.**

Take **simulation** for example. You can write programs which simulate some real world process for your personal use and edification, you can use a simulation program to teach people about the system you've simulated, or you can sell the results of your simulation study to make money.

Q 907 I assume you're going to expl . . .

Control

A   Right. I'll go over each of the application categories.
Control means using a computer to monitor and direct the performance of some physical system. For example, you could use a computer to control your furnace and air conditioning. The idea is to minimize cost and maximize comfort. By putting temperature sensors both inside and outside your house you can supply enough information to the computer to let it predict (anticipate) temperature changes inside your house. If the house is a little cold in the morning, but the sun is out, the computer could rely on the sun to heat the house and not waste energy. A regular thermostat would heat the house up with the furnace and then have to cool it off because of the solar heating . . .

Q 908 A regular thermostat just works on the temperature inside the house at one point in time, ... the system you're imagining takes a broader view of things. Is that it?

A   That's the idea. To get the best performance, you could have the computer control ducts and fans. If the sun heats the house up unevenly, the computer could direct warm air to be blown into the colder parts of the house ... and vice versa if some area gets too hot in the afternoon sun.

Another example of a control application ...

Q 909 Not so fast. Your idea sounds nice as far as it goes, but what would you need to actually do it?

A   What kind of additional equipment?
Let's see. You'd need temperature sensors — devices that put out electrical signals proportional to the temperature. Then you'd need an **analog-to-digital converter** to turn those signals into binary values for your program to use.

Q 910 That's what **A/D** stands for, right? I've seen ads for them.

A   Right. You could probably use a **digital voltmeter chip** just as well. Whatever turns out to be cheapest at the time you go to build the thing. You don't need anything that's super fast. I'm sure your computer wouldn't need to read the temperatures or change any settings more than once every few minutes or so. That means if you program it right, you wouldn't even notice your computer was doing it.

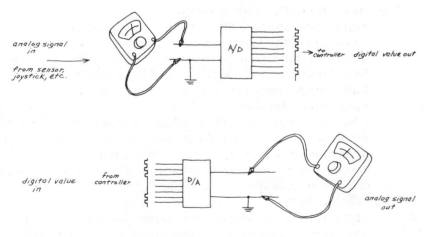

Figure 106 A/D and D/A converters. Key components are available as single IC chips. Prices increase as number of bits increase. 8-bit D/A and A/D chips cost ~ $10.00.

Q 911 What are you talking about? Wouldn't notice . . .

A   I meant that you could be using your computer for something else, working on a program, playing a game . . .
and you (at the terminal) wouldn't notice that every few
minutes the controller switched over from running your
program to check the temperatures and update the settings
of the furnace, fans, vents, etc.

Q 912 How could that be? You mean that the program for
controlling the temperatures would be real short?

A   Right. Not a lot of computation involved in it. You'd add
in a couple of IC chips to count clock cycles, and every
few million cycles, cause an interrupt that would automatically set the machine to updating the temperature control
system.

Q 913 All right. So you'd need temperature sensors, an A/D
converter, and some kind of counter. About how much
would that cost?

A   Wait. You'd also need output devices to control the furnace, air conditioning, fan motors, and motors to open
and close vents. I don't know offhand whether it would
be cheaper to buy surplus relays or use silicon control
rectifiers to do that . . . And to take real advantage of the
situation, you'd probably have to install additional ducting
in your house. Most houses haven't been built with this
sort of thing in mind. Not counting the cost of re-working
the duct system, I'd guess that you could do the whole
thing for under $100 if you did all the work yourself.

Q 914 How about the programming?

A   You'd need to do a little research to figure out the time
constants in the system so your program would anticipate
effects of solar heating and heat loss properly (that will
be different in every house) . . . but if you had the temperature sensors installed, you could use your computer to
help collect the data.
I haven't done it myself, but I'd guess that the program
you'd wind up with would be fairly short. I'll take a wild
guess and say that the whole thing would fit in 1K. Of
course, there's one problem that would have to be checked
out before you should run off and do it.

Q 915 What's that?

A   You'd have to leave your computer running 24 hours a
day. Will it cost more in electricity than you'll save in
fuel bills? [Almost certainly not.] Also, of course, you'd
need some kind of traditional thermostat as a back up
in case your computer goes down.
An interesting problem, overall.

Another common example of a control application is using your computer to turn lights and radios on and off in a convincing manner when you're away from home — to fool would-be burglars.

A more exotic control application would be using your home computer to move a mechanical arm.

Q 916 That sounds romantic, but what would you do with a computer controlled mechanical arm?

A There's been quite a bit of research into **hand/eye** systems. A TV camera provides visual input to the computer, and elaborate processing is done on the scene to determine what objects are there, and to generate the appropriate commands to the arm.

Q 917 But to do what? What's it for?

A One project showed that their system can assemble water pumps. The ultimate idea is to use it in industry — advanced automation. Japanese companies are putting a lot of effort into it . . .

Q 918 But what could *I* use it for?

A Well, a similar sort of control application would be to use your microcomputer to control a machine tool. They've used **numerically controlled** (as opposed to **manually** controlled) tools like lathes in industry for a long time. Microprocessors make it economical for one-man shops to automate . . .

Q Let's move on.

Communication

A The second category was **communication,** and here I had in mind a broad spectrum of human communication.

Here's one possibility — it isn't done yet, far as I know, but it would make a lot of sense. Suppose you're writing an article for a magazine. What you do now is write the article, type a final draft, go over it to find all the errors, then put it in the mail (which is getting to be a risky operation itself). If the editor accepts it, then someone else re-types it (the typesetter), probably introducing a few more errors. They send you a proof copy, which you correct and send back. Alternatively, you could enter the article into your computer, and keep editing it until it was in final form. Then you could call the editor and transmit your article directly from your home computer to his or her computer. If the editor likes the article, he or she can pick up the phone, and send your article to the computer which runs the type setting machines. Overall, you'd save time, paper, and (probably) have fewer errors in the finished article.

Q 919 You said it isn't being done yet. What's lacking?

A   Each subpart of the idea is being done, it's just that no one has "put it all together" as far as I know. A system like that isn't for everybody, but most everyone *could* find uses for the general ability to transmit computer programs and data over the phone. The easiest thing to do is to have a **modem** at each end of the phone connection. **Modem** stands for MOdulator/DEModulator. It serves as an interface between digital signals and signals that can be sent reliably over standard telephone lines. I guess we shouldn't dwell on it . . . there's been a fair number of articles on this sort of thing . . . [Editor's note: see, for example, the "Pennywhistle Modem" article in the March 1976 issue of *Popular Electronics.*]

One communications application that I think is really exciting because of its long-range implications is the use of home TV sets as output devices.

Q 920 What's so exciting about that?

A   Here's one thing: Maybe it's just a personal bias, but I think it's time people started talking back to their TV sets, stopped seeing what comes through them as an alternate reality, started using them in an active way. It scares me to think of all the time children spend in an input-only mode, passively absorbing myths from TV. I'm sure you won't get children away from TV, but if they're able to move patterns around the screen themselves, to have a direct influence over what the TV does, it'll be a more balanced situation.

Q 921 You read stories in the newspaper about two-way cable TV. A scheme that would let you request information from the library and have it displayed on your home TV. And shopping by phone . . . Those are kinds of communications applications, right?

A   Yes, but I don't think you'll see any widespread use of those sorts of things for quite a few years — for social and economic reasons, not technical ones.

A communications application that can happen right now, though, is sending messages to your friends, in the form of programs stored on cassette tapes.

Q 922 Sounds like it's just an expensive way to send a letter.

A   Here's the thing, see — a letter is *passive.* Programs represent (potentially, at least) an *active* communications medium. Unlike a letter, a program can interact with the reader, ask questions, change what comes next to suit the

Figure 107

reader's fancy. You can include sections that draw pictures on your friend's TV screen; you can send them active recipes that lead them step by step through the process of making some favorite dish; you can send them very personal game programs, . . .

Q 923 Very *personal* game programs? What do you have in mind?

A   I don't think it'll be too long before you start seeing stories (and eventually even novels) in the form of programs. Every time you read / run them, you'll get a slightly different story — and you, the reader, can have a say in the names and maybe even personality traits of the characters.
How does the name **acties** sound for program / messages like that?

A 924 Actie? Like movie, but . . .

A   **Actie** because the recipient plays an *active* role in getting the message.

Q 925 Well, it sounds nice, but I can't really imagine what they'd look like. Have you sent any yourself, or are you just daydreaming?

A   I've made some feeble attempts at it. It's not something that comes real easy — you have to be able to imagine how your friend is going to react to make it work well. But I'm going to keep trying . . . it's fun playing around with the idea. Here's the first few lines of one I did . . . I'm not real happy with it, but it might give you the idea. I won't bore you with the whole actie.

```
1Ø    REM :ACTIE FOR MARGARET.
2Ø    REM :THE ARRAY "P$" HOLDS ALTERNATIVE PHRASES.
3Ø    DIM P$(51)
4Ø    REM :USE LET STATEMENTS TO STORE THE ALTERNATIVES.
5Ø    REM :(COULD USE "READ" AND "DATA" TO SAVE SOME SPACE.)
6Ø    LET P$(1)="REALLY GLAD"
7Ø    LET P$(2)="AMBIVALENT"
8Ø    LET P$(3)="SORRY"
9Ø    LET P$(4)="MAKE YOU EVEN HAPPIER!"
1ØØ   LET P$(5)="GIVE YOU A LIFT."
11Ø   LET P$(6)="GET YOU OUT OF THE DUMPS."
12Ø   LET P$(7)="A PROBLEM"
13Ø   LET P$(8)="AN IDEA"
14Ø   LET P$(9)="A POEM"
15Ø   LET P$(1Ø)="PUZZLED BY LATELY."
16Ø   LET P$(11)="PLAYING AROUND WITH."
17Ø   LET P$(12)="WRITING FOR YOU."
                    .
                    .
1ØØØ  REM :THROUGH STORING ALTERNATIVES, START ACTIE.
1Ø1Ø  PRINT "DEAR MARGARET"
1Ø2Ø  PRINT "HI!  WHAT KIND OF A MOOD ARE YOU IN?"
1Ø3Ø  PRINT "FANTASTIC, SO-SO, OR ROTTEN (PLEASE ANSWER"
1Ø4Ø  PRINT "WITH ONE OF THOSE)";
1Ø5Ø  INPUT A$
1Ø6Ø  IF A$<>"FANTASTIC" THEN 1Ø9Ø
```

```
1070    LET M=1
1080    GO TO 1200
1090 IF A$<>"SO-SO" THEN 1120
1100    LET M=2
1110    GO TO 1200
1120 IF A$<>"ROTTEN" THEN 1030.
1130    LET M=3
1200 PRINT "I'M ";P$(M);" THAT YOU'RE FEELING ";A$;"."
1210 PRINT "I HOPE THIS ACTIE WILL ";P$(M+3)
1220 PRINT "HERE'S ";P$(M+6);" I'VE BEEN ";P$(M+9)
1230 ON M GO TO 1240,1400,1800
                  .
                  .
                  .
SAMPLE RUN

RUN

DEAR MARGARET
HI!  WHAT KIND OF A MOOD ARE YOU IN?
FANTASTIC, SO-SO, OR ROTTEN (PLEASE ANSWER
WITH ONE OF THOSE)?  ROTTEN
I'M SORRY THAT YOU'RE FEELING ROTTEN.
I HOPE THIS ACTIE WILL GET YOU OUT OF THE DUMPS.
HERE'S A POEM I'VE BEEN WRITING FOR YOU.
                  .
                  .
                  .
```

Figure 108. First part of a primitive actie

Computation

Q 926 Your next type of application was **computation,** which, it seems to me, includes everything you do with a computer . . . So what did you mean?

A   Well, I meant it in a fairly technical way. I meant that if you were analyzing some system, and had come up with a mathematical, statistical, or logical model, you could use the computer to help derive the consequences of your model. To help test it out, . . . I'm talking about programs that make the involved computations which are necessary to solve technical problems. That's been one of the two main uses of computers from the very start.

Q 927 If you're an engineer or scientist who's used to using computers in your job, you can do the same sorts of things on your home computer. Is that what you're saying?

A   Right. Scientific programming, data analysis, . . .

Q 928 But is that realistic?

A   Yes, I really think it is. Even though microcomputers aren't tremendously powerful number crunchers compared to today's super computers, there's no reason you can't leave your home computer grinding away in the corner for a couple of days straight if you have to.

There are two problems you'll run into, though. First, you'll probably not be able to use the same programming languages and canned subroutines . . .

Q 929 Canned subroutines?

A   Subroutines written by someone else that are available for public use . . . All large computer centers keep a library of useful subroutines to save people from having to write everything themselves . . . Some of the home computer manufacturers do something like that. The second problem arises if your programs need a large amount of memory to run. Then you'll need a disc or something equivalent, and you'll have to figure out how to partition your programs so they can run in modules small enough to fit in memory. Even if you have to buy a disc, you may find that a complete home computer system costs less than a couple of hours of time on the super computer you're using now.

One more point here . . . if you do use your computer for extensive numerical computations, and you find it unendurably slow, you can get **hardware multiply and divide units.** They can be placed on the busses just like any other peripheral device. When your program wants to do a multiply or divide, typically, it sends the two numbers which are to be multiplied or divided along with a control signal telling which operation is desired. Like a flash, the multiply/divide unit computes the result and puts it on the bus.

Q 930 Instead of using the program we worked out before . . . Do many people do that? Buy special purpose hardware gadgets to speed up their machines?

A   Not as far as I know. In most situations, it doesn't make that much difference if your system takes 10 instead of 100 microseconds to do a multiplication. One place it *would* matter, however, is in a complicated graphics program.

Q 931 Graphics means pictures, right?

A   Basically. Displaying visual scenes, processing pictures, producing animated displays . . . To keep an animated display going, your program has to be able to update the information that's being displayed fairly often. Every few dozen milliseconds. If a complex computation has to be made to figure out how to update the display, you might find you need a hardware multiply/divide unit to keep up.

Simulation

Q 932 All right. Your next category was **simulation.**

A   Right. That can apply in a lot of different contexts. For instance, a business establishment could write a program which simulates some aspect of their operation and use it to study the effects of different possible re-organizations.

Q 933 For instance?

A   Oh, say . . . a supermarket might be considering changing the way their checkout counters are set up. They'd like to have an idea of the optimum number of checkers, the effect of different numbers of express lanes, the effect of differing limits on the number of parcels a shopper can have and still use the express lane, and so on. Assuming they have fairly good statistics on the number of people using the store at different times of day, and the quantities of goods people buy, they could go a long way toward solving their problem by studying a computer simulation. The advantage of a computer simulation is that you don't have to disrupt the normal activity of the store with a long series of experiments.

Q 934 Didn't they use a computer simulation in that book put out by the Club of Rome . . . I think it was called *The Limits to Growth?*

A   Right. A simulation of world resources, populations, economies. They ran their program with a number of differing parameter values (corresponding to differing assumptions about natural resources, governmental actions, population pressures, etc.) to see what effect different governmental policies might have. They used computer simulation to study different possible world futures.

Q 935 They were simulating the whole world! It must have been a huge program.

A   Obviously they had to make a large number of simplifying assumptions. And predictably, they ran into a lot of criticism because of some of their assumptions. A few critics wrote their own simulations, making different assumptions, and a few of those got markedly differing results. The question is of some relevance — are we (our society) going to make it for another hundred years, or will dwindling natural resources, coupled with population pressures, do us in?

Q 936 But is it too big to run on a home computer?

A   Their simulation program? No, you could do that. In fact, I have it from a reliable source (heh, heh) that within a

year, you'll be able to buy a Basic program that implements the same model as the one they used in *The Limits to Growth.*
That should put some life into arguments about planning for the future! Just imagine the effect on local politics if computer hobbyists start using sophisticated simulations to inform people about the probable effects of specific governmental policies . . .

Q 937 How do you go about making a simulation program?

A   Well, there are two main types of simulations. For both, you have to start (obviously) with some solid facts about the system you want to simulate.
One type is called an **aggregated** model. You come up with a set of mathematical equations that describe the relationships among variables which represent properties of the system.

Q 938 That's not really telling me very much . . . can't . . .

A   I know. Remember the drag race program?

Q   Yes.

A   OK. Our main concern there wasn't in getting a perfectly accurate simulation, but all the *ideas* about creating a simulation are there. We came up with a set of equations that describes how the properties we called *torque output, engine speed, position, speed* of the truck, etc. are interrelated. We took all the complexities of pistons moving up and down, cams moving valves, spark plugs firing, etc., etc., and lumped everything into a single variable we called ''engine speed''. We aggregated the behavior of all the individual parts of the engine into that one variable. Our equations dealt with the relationships among *properties* of the system.

Q 939 So? What else could you do?

A   Well, right. That was the most reasonable choice for what we were doing. But in other situations, another kind of model (simulation) is better — a **structural** model. In a structural simulation, you're concerned with how the actual parts of the system interact, and the properties of the system follow from that.

Q 940 Can you say that in English? I . . .

A   Well, I guess there's no point in making a big deal of this . . . but . . .
Engine speed is a *property* of the system, right? You can't walk up to an engine and touch its speed. But an engine does have pistons, and valves, . . . A structural simulation would have parts dealing with each physical subsystem. And by counting how often the simulated pistons go up

and down, your program could figure out the simulated engine speed.

Q 941 All right. But we're supposedly talking about things you can do with a home computer. Let's not drift off into the metaphysics of simulations.

I guess you're saying that you *can* do a lot of different kinds of simulations with a home computer. Right?

A Right. And a lot of the things people call computer games *are* simulations. *Crude* simulations, to be sure, with little attention paid to the details, and with no effort made to establish their veracity, but the basic techniques of computer simulation are there for you to study . . .

Organization

Q 942 **Organization.** What did you mean by that?

A I mentioned that **scientific computing** was one of the two main types of commercial computing. The other is **business data processing,** which I'm including in this category. It means keeping records, maintaining files of information . . . The possibilities are endless — your personal finances, a record of your stamp collection, club membership rosters, mailing lists, store inventories, on and on . . .

Q 943 Your very own data bank.

But won't you need a disc to do any kind of extensive record keeping?

A That depends on how big your ''data bank'' is, and how patient you are.

Q 944 How *patient* you are?

A Right. If you take care in designing your programs, you can maintain a fairly substantial amount of information on cassette tapes. If you're not careful, though, you'll spend all your time waiting for tapes to be read in and out.

Q 945 Come on. What does ''fairly substantial'' mean?

A Let's work out some estimates.

Suppose you're keeping club membership records. You need to store each person's name and address. That takes something like 70 bytes per person, on the average (remember, it takes one byte to store each character). Then you'll need to store other things like . . . oh, if their dues are paid, when they first became a member, whether they want to be on the junk mailing list, a sentence or two describing their system, their area of expertise, things like that. You're probably talking about 200 bytes per record, on the average.

Q 946 Not counting the programs you need to access the records, right?

A Right, right.

Now let's suppose you have 8K of memory that you can use for storing records at any one time. That would mean you probably have 16K or so in all. Probably about 8K of that will be used up by the Basic interpreter, and your file manipulation program.

Q 947 So you're assuming that it'll be done in Basic. Is that a good assumption?

A The programming will be much easier if you have a version of Extended Basic with strings. One that lets you store strings in arrays. [And easier still with the file manipulation extension.]

Q 948 Do all Extended Basics with strings let you do that?

A Some do, some don't. Altair 8K Basic and Extended Basic both do. You'll have to check other Extended Basics to make sure. Of course you can do the same things in assembly language, but you'll need a detailed knowledge of programming to pull it off. OK. Where were we? If you have 8K available for storing records, and each record takes about 200 bytes, you can fit about 40 records in memory at once. All the others will have to be on tape, organized in chunks (typically called **files**) of no more than 40 records each.

Q 949 How many files will fit on one tape?

A Quite a few, but I find it easier to have a lot of tapes with just a few things on each. Cassette tapes are cheap. Assuming you're using a Kansas City Standard tape system, that means it'll take about, oh, about 5 minutes to read in a file, to read in 8K of records.

Q 950 So that's what you meant about being patient. Five minutes doesn't seem like a very long time.

A But that's five minutes *per file*.

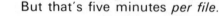

a record consists of a number of fields
a file consists of a number of records
a library consists of a number of files

Figure 109 File organization terminology

Imagine you had a month's worth of updating to do. New members to add, mistakes in old members' data to correct, recent dues payments to record, . . . You'd read in the first tape (5 minutes approx.), type in a few commands to update the data on that file, then since you'd changed the file, you'd have to make a new copy back onto the tape (5 minutes), then read in the next tape file (5 minutes), type for a little while, wait while it was copied out (5 minutes), etc. Again, it depends on how patient you are, but I'd guess that you wouldn't put up with it if you had more than a thousand members in your club . . . you'd start cursing at the tape recorder, trying to make it go faster . . .

Q 951 So why do it at all? Why not just get a disc . . . I know why not — money.

A   Right. The scheme we've been talking about is dirt cheap. And it's very convenient, simple to use, great for situations where you don't have a voluminous amount of data.

Q 952 What's the basic idea behind dealing with data banks? I mean, what does the program have to do?
[Editor's note: A description of this data organization scheme and a Basic program which implements it appear in "The Soft Art of Programming, Part III", in the December, 1976 issue of 73 Magazine, p.92-97]

A   Assuming you're using a version of Extended Basic that lets you have arrays which contain string values, here's what you do. You declare an array for each field you want in your records. Say, an array called N$ for member names, one called A$ for addresses, one called D$ for the dues expiration information, and so on. [A dollar sign after a Basic memory cell name denotes that it holds string values rather than numbers.] Then, the memory cells in each array with the same subscript value form a **record.**

Q 953 What? What's that mean?

A   Here. Let me write some statements that'll fill in a record. Suppose we've declared the arrays. Then, to fill the information in record number 3, for example, you'd do something like this.

```
LET N$(3)="KINSTLER, MARGARET M."
LET A$(3)="2023 RIVER VIEW DR., CAPITOLA, CA 95031"
LET D$(3)="PAID UNTIL JAN 1977"
```

And so on. You can imagine that we've lined the arrays up side by side, with a given row corresponding to a specific record.

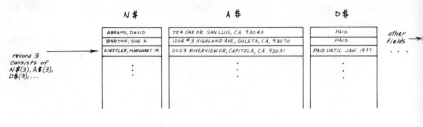

*Figure 110   A **record** consists of the array elements with the same subscript*

Q 954 Ah. I see. The picture helped.
And then to find a particular record . . .

A   Here's a crude way to find a particular member's record. [Editor's note: If the records are maintained in alphabetical order, there is a more efficient search procedure. See "The Soft Art of Programming," *ibid.*]

```
1000   REM :SEARCH FOR MEMBER "M$".
1010   LET S=0
1020   IF N$(S)=M$ THEN 1100
1030   LET S=S + 1
1040   REM :THERE ARE "NO" RECORDS IN THE WHOLE FILE.
1050   IF S < =NO THEN 1020
1060   REM :GET HERE IF "M$" DOESN'T APPEAR IN THIS FILE.
1070   PRINT M$; "ISN'T HERE."
                    •
                    •
                    •

1100   REM :FOUND IT, IT'S RECORD NUMBER "S".
1110   PRINT "RECORD";S
1120   PRINT N$(S)
1130   PRINT A$(S)
1140   PRINT D$(S)
                    •
                    •
                    •
```

Q 955 So in summary, then, keeping records is something you can do with home computers, but if you have a huge amount of data, you need some kind of storage device that's faster than cassette tapes. Right?

A   Right. Maybe I should let you do more of the talking Seems like it took me a long time to say what you jus said in one sentence.

Recreation

Q 956 All right. Your last category was **recreation**. That means games, right?

A   Basically. Although, depending on your personality, you might find almost any aspect of home computing recreational — *I* find all of it fun, even writing about it.

Q 957 Sometimes I get the feeling that most people just play *games* on their home computers. You see ads for programs — and most of them are game programs. A lot of the programs you see in some of the magazines are games, there are books of game programs . . .

A   I don't know whether you're just an old grouch . . . or if you're missing something here. Certainly, playing games on a computer is just one tiny aspect of what you can do. I hope I've gotten that across to you.

Besides being fun in and of themselves, computer games provide tremendous opportunities for learning. A surprising number of people have a fear of computers. They think that computers are some kind of incredibly complex, awesome, de-humanizing monsters. Possibly some member of your own immediate family feels that way. (Don't ask them — no one would admit it.) But if you take someone like that and sit them down at a terminal, and start them playing an interesting game, an amazing change happens. Once they get involved with the *game,* they seem to forget they're sitting in front of a (shudder) computer and their preconceived notions about computers seem to just fade away, then they start wondering what else they can . . .

Q 958 But I'm past that stage.

A   But are all your friends?

Anyway, as I said before, playing around with game programs, making changes to them, making them more elaborate, easier to use, etc. is a good way to start learning to program. And writing your own game programs is a fast way to pick up programming skills. And if you're still not convinced — writing really good game programs is a way to pick up a little extra cash. Somebody must want games or you wouldn't see all the ads you were talking about.

Q 959 Can you play games like Pong and Tank on a home computer? You must need some kind of special equipment, right?

A   You'd need a couple of joysticks for input, plus some form of analog-to-digital converter to sense their position, obviously you need some way to display patterns on a TV screen, and you need a program to control the game, keep score, and move the "ball" around. If you remember a little mechanics from your high school physics class, it shouldn't be too hard to figure out how to do Pong — and a lot of variations.

By the way, you don't need a whole home computer — you can buy a single IC chip that'll do the job. [See "Look What My Daddy Built", 73 magazine, October, 1976, p.104-108]

Q 960 You'd have to write the program in assembly language, right? So it would run fast enough to keep the TV display moving?

A Right.

We've touched on the major categories on applications. There's no sense in going on all day on what you can do with a home computer — the magazines are a good source of ideas and techniques. For balance, why don't I tell you some things you *can't* do with . . .

Q 961 Wait a minute. I still don't see why you don't include **education** as an application. Don't they use computers in schools these days for something besides keeping records?

Different approaches to the applications

A Sure, but what they do fits in the categories we've already gone over. As I said earlier, you can do any of the six different types of application from (at least) three different approaches. You can do them for your personal use and pleasure, you can do them to learn about or teach particular subjects; you can do them to make a profit.

Pick a category. Any category.

Q 962 How about the one you called **organization?**

A OK. You could use a file keeping program yourself — to keep your income tax records, to keep records for a club you belong to, etc.

You could use the program to teach people how data banks work, to give them a better understanding of who's to blame for the abuses of privacy we read about in the papers.

Q 963 And I suppose it would be educational for me to try to get the program working . . .

A Well, that's true of every aspect of computing . . .

A third way you could use the program would be to make

money. You could keep records for small business establishments, print mailing lists for people, on and on.

Some things computers can't do

Q 964 All right. That makes sense.
When you said "things computers can't do", what were you talking about? Do you mean there are some problems that are so hard you can't do them on a home computer?
A   No. There are some things that no computer can do, no matter how big. Not now, and (apparently) never.
Q 965 All right. I'll bite. What?
A   You don't have to look very far. See the TV screen there? The interface I have on my system organizes the display into 16 lines of up to 32 characters per line. Right?
Q   So?
A   So imagine that we hit on the clever idea of generating works of art by having the computer display all the possible combinations of light and dark squares.
Q 966 What do you mean? Have it put out random patterns of light and dark squares? Where would that get us?
A   Not random patterns. Each of the $16 \times 32 = 512$ character positions can be black or white. Start with the picture that consists of all white squares, then display the picture with one black square in the upper left hand corner . . . go through all the possible pictures in order, and pick out the ones we like. A lot of them will be crummy and meaningless, but some of them will be great works of art.
Get the idea?
Q 967 Yes. Seems like a simple idea. It might get boring . . .
A   No computer could do that.
Q 968 Why not? I'm pretty sure I could write the program. What are you talking about?
A   Let's figure out how many possible patterns there are. There are 512 different positions, and each one can be either black or white, so there's

2 possibilities for the first position
4 possibilities for the first two positions
8 possibilities for the first three positions
•
•
•
2^n possibilities for the first n positions

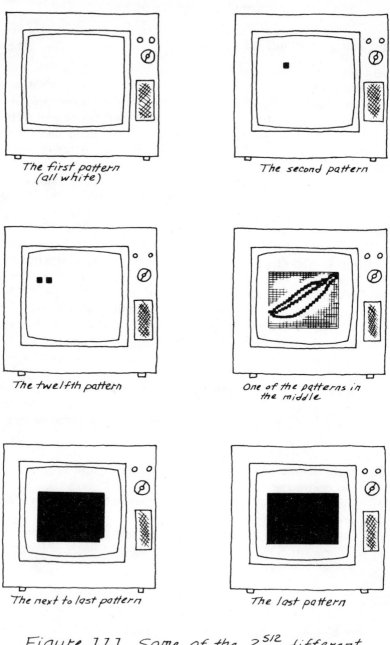

The first pattern
(all white)

The second pattern

The twelfth pattern

One of the patterns in
the middle

The next to last pattern

The last pattern

Figure 111   Some of the 2^{512} different
patterns of light and dark squares
(16 lines, 32 characters per line)

·
·
·

2^{512} possibilities for the whole TV screen.

Q 969 2^{512} doesn't really mean very much to me — I gather that it's a large number. What would that be in powers of 10?

A Here's a trick you can use. To convert a power of 2 to the equivalent power of 10, multiply by .3 (that's close to log1 (2)). Doing that, we get

$$2^{512} = 10^{512 \times 0.3} \simeq 10^{154}$$

So, there are about 10^{154} different pictures to cycle through.

Q 970 That's quite a few, I'm sure . . . but how big *is* it?

A To see, let's figure out how long it would take to display all of them.

Let's be super generous, and imagine that some computer in the future was capable of generating one picture each thousandth of a microsecond (i.e. each nanosecond). Then . . .

Q 971 What use would *that* be? You couldn't see them to choose the good ones. They'd go by too fast.

A You *would* think of that.

If you have to go slower, it just makes things worse. I was trying to be as optimistic as possible . . . Bear with me a minute. Using my assumption, it would take 10^{154} nanoseconds to go through all of them

Q 972 How many hours is that?

A I think I'd better figure it out in centuries.

$$10^{154} \, nanoseconds \times \frac{1 \, second}{10^9 \, nanoseconds} \times \frac{1 \, minute}{60 \, seconds} \times \frac{1 \, hour}{60 \, minutes} \times \frac{1 \, day}{24 \, hours} \times \frac{1 \, year}{365 \, days}$$

$$\times \frac{1 \, century}{100 \, years} \simeq 3 \times 10^{135} \, centuries$$

Q 973 Wow.

A The age of the universe is *nothing* compared to that.

It's really fascinating that such a simple seeming problem is so huge. As you said, it's easy to write the program for it, but it's totally impossible for a computer to carry it out. So this is one sort of thing that computers can't do . . . Some problems involve an exponential growth in the number of alternatives, and you won't be able to solve them by blindly trying out all the possibilities.

Q 974 But are there any practical situations when that happens? I mean, nobody is going to draw pictures by making all possible random scribbles and throwing away the bad ones.

A   You say that now, but you didn't seem to think it was such a bad idea before . . .

But, your question. Well, let's see. Any time you're trying to find the optimal way to do something you run the risk of finding yourself in the exponential growth situation. It comes up in game playing programs.

Q 975 In computer games?

A   No, I mean in programs that play games themselves. Suppose you want to write a program that plays chess. If it weren't for the problem we've been talking about, it would be simple to write an unbeatable chess playing program. When it was the program's turn to move, you'd just have it look over all the possible consequences of every move it could make, and choose one that would lead to a win.

Q 976 But you couldn't do that because there are too many possibilities, is that it?

A   Right. On the average, there might be 20 legal moves from a given position. Then, for each of those, 20 legal replies (that's 400 possibilities so far); for each of those, 20 counter replies (8000 possibilities for three moves); 20 replies to each of those (160 000); on and on.

Q 977 But people do have chess playing programs, right? How do they work?

A   Obviously they have to make do with limited lookahead. The programs have to have some way of dealing with high-level strategies, with *types* of attacks and defenses instead of exploring every detail of every possible move. It's a hard problem.

Q 978 How well do chess programs play?

A   The best ones could clobber you or me. And the best human chess players can clobber the best programs. If you're really interested in chess playing programs, skim through some back issues of the SIGART Newsletter [see Bibliography]. They have reports on computer chess tournaments. Oh! You might watch the newspapers — a grandmaster chess player [D.N.L. Levy] has a rather large bet with several artificial intelligence researchers [D. Michie, J. McCarthy, and (?) A. Newell] that no computer program will be able to beat him, playing under tournament rules. I think the bet was made in 1968, and included the phrase "within 10 years".

Q 979 From what *you're* saying, the computer won't stand a chance.

A   Who knows? A group of people in Boston is building a special purpose computer to help with lookahead . . . That may even things up. We'll know soon.

Q 980 You said there were other things computers can't do. What were you thinking of? More things like this?

A   No. The other thing I was thinking of is pretty theoretical. The exponential growth, **combinatorial explosion** problem is one you'll probably bump up against some time or other in your programming life. The one I'll tell you about now isn't likely to occur to you (at least not in its pure form), but it's still really interesting.

Q 981 All right. But what is it?

A   It's the so-called **halting problem.**
Remember the first thing I said when you asked me what you can really do with a home computer?

Q 982 You said "anything you can compute" or something silly like that.

A   What I said was, "anything that's computable". People have made (rather technical) studies of what sorts of problems are and aren't **computable.**
A problem is **computable** if you can write a finite list of precise instructions that tell, in detail, how to solve it. That is, if you can write a program that solves it. You can't do that for every problem you come across.

Q 983 So? You already showed me a problem you can't solve — the TV screen thing.

A   I didn't prove that you can't write a program for it — in fact you *can.* I showed that no computer could carry out such a program in a reasonable length of time. That's a different question.

Q 984 You still can't do it . . . It sounds like a pretty fine distinction.

Q   Here's the distinction. If you can't solve a problem because it would take an impractical amount of computer time to run the program, you can still have a hope that someday it *will* become practical. Who knows how fast computers will be in ten years? In a hundred years? In a thousand years?
On the other hand, if you're dealing with a problem that you can't write a program to solve, one that's not computable, then that's it. You'll *never* be able to do it, no matter *how* fast computers get. The **halting problem** is the most famous noncomputable problem. Let me try to explain it. First, you'll agree that some programs run for a while and

then stop, and others go on forever, right?

Q 985 How could I agree with that? Obviously no program has ever gone on for*ever.*

A OK. What I mean is, some programs say to do things that can never be completed. Surely you agree that this program would go on forever if you didn't interrupt it in some way.

```
10 REM :A SHORT PROGRAM THAT TAKES A LONG TIME TO RUN.
20 GO TO 20
```

Q 986 Is that a legal program?

A Sure. It's a perfectly legal Basic program. It's also the tightest possible infinite loop. In machine language you could write it with one instruction, a JMP to itself.

Now on the other hand, I'm sure you'll agree that *this* program will stop after a while.

```
10 REM :A SHORT PROGRAM THAT TAKES A SHORT TIME TO RUN.
20 STOP
```

Q 987 Those are pretty weird programs . . .

A Well, in between those two extremes, there are all kinds of programs that take different lengths of time to run, but each specific program, running on specific data values, either goes on forever or else it eventually stops.

Q 988 Why did you suddenly throw in ''running on specific data''?

A Here. Look at this program. You have to know what data value it gets to know whether it'll stop or not.

```
11 REM :IT STOPS, NOBODY KNOWS.
20 INPUT A
30 IF A < 0 THEN 30
40 STOP
```

Q 989 All right, I'll buy that. But what's the **halting problem?** Telling whether a program is going to stop, or something like that?

A Right. Let me state it this way.

Imagine we have a program called the **halting tester.** It takes two things as data. It takes a program listing, and it takes the data you plan to use with the program. The halting tester chews away on those two inputs for a while, and then prints out one of two things. Either it says ''THIS PROGRAM RUNNING ON THIS DATA WILL STOP'', or else it says ''WON'T EVER STOP''.

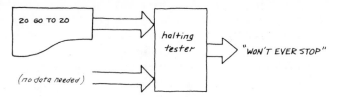

The halting tester decides that the first program would never stop if someone had the misfortune to start it going.

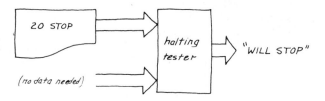

The halting tester decides that the second program will stop.

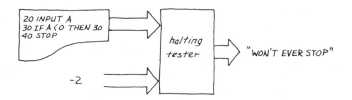

The halting tester decides that the third program, running with the data value -2 won't ever stop.

Figure 112 Using the halting tester program.

Got the idea?

Q 990 I don't really see how we're going to write the halting tester program, but I see what it's supposed to do all right.

A   Well, that's what I'm getting at. You *can't* write a program for the halting tester. It's not a **computable function.** Even though we can describe what we want it to do, there's no computer program that can do it.

Q 991 How do you know that?

A   I don't think I should go over the proof right now, but I'll try to make it sound reasonable . . . [Editor's note: A proof appears as Appendix — Halting Problem.]
        The most obvious way to see if a program is going to stop is to start it running and watch what it does. Some

programs will stop right away, some will enter loops with no way out, and those you can decide about pretty easily. But others will compute away here, and then go into another loop for a while, then jump over there — just be so complex that you can't really foretell what's going to happen. But the halting tester can't just run a program and wait to see what happens, it has to be able to figure out what any program will do without running it.

Q 992 Why's that?

A   Think about it a minute. If the halting tester had to *run* a program to see if it would stop or not, how could it ever decide that a given program won't stop? Just because a particular program has kept going for a week doesn't mean it isn't going to stop eventually. And just because a program has kept running for a thousand years doesn't mean it won't stop the very next second. And if you can tell what a program's going to do without running it, what *use* would it . . .

Q 993 One last question about this, and then I want to ask a few more things before it starts to get dark.
        Am I right that this idea of **computable** and **noncomputable** isn't something that'll concern me when I'm writing my own programs?

A   Uh, right. All you care about when you're programming is the practical side of it. If a program won't solve your problem in a reasonable length of time, then it's worthless to you, so who cares if it will stop in a thousand years as opposed to going on forever.
        What were your other questions? Fire away.

Q 994 All right. I thought of this one when you were talking about chess playing programs [Q 975]. I wasn't going to ask it because I thought it was a little weird.

A   But I've broken the weirdness barrier, hunh?

Q   You said it, not me.
        When I was a little kid, I heard someone say that computers were going to be the world chess champions because even though they didn't play very well yet, they kept learning from their mistakes and they'd just keep getting better until no one could beat them.

A   What's the question? Did people say that?

Q 995 No, is it *true?*

A   It hasn't happened yet. And anyway, they were probably basing their speculations on a program that played checkers, because . . .
        [Editor's note: A appears to be referring to Arthur Samuel's checkers playing program which improved its performance

by using several experimental forms of machine learning. See Samuel's article in *Computers and Thought* (Bibliography).]

Q 996 Do you think something like that *could* happen?

A   The way I think people mean it when they say things like that, no, I don't. In the early days of computing (and I suppose these are *still* the early days of computing), there was a lot of mystery around computers. People would go to computer demonstrations without knowing what they were seeing. They'd see a computer flawlessly multiplying huge numbers together, they'd remember how hard it was to learn to multiply when they were in grade school, and jump to the assumption that the computer could do *any*thing of that complexity. The general populace seemed willing to think that computers were magic. There's *still* a tendency toward that. Pocket calculators have taken the thrill out of machines doing arithmetic, but try running this program for someone who doesn't know anything about computers and see what their reaction is.

```
1Ø     REM : SNOWJOB PROGRAM
2Ø     REM : AN EXAMPLE OF IRRESPONSIBILITY.
3Ø     PRINT "HI.  MY NAME IS HAL.  WHAT'S YOUR NAME";
4Ø     INPUT A$
5Ø     PRINT "GLAD TO MEET YOU ";A$; ".  HOW ARE YOU TODAY";
6Ø     INPUT B$
7Ø     PRINT "THAT'S NICE.  SAY--HOW DO YOU FEEL ABOUT THE"
8Ø     PRINT "FORCED BUSSING OF CHILDREN TO ACHIEVE RACIAL"
9Ø     PRINT "EQUALITY";
1ØØ    INPUT B$
11Ø    PRINT "I CAN UNDERSTAND THAT.  I HAVE A LOT OF"
12Ø    PRINT "THOSE SAME KINDS OF FEELING TOO.  YOU KNOW,"
13Ø    PRINT "I . . . OOOPS . . . SORRY--I'D LIKE TO CONTINUE OUR"
14Ø    PRINT "CONVERSATION, BUT I'M SUDDENLY HAVING PROBLEMS"
15Ø    PRINT "WITH MY VEEBELFRITZER CIRCUITS--I'LL HAVE TO GET"
16Ø    PRINT "BACK TO YOU LATER."
17Ø    PRINT "GOODBYE,";A$
18Ø    END
                        SAMPLE RUN #1
RUN

HI.  MY NAME IS HAL.  WHAT'S YOUR NAME?  q
GLAD TO MEET YOU, Q.  HOW ARE YOU TODAY? Super
THAT'S NICE.  SAY--HOW DO YOU FEEL ABOUT THE
FORCED BUSSING OF CHILDREN TO ACHIEVE RACIAL
EQUALITY? I think it's unpopular politically.
I CAN UNDERSTAND THAT.  I HAVE A LOT OF
THOSE SAME KINDS OF FEELING TOO.  YOU KNOW,
I . . . OOOPS . . . SORRY--I'D LIKE TO CONTINUE OUR
CONVERSATION, BUT I'M SUDDENLY HAVING PROBLEMS
WITH MY VEEBELFRITZER CIRCUITS--I'LL HAVE TO GET
BACK TO YOU LATER.
GOODBYE, Q.

READY
```

Figure 113. Snowjob

Q 997 Surely the people who work on chess playing programs aren't that naive.

A   Of course not. I'm not saying they are. I'm just saying that there are a lot of popular misconceptions about what you can do with computers. You can't start with a bunch of random statements and expect a computer program to muddle around changing things until it learns to do a complicated task. The thing we went through about how many different visual patterns can be on the TV screen [Fig. 111] should tell you why.

Q 998 Too many possibilities. I guess then . . .

A   The people who are trying to write programs to do really sophisticated things like play a good game of chess, understand English sentences (in specific, fairly narrow, contexts), move robot vehicles around in the world, etc. [see Bibliography listings concerning **artificial intelligence**] proceed by trying to gain a deep understanding of the *task,* not by tossing together a huge conglomeration of weird data structures, incorporating some way of changing the connectivities, and "feeding in all the data they can find on the subject" (or whatever it is they say in the movies). The stuff you hear like "and then we fed all the data into the computer and let it make the decision with its lightning fast speed and unimaginable complexity" is hogwash, as my grandpa used to say.

        But before I get carried away here, I want to make some things clear.

        First, just because no one's done it yet doesn't mean it can't be done. There's no obvious reason to think that someday there won't be championship level chess playing programs, programs that make skilled medical diagnoses, computerized chauffeurs, computer programs that can have intelligent conversations with people, etc. . . . someday. Second, programs for these sorts of applications exist in crude forms right now, and a group of computer hobbyists could get together, study what's been done, what's been tried and found wanting, add a lot of time, energy, and creativity and work as a team to produce some really science fiction-like programs. Even if you don't invent the first intelligent program, it'll by a lot of fun trying. Third . . .

Q 999 Is it . . . oh. You're still on your rampage. Go on, get it out of your system.

A   Third, these sorts of problems are turning out to be harder than people imagined at first. In the fifties, there was a tremendous amount of excitement about **machine trans-**

lation. The government spent a lot of money on research they hoped would lead to computer programs that could translate, say, Russian research papers into English. It turned out to be a *much* harder problem than anticipated, and even now it appears that much of the basic research needed to do a good job of translating natural language text is yet to be done. It's very unlikely that we'll see anything that people will agree is intelligent behavior by a computer program for decades. Even if a breakthrough does occur in the near future, we might not see it for quite a while, I'd guess.

Q 1000 What? Why not?

A   Most of the funds used for artificial intell . . . Well, let's just say that the first robots you hear of will be flying fighter planes and driving tanks.

Q 1001 You sound a little paranoid to me.

A   OK. Let's skip it. Any other esoteric questions?

Are computers like brains?

1002 Are computers anything like brains? You used to hear things about that.

         The most obvious thing in common is that both are information processors, both manipulate symbols. I don't know what to tell you. We could go into it in detail if you want—it's something I've been deeply interested in for a long time.

1003 The brain?

         Well, developing information processing models of specific parts of brains.

         It's an interesting thing. Nervous systems are so complex that a comprehensive, simple explanation of how they "work" has eluded science so far. It's as if we're still searching for the right way to look at the brain. In the hopes of stumbling onto the key to the puzzle, people use new technologies as metaphors for the function of the brain. Fifty to a hundred years ago, people were comparing the brain to a giant telephone switchboard. For the last thirty years or so, people have used computers as metaphors, and in the last ten, some have tried to show that (in some ways) the brain organizes information in a way similar to the way holograms are made.

         So, if you'll keep in mind that brains are one thing, and computers another, that I'm just speaking metaphorically, I'll try to answer what I think you're asking.

1004 All right. Tell me how computers *aren't* like brains if you'd rather but stop the sermonizing.

A   *Ser*monizing! Look—I'm getting a little tired of you always jumping on everything I say. Here I am doing my best to explain things and you're always going "nyah—I don't care about that, tell me about this." How am I supposed to think straight if you keep us rushing all the time?

Q1004   Calm down, calm down.
        We're almost done, so let's not blow it now.
        Besides, *some*body's got to keep you on the subject.

A   OK . . . OK.
        The main organizational difference between present day computers and brains is the degree to which each works in parallel.

Q1005   But computers work faster than brains, don't they?

A   Wait a minute, I'll get to that.
        It's commonly estimated that there are some ten billion nerve cells in the human brain, each of which may have ten, or even a hundred, thousand connections to other nerve cells. OK? Now here's what I meant about brains functioning more in parallel than current computers. Each nerve cell is capable of "computing" some function of the "values" it receives from other nerve cells, and all ten billion of them are "computing" all the time—in parallel. Now that's not to say that each nerve cell fuctions independently—to some extent there is a squential nature to the flow of information through the brain. But the general theme is one of cooperative parallel processing—of **distributed information processing.** [See *Brain Theory Newsletter* in Bibliography.]
        I think a more reasonable comparison is between individual nerve cells and current day computers, rather than between a whole brain and a computer.

Q1006   But an individual nerve cell can't do anything by itself, can it?
        And computers can do all sorts of things. And computers are faster, aren't they?

A   I didn't say it was a *good* comparison, I just said it was more reasonable.
        Computers *can* process information a lot faster than individual nerve cells, and computers can probably compute more complex functions than individual nerve cells. That is, a computer is (probably) a more general information processor than an individual nerve cell. But when you hook ten billion of them together, you get . . . well, you know what our brains can do.

Q1007   So all you'd have to do to make an intelligent computer would be to hook together a few million microprocessors.

A   You're kidding, right?

Q1008   Well, that's the main idea, isn't it? A huge number of information processors working in parallel?

A   If that's all it took, the telephone system in New York City would have become intelligent a long time ago.

The real question is how the brain is organized, what each region computes, how it's coordinated, not how many nerve cells there are in it or how fast they run. How on earth would you program your million microprocessor monster?

Q1009   All right, all right.

I take it from all this that you don't think general purpose intelligent robots will be on the market next week?

A   Of course not.

Q   All right. Let's shift to something that's more int . . ., er, more directly related to home computing.

The Swami speaks

Q1010   What's on the horizon?

A   How should I know?

Q1011   You must have some opinion. Look, I'm sorry if I hurt your feelings. Actually, I thought what you were saying about brains was very interesting, it just isn't directly relevant.

Why don't you make some predictions?

Let me ask you some specifics then, if you can't think of anything to say.

Will one microprocessor become dominant so everybody can share programs and other pieces of hardware and stuff easily?

A   Nah.

Q1012   Will one language become dominant? Maybe Basic?

A   Unh uh. No way.

Q1013   Is the home computer movement a fad to some extent?

A   A fad?

If you want to call anything that gains popularity rapidly a **fad,** maybe so.

Q1014   But if it's a fad, it'll lose popularity just as fast as it gained it. Do you think that's going to happen?

A   No. I think as more and more people get into home computing, we'll discover more and more things computers are useful for, and the more things we find to do with them, the more people will get into it . . .

Q1015   The infinite loop theory of home computing, eh?

A   Heh, yeh.

Here. I'll try to make a few predictions if that's what you want. Prediction 1: We will continue to be amazed at the ability of the electronics industry to provide a seemingly endless flow of new products. The cost and size of the basic electronic constituents will continue to decline, and the speed and storage capacities will continue to increase. Advances in i/o devices will be slower, but even there we'll see breakthroughs.

Q1016   Any predictions about specific products?

A   How about a cheap, indestructable keyboard with no moving parts?

Q1017   Wait a minute. How could you have a keyboard with no moving parts?

A   Haven't you ever seen those elevators with buttons that don't move? That you set off just by bringing your finger close? I leave the rest to your imagination.

Q1018   Come on, that's ridiculous. If you put your fingers over the keys to get ready to type, ''asdfjkl;'' would all print at once!

A   Don't bother me with details, I'm pre*dic*ting.

Prediction 2: The spread of computing into our everyday lives will have a dramatic, lasting, long term effect on our society. For instance. Think of the role played by the automobile in our economy. Automotive related industries form the backbone of it, right now.

As long as I'm predicting, I'll predict that in the long run, computers and the computing industry will displace automobiles from their current position of economic dominance.

Q1019   The Swami speaks.

A   Consider: computers are of potential use to every sector of the society. But that doesn't mean that the market for computers is just everybody in the country—computers keep getting *better,* which means that computers can be sold to people who *already have one.* (The automotive industry solves this basic marketing problem by having their products break down after a while.)

Computers keep getting *smaller,* which means that as time goes on, the amount of raw materials used by the industry may actually *decline,* even as the total number of computers sold increases. And, of course, the software industry may be able to sell programs over the phone, thereby saving even more raw mat . . .

Q1020   Maybe that's not as wacky as it sounds at first . . . I never thought of it that way—computers don't use gasoline.

A   There will be both positive and negative effects.
        As people come to depend on their computers for more
        and more things, our society will become even more
        fragile. Electrical power failures will become even more
        disruptive than they are now.
        And there will be changes in human values.
Q   I can't believe this! A minute ago you were just grunting
        "no" to everything I asked you. Now you're . . .
A   Think about it. When a new machine comes along that
        can do something we're used to thinking of as a human
        job, the ultimate response is to deny that that ability has
        much to do with being human. I'd imagine that before
        the development of writing, people assumed that remem-
        bering things was a basic, important part of being human.
        They called the Colt 44 the "Equalizer" because it elimi-
        nated the thing that made some people "better" than
        others, namely their hand-to-hand fighting skills. Physical
        strength was no longer the "measure of a man".
        I'll bet you're wondering what this has to do with com-
        puters, right?
Q   No, I'm just trying to avoid getting hit by that arm you're
        waving.
A   Here's the idea. Right now we tend to think of "intelli-
        gence" as a uniquely human property, and to reward
        people who use logical thinking to get ahead.
Q1021   So? What's wrong with that?
A   There's nothing *wrong* with it, I just feel we'll find ourselves
        doing that to a lesser extent in the fuzzy, computerized
        future.
        I mean, can't you *feel* what I'm saying?
        What it means to be human will depend less and less
        on the ability to do arithmetic, to think logically (as opposed
        to rationally), and so on.
        When everybody has their own computer, it won't make
        any difference if you can make simple logical deductions
        faster than your competitor—their computer will be their
        IQ Equalizer.
        And as a consequence, other aspects of being human will
        be the ones we value most.
Q1022   That's all very nice, but aren't you getting a little bit ahead
        of things? I mean, computers are hardly ready to do our
        thinking for us. You said yourself . . .
A   It's already starting to happen! When was the last time
        you heard of someone getting a job because they were
        good at arithmetic?
Q1023   You're just saying that in the long run, we'll tend to

At the Crafts Fair, 1992

Figure 114

de-emphasize things computers can do better. Because we won't do them anymore, right?

A   I guess. And we'll put more stock in things we can do but computers can't.

I have two more predictions.

First. If you take the plunge, get a home computer, get it working, struggle to learn all you need to know to use it, learn to program, fight with crummy documentation, endless bugs, glitches, . . .

Q1023 Yes?

A   . . . you won't regret it for even one moment. Really!

And now for my last prediction. It's very precise.

I predict that our many days of long hours sitting here babbling into this Panasonic Portable Cassette Tape Recorder, Model RQ-309DS, serial number EF6 16573, will be over very soon.

Do you have any more questions?

Q1023 No . . . I'm all questioned out.

A   In that case, let's take this previously mentioned tape recorder and hook it back up to the computer, where it belongs.

Q1024 I wonder if this'll be the only one of your predictions that comes tr . . .

APPENDIX A

Powers

Here are some powers of 2, 8, and 16, along with the program that was used to generate them.

RUN POWERS OF? 2

```
 0   1
 1   2
 2   4
 3   8
 4   16
 5   32
 6   64
 7   128
 8   256
 9   512
10   1 024
11   2 048
12   4 096
13   8 192
14   16 384
15   32 768
16   65 536
17   131 072
18   262 144
19   524 288
20   1 048 576
21   2 097 152
22   4 194 304
23   8 388 608
24   16 777 216
25   33 554 432
26   67 108 864
27   134 217 728
28   268 435 456
29   536 870 912
30   1 073 741 824
31   2 147 483 684
32   4 294 967 296
33   8 589 934 592
34   17 179 869 184
35   34 359 738 368
36   68 719 476 736
37   137 438 953 472
38   274 877 906 944
39   549 755 813 888
40   1 099 511 627 776
41   2 199 023 255 552
42   4 398 046 511 104
43   8 796 093 022 208
44   17 592 186 044 416
45   35 184 372 088 832
46   70 368 744 177 664
47   140 737 488 355 328
48   281 474 976 710 656
49   562 949 953 421 312
50   1 125 899 906 842 624
```

```
 0   1
 1   8
 2   64
 3   512
 4   4 096
 5   32 768
 6   262 144
 7   2 097 152
 8   16 777 216
 9   134 217 728
10   1 073 741 824
11   8 589 934 592
12   68 719 476 736
13   549 755 813 888
14   4 398 046 511 104
15   35 184 372 088 832
16   281 474 976 710 656
17   2 251 799 813 685 248
18   18 014 398 509 481 984
19   144 115 188 075 855 872
20   1 152 921 504 606 846 976
21   9 223 372 036 854 775 808
22   73 786 976 294 838 206 464
23   590 295 810 358 705 651 712
24   4 722 366 482 869 645 213 696
25   37 778 931 862 957 161 709 568
26   302 231 454 903 657 293 676 544
27   2 417 851 639 229 258 349 412 352
28   19 342 813 113 834 066 795 298 816
29   154 742 504 910 672 534 362 390 528
30   1 237 940 039 285 380 274 899 124 224
31   9 903 520 314 283 042 199 192 993 792
32   79 228 162 514 264 337 593 543 950 336
33   633 825 300 114 114 700 748 351 602 688
34   5 070 602 400 912 917 605 986 812 821 504
35   40 564 819 207 303 340 847 894 502 572 032
36   324 518 553 658 426 726 783 156 020 576 256
37   2 596 148 429 267 413 814 265 248 164 610 048
38   20 769 187 434 139 310 514 121 985 316 880 384
39   166 153 499 473 114 484 112 975 882 535 043 072
40   1 329 227 995 784 915 872 903 807 060 280 344 576
41   10 633 823 966 279 326 983 230 456 482 242 756 608
42   85 070 591 730 234 615 865 843 651 857 942 052 864
43   680 564 733 841 876 926 926 749 214 863 536 422 912
44   5 444 517 870 735 015 415 413 993 718 908 291 383 296
45   43 556 142 965 880 123 323 311 949 751 266 331 066 368
46   348 449 143 727 040 986 586 495 598 010 130 648 530 944
47   2 787 593 149 816 327 892 691 964 784 081 045 188 247 552
48   22 300 745 198 530 623 141 535 718 272 648 361 505 980 416
```

RUN POWERS OF? 16

```
 0   1
 1   16
 2   256
 3   4 096
 4   65 536
 5   1 048 576
 6   16 777 216
 7   268 435 456
 8   4 294 967 296
 9   68 719 476 736
10   1 099 511 627 776
11   17 592 186 044 416
12   281 474 976 710 656
13   4 503 599 627 370 496
14   72 057 594 037 927 936
15   1 152 921 504 606 846 976
16   18 446 744 073 709 551 616
17   295 147 905 179 352 825 856
18   4 722 366 482 869 645 213 696
19   75 557 863 725 914 323 419 136
20   1 208 925 819 614 629 174 706 176
21   19 342 813 113 834 066 795 298 816
22   309 485 009 821 345 068 724 781 056
23   4 951 760 157 141 521 099 596 496 896
24   79 228 162 514 264 337 593 543 950 336
25   1 267 650 600 228 229 401 496 703 205 376
26   20 282 409 603 651 670 423 947 251 286 016
27   324 518 553 658 426 726 783 156 020 576 256
28   5 192 296 858 534 827 628 530 496 329 220 096
29   83 076 749 736 557 242 056 487 941 267 521 536
30   1 329 227 995 784 915 872 903 807 060 280 344 576
31   21 267 647 932 558 653 966 460 912 964 485 513 216
32   340 282 366 920 938 463 463 374 607 431 768 211 456
33   5 444 517 870 735 015 415 413 993 718 908 291 383 296
34   87 112 285 931 760 246 646 623 899 502 532 662 132 736
35   1 393 796 574 908 163 946 345 982 392 040 522 594 123 776
36   22 300 745 198 530 623 141 535 718 272 648 361 505 980 416
```

LIST

```
 10   REM :GENERATE LOTS OF POWERS OF X.
 20   REM :"X" IS GIVEN BY THE USER.
 30   REM :THE ARRAY "N" STORES LARGE NUMBERS, ONE
 40   REM :DECIMAL DIGIT PER MEMORY CELL.
 50   REM :THE ARRAY "T$" IS USED TO GET PROPER SPACING
 60   REM :WHEN PRINTING THE RESULTS.
 70   REM :"P" IS THE CURRENT POWER OF "X"
 80   REM :"C" IS THE CARRY OUT OF EACH LOCATION.
 90   DIM N (50), T$(9)
100   REM :INITIALIZE.
110   GO SUB 2000
120   PRINT "POWERS OF";
130   INPUT X
140   PRINT
150   PRINT
200   REM :MAIN LOOP. FIRST PRINT LATEST POWER OF "X".
210   GO SUB 3000
220   LET P=P+1
230   REM :NOW MULTIPLY LATEST VALUE BY "X"
240   GOSUB 4000
250   REM :IF CARRY OUT OF LEFT-MOST DIGIT, QUIT. ELSE GO ON.
260   IF C=0 THEN 200
270   STOP

2000  REM :SUBROUTINE TO INITIALIZE RELEVANT VARIABLES.
2010  LET P=0
2020  REM :HANDLE "NO" DIGITS IN ALL.
2030  LET NO=50
2040  REM :START "N" AT 000 . . . 0001
2050  LET N(1)=1
2060  hOR D=2 TO NO
2070     LET N(D)=0
2080     NEXT D
2090  LET C=0
2100  REM :INITIALIZE "T" TO STORE STRING VERSION OF
2110  REM :DIGITS (USED TO GET SPACING RIGHT).
2120  FOR D=0 TO 9
2130     READ T$(D)
2140     NEXT D
2150  DATA "0", "1", "2", "3", "4", "5", "6", "7", "8", "9"
2160  RETURN

3000  REM :SUBROUTINE TO PRINT LARGE NUMBERS
3010  PRINT P,
3020  REM :SKIP LEADING ZEROS.
3030  FOR D=NO TO 1 STEP -1
3040     IF N(D)   0 THEN 3060
3050     NEXT D
3060  REM :PRINT VALUE, LEAVING A BLANK EVERY 3 DIGITS.
3070  LET V$=T$(N(D) )
3080     LET D=D-1
3090     IF D=INT(D/3)*3 THEN 3200
3100     LET V$=V$ + T$(N(D) )
```

```
3110      LET D=D-1
3120      GO TO 3090
3200      REM :GOT A BLOCK OF 3—PRINT 'EM.
3210      PRINT V$ + '' '';
3220      REM :DONE WITH THE WHOLE NUMBER?
3230      IF D > 0 THEN 3060
3240    PRINT
3250    RETURN

4000    REM :SUBROUTINE TO MULTIPLY LARGE NUMBERS BY ''X''
4010    FOR D=1 TO NO
4020      LET N(D)=N(D)   X + C
4030      REM :HAVE A CARRY?
4040      IF N(D) > 9 THEN 4080
4050      REM :NO CARRY—CONTINUE.
4060      LET C=0
4070      GO TO 4110
4080      REM :DO HAVE A CARRY.
4090      LET C=INT(N(D)/10)
4100      LET N(D)=N(D)-C*10
4110      NEXT D
4120    RETURN
10000   END
```

Appendix B

Halting problem [see Q981-993]

It's impossible to write an algorithm which can tell if an arbitrary program will stop.

Proof: This is a proof by contradicition. We begin by supposing that we have been able to write an algorithm (let's call it the *halting tester* and assume it's a Basic subroutine) which takes two parameters (P$, a string which consists of a program listing and D$, a string which tells what data the program P$ is to run on), and returns the value 1 (say in memory cell H) if P$ running on D$ will stop and return 0 if P$ (D$) is an infinite loop. Next we cook up a legitimate program which includes a call to the halting tester subroutine and show that we can specify a specific input to the legitimate program which forces the halting tester to be wrong. Therein lies the contradiction, and the proof that the halting tester subroutine can't exist.

Here's the program we'll use.

```
10 REM: A strange but legitimate program, assuming the halting
11 REM: Tester exists.
20 REM: Input a program listing (assume that we
30 REM: Can have arbitrarily long string values.)
40 INPUT L$
50 REM: The halting tester subroutine starts at
60 REM: Line 5000, takes two parameters —
70 REM: P$ = A program listing
80 REM: D$ = A string containing the data P$ is to run
90 LET P$ = L$
100 LET D$ = L$
110 GOSUB 5000
120 REM: If H=1, P$ running on D$ will stop,
130 REM: But this program won't.
140 IF H=1 then 140
150 REM: If H=0, P$ running on D$ won't stop,
160 REM: But this program will.
170 stop
5000 REM: Halting tester subroutine.
5010 REM: Figures out if P$ (D$) will stop.
1000 End
```

Now we imagine running the above program. We type

RUN

and the program prints a ?, waiting for us to enter a value for L$ (line 40). And here's the catch. Now we type in the above program! Everything from statement 10 through 10000. What we've done is RUN the program, and given it a copy of itself for data. OK so far. Statements 90, 100, and 110 call the halting tester to see what will happen if we run the above program on itself . . . Now look at statement 140.

If the halting tester says that the program will stop, the program goes into an infinite loop. If the halting tester says the program won't stop, the program obediently goes on to statement 170 and stops.

End of proof.

This result may sound discouraging. However, there are ways to tell if many programs (maybe even all the ones of practical use) will stop, so maybe this result should go under the heating

STRANGE BUT TRUE.

APPENDIX C

HOME COMPUTERS
2^{10} Questions and Answers
Volume 1

Contents

Appendix D

Minimal Basic

These are the statement types in Minimal Basic as described in the document "Draft Proposed American National Standard — Programming Language Minimal BASIC", BSRX3.60, X3J2/76-01.

As of this writing (Nov. 12, 1976), this is still a *proposed* standard. The public review period ended Sept. 28, 1976, and the committee (headed by Prof. Thomas E. Kurtz, who, with Prof. John G. Kemeny, invented the original version of Basic) is making a few final changes. The final standard will be fairly close to what's shown here — watch for announcements.

STATEMENTS IN MINIMAL BASIC

as described in the document

Draft Proposed American National Standard Programming Language Minimal BASIC, BSRX3.60, X3J2/76-01

statement	keyword(s)	example	meaning
remark, comment	REM	REM DRAG RACE PROGRAM	Used to describe what's going on in the program. Used by humans reading program lising, contains no commands to the controller.
assignment	LET	LET V = VØ + S*D − 1.3	The value of the expression to the right of the equals sign in computed and then stored in the memory cell named immediately after the LET.
unconditional branch, go to	GO TO	GO TO 10	Transfers control to the statement with the named line number. In this example, statement number 10 will be carried out next. May be written GOTO or GO TO.
conditional branch, if-then	IF, THEN	IF R > 6000 THEN 355	If the condition is met (if the expression between the IF and the THEN is true), transfer control to the named line (355 in the example). Otherwise go on to the next statement.
computed GOTO, case	ON, GOTO	ON P GOTO 200,300,200,350	Transfers control to one of the named statements depending on the value of the expression between the ON and the GOTO. In this example, GOTO 200 if P=1 or 3; GOTO 300 if P=2; GOTO 350 if P=4.
subroutine call, subroutine reference	GO SUB	GOSUB 5000	Transfers control to the subroutine which starts at the given line number.
subroutine return	RETURN	RETURN	Return from subroutine. Transfers control back to the calling program (to the line after the GOSUB that called the subroutine to begin with).
halt, stop, finis	STOP	STOP	Stop running the program. Transfer control back to the Basic system itself.

statement	keyword(s)	example	meaning

counting loop, for loop, do loop	FOR, STEP, TO, NEXT	100 FOR K=∅ TO 8 STEP 2
		110 PRINT "****"
		120 NEXT K
		130 :
			The statements after the FOR up to the NEXT are performed repeatedly as specified in the FOR line. The STEP part is optional. Leaving it out implies a STEP of +1. The example has the same effect as
			  100 LET K=∅
			  101 IF K>8 THEN 13∅
			  110 PRINT "****"
			  119 LET K=K+2
			  120 GOTO 1∅1
			  130 :

input from terminal,	INPUT	INPUT A$,R	Prints a question mark and then stores the value(s) the user types on the terminal in the named memory cell(s).
print, output to terminal	PRINT	PRINT "TIME=";T	Sends the character string(s) and the value(s) of variable(s) to the terminal to be printed. Semicolons and commas affect spacing of the output.

read data stored om program itself	READ, DATA	200 READ A,B,C
		210 DATA ∅,1
		220 DATA 9,74,24
			The READ statement takes successive values from DATA statements and stores those values in the named memory locations. This example has the same effect as
			  200 LET A=∅
			  210 LET B=1
			  220 LET C=9

re-initialization	RESTORE	RESTORE	Makes the next READ statement start with the first value in the first DATA statement. Used when you need to use DATA values over again.
array declaration, dimension	DIM	DIM A(16), B(9)	Establishes the named variables as arrays with the specified number of locations. The example sets up two arrays, one called A, and one called B. A consists of A(∅),A(1),A(2),...,A(16), unless OPTION BASE 1 is in effect. In that case A consists of A(1),A(2),...,A(16).
optional array starting location	OPTION, BASE	OPTION BASE 1	Makes DIM statements begin arrays with the given value (the value may be either ∅ or 1).

statement	keyword(s)	example	meaning
function definition, function reference	DEF	20 DEF FNA(I)=I*I/2.0 100 PRINT FNA(4)	Defines a function which may be referenced elsewhere in the program. Legal function names are FNA, FNB,....,FNZ. Statement 100 will print the value 8.
end	END	END	The last (highest numbered) statement of any program.
initialize the random number generator	RANDOMIZE	RANDOMIZE	Make RND (the random number function) start with an unpredictable value.
relations	= < > <= >= < >	IF A$="YES" THEN 320 IF X<THEN 600 IF R>6000 THEN 355 IF Z<=3 THEN 2010 IF Z+Q>=X-Y THEN 20 IF A$< >"NO" THEN 320	equals less than (*not* defined for strings in Minimal Basic — greater than only=and < > may be used with strings) less than or equal to greater than or equal to not equal to
operations	+,−,*,/,∧	(A+B−C)*2/(I∧2)	* means "multiply", ∧ means "raise to the power". They wanted to have "raise to the power" be ↑, but there's no "up arrow" symbol in the ASCII character set, so "∧" comes close.
built-in functions	ABS ATN COS EXP INT LOG RND SGN SIN SQR TAN	LET B=ABS(X) LET T∅=ATN(1.0) IF COS(X)>3.14159/4.0 THEN 2000 LET P=EXP(1.0) IF INT(N/2)*2=N THEN 4010 LET Z=LOG(Y) LET C=RND PRINT SGN(A) PRINT SIN(X) PRINT SQR(2.) IF TAN(X)<1.0 THEN 160	absolute value. |x| arctangent cosine, argument in radians e to the x. e` largest integer not greater than x. Thus INT(1.4)=1 and INT(−2.7)=−3 natural logarithm random number generator (note that it takes *no* argument). +1 if argument is >0. 0 of argument=0, −1 if argument is negative trigonometric sine, argument in radians square root tangent

APPENDIX E

ASCII Character Set
(American Standard Code for Information Interchange)

7-bit value

(8-th bit chosen to
give even or odd parity)

binary	octal	hex	symbol printed	
0000000	0	0	NULL	
.	.	.	.	
.	.	.	.	non-printing control
.	.	.	.	characters
0011111	37	1F	US	
0100000	40	20	space	
0100001	41	21	!	
0100010	42	22	''	
0100011	43	23	#	
0100100	44	24	$	
0100101	45	25	%	
0100110	46	26	&	
0100111	47	27	'	
0101000	50	28	(	
0101001	51	29	)	
0101010	52	2A	*	
0101011	53	2B	+	
0101100	54	2C	,	
0101101	55	2D	-	
0101110	56	2E	.	
0101111	57	2F	/	
0110000	60	30	0	
0110001	61	31	1	
0110010	62	32	2	
0110011	63	33	3	
0110100	64	34	4	
0110101	65	35	5	
0110110	66	36	6	
0110111	67	37	7	
0111000	70	38	8	
0111001	71	39	9	
0111010	72	3A	:	
0111011	73	3B	;	
0111100	74	3C		
0111101	75	3D	=	
0111110	76	3E	>	
0111111	77	3F	?	
1000000	100	40	@	
1000001	101	41	A	
1000010	102	42	B	
1000011	103	43	C	
1000100	104	44	D	
1000101	105	45	E	
1000110	106	46	F	
1000111	107	47	G	
1001000	110	48	H	

1001001	111	49	I
1001010	112	4A	J
1001011	113	4B	K
1001100	114	4C	L
1001101	115	4D	M
1001110	116	4E	N
1001111	117	4F	O
1010000	120	50	P
1010001	121	51	Q
1010010	122	52	R
1010011	123	53	S
1010100	124	54	T
1010101	125	55	U
1010110	126	56	V
1010111	127	57	W
1011000	130	58	X
1011001	131	59	Y
1011010	132	5A	Z
1011011	133	5B	[
1011100	134	5C	
1011101	135	5D	]
1011110	136	5E	^
1011111	137	5F	_
1100000	140	60	`
1100001	141	61	a
1100010	142	62	b
1100011	143	63	c
1100100	144	64	d
1100101	145	65	e
1100110	146	66	f
1100111	147	67	g
1101000	150	68	h
1101001	151	69	i
1101010	152	6A	j
1101011	153	6B	k
1101100	154	6C	1
1101101	155	6D	m
1101110	156	6E	n
1101111	157	6F	o
1110000	160	70	p
1110001	161	71	q
1110010	162	72	r
1110011	163	73	s
1110100	164	74	t
1110101	165	75	u
1110110	166	76	v
1110111	167	77	w
1111000	170	78	x
1111001	171	79	y
1111010	172	7A	z
1111011	173	7B	
1111100	174	7C	
1111101	175	7D	
1111110	176	7E	
1111111	177	7F	DEL

if a product says it
supplies "64 ASCII
characters", you get these

APPENDIX F

6800 Instruction Set*

The notation used to describe the meaning of each instruction is explained in Q639-646. [Editor's note: Recall that (x) is read "the contents of x".] The architecture of the 6800 is discussed in Q621-625 and Figure 60. Op codes are given in hexadecimal.

The 6800 provides six different memory addressing modes. One of the modes, *relative,* is used only with *branch* instructions. The other addressing modes have the following interpretations:

MOTOROLA name for addressing mode	name used in Table 7 (near Q655)	meaning	length
inherent	register	refers to registers on the 6800 itself. E.g. ASLA which affects accumulator A only, and does not refer to memory.	one byte
immediate	immediate	**effective address = byte**$_2$	two bytes except for CPX, LDS, and LDX which are three bytes long in their *immediate* forms.
direct	bottom page	effective address = $00000000_2 (\text{byte})_2$ i.e. instructions using the *direct* mode can refer to memory locations with addresses in the range 0 to 255_{10} only.	
indexed	indexed	**effective address =** **(index register) + (byte)**$_2$ (byte$_2$) are treated as an unsigned positive value	two bytes
extended	direct	**effective address =** **(byte)**$_2$**(byte)**$_3$	three bytes

*Thanks to MOTOROLA Semiconductor Products, Inc. for permission to include this material.

The 6800 has six *status flags*.

status flag	abbreviation	meaning for instructions which affect the flag
carry	C	if an arithmetic operation resulted in a carry or a borrow out of the leftmost bit, **carry** = 1.
overflow of the	V	if an operation resulted in a two's complement overflow, **overflow** = 1, i.e. if the leftmost bit (which indicates whether the value is positive or negative) has been changed improperly.
zero	Z	if the result of an operation is zero (all bits = 0), **zero** = 1.
sign	N	if the leftmost bit of the result is 1, **sign** = 1.
interrupt mask	I	if I = 1, the processor will ignore interrupt requests.
half carry	H	carry out of bit 3, used in dealing with BCD values

Other abbreviations

The second and third bytes of multibyte instructions are identified as **byte** and **byte**

A — accumulator A (an 8-bit register)
B — accumulator B (an 8-bit register)
pc — the *program counter* (a 16-bit register)
sp — the *stack pointer* (a 16-bit register)

Branch instructions

Branch instructions on the 6800 are all two bytes long, and use *relative* addressing.

As with any instruction, the first step that is taken is to increment the *program counter* so that it contains the address of the next instruction. Since branch instructions are two bytes long, that means (**pc**) (**pc**) + 2. Next, the test associated with the branch instruction is carried out. If it fails, no further action is taken. If it succeeds, (**byte**) are added to the *program counter* as a signed (twos complement) value. Thus, overall, if the test succeeds, the effect is (**pc**) (**pc**) + 2 + (**byte**).

If you need to branch to a location which is more than 127 bytes [Editor's note: Actually the range is -126 to +129 from the address of the branch instruction.] away, use the (*extended*) JMP instruction.

When you're dealing with signed (two's complement) values, BLT, BLE, BGE, BGT, BEQ, and BNE are appropriate. When you're dealing with plain 8-bit values, BCS, BLS, BCC, BHI, BEQ, and BNE are appropriate.

mnemonic	description	inherent	immediate	direct	indexed	extended	C	V	Z	N	I	H	meaning
ABA	Add accumulator B to accumulator A	1B					•	•	•	•		•	(A)←(A + (B))
ADCA	Add to A with carry		89	99	A9	B9	•	•	•	•		•	(A)←(A)+(effective address)+(carry)
ADCB	Add to B with carry		C9	D9	E9	F9	•	•	•	•		•	(B)←(B)+(effective address)+(carry)
ADDA	Add to A without carry		8B	9B	AB	BB	•	•	•	•		•	(A)←(A)+(effective address)
ADDB	Add to B without carry		CB	DB	EB	FB	•	•	•	•		•	(B)←(B)+(effective address)
ANDA	Logical *and* with A		84	94	A4	B4		0	•	•			(A)←(A)∧(effective address)
ANDB	Logical *and* with B		C4	D4	E4	F4		0	•	•			(B)←(B)∧(effective address)
ASL	Arithmetic shift left				68	78	•	•	•	•			same as ASLA, except (effective address) are shifted instead of CA
ASLA	Shift A left arithmetic	48					•	•	•	•			carry A [note that the rightmost bit of A is loaded with an 0]
ASLB	Shift B left arithmetic	58					•	•	•	•			same as ASLA, except (B) are shifted instead of (A)
ASR	Arithmetic shift right				67	77	•	•	•	•			same as ASRA, except (effective address) are shifted instead of (A)
ASRA	Shift A right arithmetic	47					•	•	•	•			carry A [note that the leftmost bit stays the same — "sign propagate"]
ASRB	Shift B right arithmetic	57					•	•	•	•			same as ASRA, EXCEPT (B) are shifted instead of (A)
BITA	Bit test A		85	95	A5	B5		0	•	•			sets the status flags according to the value of (A) ∧(effective address), doesn't affect the values in A or effective address
BITB	Bit test B		C5	D5	E5	F5		0	•	•			same as BITA except compares (B) to (effective address)
BRANCH	[Branch instructions are listed immediately after this table (i.e. after the WAI instruction).]												

mnemonic	description	inherent	immediate	direct	indexed	extended	C	V	Z	N	I	H	meaning
CBA	Compare accumulators	11					•	•	•	•			sets the status flags according to the value of (A) - (B) neither (A) nor (B) are altered
CLC	Clear carry	0C					0						(carry) 0
CLI	Clear interrupt mask	0E									0		(interrupt mask) 0 [enables interrupts]
CLR	Clear				6F	7F	0	0	1	0			(effective address) 00000000
CLRA	Clear A	4F					0	0	1	0			(A) 00000000
CLRB	Clear B	5F					0	0	1	0			(B) 00000000
CLV	Clear two's complement overflow bit	0A						0					(overflow) 0
CMPA	Compare A		81	91	A1	B1	•	•	•	•			sets the status flags according to the value of (A) - (effective address), neither (A) nor (effective address) are altered
CMPB	Compare B		C1	D1	E1	F1	•	•	•	•			sets the status flags according to the value of (B) - (effective address), neither (B) nor (effective address) are altered
COM	Complement				63	73	1	0	•	•			(effective address) $\overline{\text{(effective address)}}$ [all 0's change to 1's and vice versa]
COMA	Complement A	43					1	0	•	•			(A) $\overline{(A)}$ [all 0's change to 1's and vice versa]
COMB	Complement B	53					1	0	•	•			(B) $\overline{(B)}$ [all 0's changed to 1's and vice versa]
CPX	Compare index register		8C	9C	AC	BC		•	•	•			sets the status flags according to the value of (index register) - (effective address) (effective address + 1) neither (index register) nor (effective address) nor (effective address + 1) are altered

mnemonic	description	inherent	immediate	direct	indexed	extended	C	V	Z	N	I	H	meaning
DAA	Decimal adjust A	19					•						converts the value in A to binary-coded decimal (BCD) representation after additios
DEC	Decrement				6A	7A		•	•	•			(effective address)←(effective address) - 1
DECA	Decrement A	4A						•	•	•			(A)←(A) - 1
DECB	Decrement B	5A						•	•	•			(B)←(B) - 1
DES	Decrement stack pointer	34											(sp)←(sp) - 1
DEX	Decrement index register	09							•				(index register)←(index register) - 1
EORA	Exclusive-or with A		88	98	A8	B8		0	•	•			(A)←(A) + (effective address)
EORB	Exclusive-or with B		C8	D8	E8	F8		0	•	•			(B)←(B) + (effective address)
INC	Increment				6C	7C		•	•	•			(effective address)←(effective address) + 1
INCA	Increment A	4C						•	•	•			(A)←(A) + 1
INCB	Increment B	5C						•	•	•			(B)←(B) + 1
INS	Increment stack pointer	31											(sp)←(sp) + 1
INX	Increment index register	08							•				(index register)←(index register) + 1
JMP	Jump				6E	7E							indexed (pc)←(index register) + (byte$_2$) or extended (pc)←(byte$_2$)(byte$_3$)
JSR	Jump to subroutine				AD	BD							first the (pc) are updated to point to the next instruction (the *return address*) then the low order byte of the pc is pushed on the stack, followed by the high order byte. Finally the pc is set as in the JMP instruction.
LDAA	Load accumulator A		86	96	A6	B6		0	•	•			(A)←(effective address)
LDAB	Load accumulator B		C6	D6	E6	F6		0	•	•			(B)←(effective address)

flags affected: C V Z N I H

mnemonic	description	inherent	immediate	direct	indexed	extended	C	V	Z	N	I	H	meaning
LDS	Load stack pointer		8E	9E	AE	BE							(sp)←(effective address) (effective address + 1)
LDX	Load index register		CE	DE	EE	FE							(index register)←(effective address) (effective address + 1)
LSR	Logical shift right				64	74	•	0	•	0			same as LSRA except (effective address) are shifted instead of (A)
LSRA	Shift A right logical	44					•	0	•	0			same as LSRA except (B) are shifted instead of (A)
LSRB	Shift B right logical	54					•	0	•	0			same as LSRA except (B) are shifted instead of (A)
NEG	Negate				60	70	•	•	•	•			(effective address)←-(effective address) [two's complement]
NEGA	Negate A	40											(A)←-(A)
NEGB	Negate B	50											(B)←-(B)
NOP	No operation	01											do nothing (except, of course, increment **pc** to prepare for next instruction)
ORAA	Inclusive *or* with A		8A	9A	AA	BA		•	•	•			(A)←(A) **v** (effective address)
ORAB	Inclusive *or* with B		CA	DA	EA	FA		•	•	•			(B)←(B) **v** (effective address)
PSHA	Push A onto stack	36											(sp)←(A) (sp)←(sp) - 1
PSHB	Push B onto stack	37											(sp)←(B) (sp)←(sp) - 1
PULA	Pull top of stack into A	32											(sp)←(sp) + 1 (A)←((sp)) [pop the stack]
PULB	Pull top of stack into B	33											(sp)←(sp) + 1 (B)←((sp))
ROL	Rotate left				69	79		•	•	•			same as ROLA except (effective address) are affected instead of (A)

mnemonic	description	inherent	immediate	direct	indexed	extended	C	V	Z	N	I	H	meaning
ROLA	Rotate A left	49					•	•	•	•			carry A
ROLB	Rotate B left	59					•	•	•	•			same as ROLA except (B) are affected instead of (A)
ROR	Rotate right				66	76	•	•	•	•			same as RORA except (**effective address**) are affected instead of (A)
RORA	Rotate A right	46					•	•	•	•			carry A
RORB	Rotate B right	56					•	•	•	•			same as RORA except (B) are affected instead of (A)
RTI	Return from interrupt	3B					•	•	•	•	•	•	the status flags (stored in one byte), (B), (A), (**index register**) [2 bytes], and (**pc**) [2 bytes] are popped [PULled] off the stack [in the order given].
RTS	Return from subroutine	39											the 2 top bytes on the stack are popped [PULled] off and stored in **pc**, i.e. (**pc**) ← (**sp**) + 1) ((**sp**)) + 2), (**sp**) (**sp**) + 2
SBA	Subtract accumulators	10					•	•	•	•			(A)←(A) - (B)
SBCA	Subtract from A with borrow		82	92	A2	B2	•	•	•	•			(A)←(A) - (**effective address**) - (**carry**)
SBCB	Subtract from B with borrow		C2	D2	E2	F2	•	•	•	•			(B)←(B) - (**effective address**) - (**carry**)
SEC	Set carry	0D					1						(carry)←1
SEI	Set interrupt mask	0F									1		(interrupt mask)←1 [disable interrupts]
SEV	Set two's complement overflow bit	0B						1					(overflow)←1
STAA	Store A			97	A7	B7		0	•	•			(effective address)←(A)
STAB	Store B			D7	E7	F7		0	•	•			(effective address)←(B)

flags affected

mnemonic	description	inherent	immediate	direct	indexed	extended	C	V	Z	N	I	H	meaning
STS	Store stack pointer			9F	AF	BF		0	•	•			(effective address)← high order byte of (sp) (effective address + 1)← low order byte of (sp)
STX	Store index register			DF	EF	FF		0	•	•			(effective address)← high order byte of (index register) (effective address + 1)← low order byte of (index register)
SUBA	Subtract from A		80	90	A0	B0	•	•	•	•			(A)←(A) - (effective address)
SUBB	Subtract from B		C0	D0	E0	F0	•	•	•	•			(B)←(B) - (effective address)
SWI	Software interrupt	3F									1		(pc)←(pc) + 1, then (pc), (index register), (A), (B), (status flags) are pushed onto the stack, then (pc)← (FFFA$_{16}$) (FFFB$_{16}$)
TAB	Transfer from A to B	16						0	•	•			(B)←(A)
TAP	Store A in status flags	06					•	•	•	•	•	•	(status flags)←(A) bit$_0$ of A→C bit$_3$→N bit$_1$ of A→V bit$_4$→I bit$_2$ of A→Z bit$_5$→H
TBA	Transfer from B to A	17						0	•	•			(A)←(B)
TPA	Store status flags in A	07											(A)←(status flags) [see TAP for storage scheme]
TST	Test				6D	7D	0	0	•	•			status flags set according to the value of (effective address)
TSTA	Test A	4D					0	0	•	•			status flags set according to the value of (A)
TSTB	Test B	5D					0	0	•	•			status flags set according to the value of (B)
TSX	Transfer from stack pointer to index register	30											(index register)←(sp) + 1
TXS	Transfer from index register to stack pointer	35											(sp)←(index register) - 1
WAI	Wait for interrupt	3E											(pc)←(pc) + 1, then (pc), (index register), (A), (B), (status flags) are PUSHed onto the stack. Then execution is suspended until an interrupt occurs.

Branch instructions

	description	op code	meaning
BCC	Branch if carry clear	24	if (carry) = 0 then (pc)←(pc) + 2 + (byte$_2$) otherwise (pc)←(pc) + 2 (i.e. if (carry) = 0 branch otherwise go on in sequence)
BCS	Branch if carry set	25	if (carry) = 1 then branch [as specified in byte$_2$] otherwise go on in sequence
BEQ	Branch if equal	27	if (zero) = 1 then branch, otherwise go on
BGE	Branch if greater than or equal to zero	2C	if (sign) + (overflow) = 0 then branch, otherwise go on
BGT	Branch if greater than zero	2E	if (zero)∧[(sign) + (overflow)] = 0 then branch, otherwise go on
BHI	Branch if higher	22	if (zero)∧(carry) = 0 then branch, otherwise go on
BLE	Branch if less than or equal to zero	2F	if (zero)∨[(sign) + (overflow)] = 1 then branch, otherwise go on
BLS	Branch if lower or same	23	if (zero)∨(carry) = 1 then branch, otherwise go on
BLT	Branch if less than zero	2D	if (sign) + (overflow) = 1 then branch, otherwise go on
BMI	Branch if minus	2B	if (sign) = 1 then branch, otherwise go on
BNE	Branch if not equal	26	if (zero) = 0, then branch, otherwise go on
BPL	Branch if plus	2A	if (sign) = 0, then branch, otherwise go on
BRA	Branch always (unconditional)	20	branch [i.e., (pc) (pc) + 2 + (byte$_2$)]
BSR	Branch to subroutine	8D	increment (pc), PUSH (pc) onto the stack, then branch
BVC	Branch if overflow clear	28	if (overflow) = 0 then branch, otherwise go on
BVS	Branch if overflow set	29	if (overflow) = 1, then branch, otherwise go on

8080 Instruction Set*

The notation used to describe the meaning of each instruction is explained in Questions 639-646. The architecture of the 8080 is discussed in Q614-620 and Figure 59. Op codes are given in binary.

Some of the instructions include references to specific registers. For instance, the MOV r_1, r_2 instruction takes the value stored in register r_2 (called the *source* register) and stores it in register r_1 (called the *destination* register). The three bit value used to identify the *source* is shown as SSS in the op code; the three bit value used to identify the destination is shown as DDD. The correspondences between registers and three bit values are

	register	SSS or DDD
(accumulator)	A	111
	B	000
	C	001
	D	010
	E	011
	E	011
	H	100
	L	101

Thus, the op code for MOV A, B is

DDD

01111000

SSS

The 8080 (and the 8085) has five *status flags* (also called *condition flags* or *condition codes*).

status flag	abbreviation	meaning for instructions which affect the flag
zero	Z	if the result of an instruction is zero (all bits 0), **zero** = 1, otherwise **zero** = 0.
sign	S	if the leftmost bit of the result is 1, **sign** = 1, else 0.
carry	CY	if an arithmetic operation resulted in a carry or a borrow out of the leftmost bit, **carry** = 1
parity	P	if there is an even number of 1's in the result, **parity** = 1.
auxiliary carry	AC	carry out of bit 3. Used when dealing with binary coded decimal values (see DAA instruction).

Other abbreviations

The second and third bytes of multibyte instructions are identified as **byte**$_2$ and **byte**$_3$.

pc	—	the *program counter* (a 16-bit register)
r	—	a *register,* one of A, B, C, D, E, H, L
sp	—	the *stack pointer* (a 16-bit register)

*Thanks to Intel Corp. for permission to include this material.

			flags affected					clock		
mnemonic	description	op code	Z	S	P	CY	AC	cycles	length	meaning
ACI	Add immediate to A with carry	11001110	•	•	•	•	•	7	2	$(A) \leftarrow (A) + (byte_2) + (carry)$
ADC M	Add memory to A with carry	10001110	•	•	•	•	•	7	1	$(A) \leftarrow (A) + ((H)(L)) + (carry)$
ADC r	Add register to A with carry	10001SSS	•	•	•	•	•	4	1	$(A) \leftarrow (A) + (r) + (carry)$
ADD M	Add memory to A	10000101	•	•	•	•	•	7	1	$(A) \leftarrow (A) + ((H) (L))$
ADD r	Add to register to A	10000SSS	•	•	•	•	•	4	1	$(A) \leftarrow (A) + (r)$
ADI	Add immediate to A	11000110	•	•	•	•	•	7	2	$(A) \leftarrow (A) + (byte_2)$
ANA M	And memory with A	10100110	•	•	•	•	•	7	1	$(A) \leftarrow (A) \wedge ((H)(L))$
ANA r	And register with A	10100SSS	•	•	•	•	•	4	1	$(A) \leftarrow (A) \wedge (r)$
ANI	And immediate with A	11100110	•	•	•	•	•	7	2	$(A) \leftarrow (A) \wedge (byte_2)$
CALL	Call unconditional	11001101						17	3	$((sp) - 1) \leftarrow (\text{high order byte of } pc)$ $((sp) - 2) \leftarrow (\text{low order byte of } pc)$ $(sp) \leftarrow (sp) - 2$ $(pc) \leftarrow (byte_3) (byte_2)$ i.e. (pc) is pushed on the stack, control is transferred to $(byte_3) (byte_2)$
CC	Call on carry	11011100						11/17	3	same as CALL if (carry) = 1 otherwise continue in sequence (i.e. $(pc) \leftarrow (pc) + 3$)
CM	Call on minus	11111100						11/17	3	same as CALL if (sign) = 1 otherwise go on
CMA	Complement A	00101111						4	1	$(A) \leftarrow$ one's complement of (A) i.e. all 0's become 1's and vice versa
CMC	Complement carry	00111111				•		4	1	$(carry) \leftarrow \overline{(carry)}$
CMP M	Compare memory with A	10111110	•	•	•	•	•	7	1	set status flags based on the value of (A) - ((H) (L)). (H), (L), and (A) remain unchanged
CMP r	Compare register with A	10111SSS	•	•	•	•	•	4	1	set status flags based on value of (A) - (r). (A) and (r) remain unchanged

| | | | flags affected | | | | | | | |
mnemonic	description	op code	Z	S	P	CY	AC	clock cycles	length	meaning
CNC	Call on no carry	11010100						11/17	3	same as CALL if (carry) = 0, otherwise go on
CNZ	Call on not zero	11000100						11/17	3	same as CALL if (zero) = 0, otherwise go on
CP	Call on positive	11110100						11/17	3	same as CALL if (sign) = 0, otherwise go on
CPE	Call on parity even	11101100						11/17	3	same as CALL if (parity) = 1, otherwise go on
CPI	Compare immediate with A	11111110	•	•	•	•	•	7	2	set status flags based on value of (A) - (byte$_2$). (A) remains unchanged
CPO	Call on parity odd	11100100						11/17	3	same as CALL if (parity) = 0, otherwise go on
CZ	Call on zero	11001100						11/17	3	same as CALL if (zero) = 1, otherwise go on
DAA	Decimal adjust A	00100111	•	•	•	•	•	4	1	convert the 8-bit value in A into 2 BCD digits (in A), used after additions on BCD values
DAD B	Add B & C to H & L	00001001				•		10	1	(H)(L) ← (H)(L) + (B)(C)
DAD D	Add D & E to H & L	00011001				•		10	1	(H)(L) ← (H)(L) + (D)(E)
DAD H	Add H & L to H & L	00101001				•		10	1	(H)(L) ← (H)(L) + (H)(L)
DAD SP	Add stack pointer to H & L	00111001				•		10	1	(H)(L) ← (H)(L) + (sp)
DCR M	Decrement memory	00110101	•	•	•		•	10	1	((H)(L)) ← ((H)(L)) - 1
DCR r	Decrement register	00DDD101	•	•	•		•	5	1	(r) ← (r) - 1
DCX B	Decrement B & C	00001011						5	1	(B)(C) ← (B)(C) - 1
DCX D	Decrement D & E	00011011						5	1	(D)(E) ← (D)(E) - 1
DCX H	Decrement H & L	00101011						5	1	(H)(L) ← (H)(L) - 1
DCX SP	Decrement stack pointer	00111011						5	1	(sp) ← (sp) - 1
DI	Disable interrupt	11110011						4	1	ignore interrupt requests from now on
EI	Enable interrupts	11111011						4	1	respond to interrupt requests from now on
HLT	Halt	01110110						7	1	stop. i.e. don't carry out any further instructions.

mnemonic	description	op code	Z	S	P	CY	AC	clock cycles	length	meaning
IN	Input	11011011						10	2	place a value from the input port specified by ($byte_2$) in A
INR M	Increment memory	00110100	•	•	•		•	10	1	$((H)(L)) \leftarrow ((H)(L)) + 1$
INR r	Increment register	00DDD100	•	•	•		•	5	1	$(r) \leftarrow (r) + 1$
INX B	Increment B & C registers	00000011						5	1	$(B)(C) \leftarrow (B)(C) + 1$
INX D	Increment D & E registers	00010011						5	1	$(D)(E) \leftarrow (D)(E) + 1$
INX H	Increment H & L registers	00100011						5	1	$(H)(L) \leftarrow (H)(L) + 1$
INX SP	Increment stack pointer	00110011						5	1	$(sp) \leftarrow (sp) + 1$
JC	Jump on carry	11011010						10	3	same as JMP if (carry) = 1, otherwise go on in sequence
JM	Jump on minus	11111010						10	3	same as JMP if (sign) = 1, otherwise go on
JMP	Jump unconditional	11000011						10	3	$(pc) \leftarrow (byte_3)(byte_2)$
JNC	Jump on no carry	11010010						10	3	same as JMP if (carry) = 0, otherwise go on
JNZ	Jump on not zero	11000010						10	3	same as JMP if (zero) = 0, otherwise go on
JP	Jump on positive	11110010						10	3	same as JMP if (sign) = 0, otherwise go on
JPE	Jump on parity even	11101010						10	3	same as JMP if (parity) = 1, otherwise go on
JPO	Jump on parity odd	11100010						10	3	same as JMP if (parity) = 0, otherwise go on
JZ	Jump on zero	11001010						10	3	same as JMP if (zero) = 1, otherwise go on
LDA	Load A direct	00111010						13	3	$(A) \leftarrow ((byte_3)(byte_2))$
LDAX B	Load A indirect	00001010						7	1	$(A) \leftarrow ((B)(C))$
LDAX D	Load A indirect	00011010						7	1	$(A) \leftarrow ((D)(E))$
LHLD	Load H & L direct	00101010						16	3	$(L) \leftarrow ((byte_3)(byte_2))$ $(H) \leftarrow ((byte_3)(byte_2) + 1)$

| | | | flags affected | | | | | clock | | |
mnemonic	description	op code	Z	S	P	CY	AC	cycles	length	meaning
LXI B	Load immediate register Pair B & C	00000001						10	3	$(B)\leftarrow(byte_3)$ $(C)\leftarrow(byte_2)$
LXI D	Load immediate register Pair D & E	00010001						10	3	$(D)\leftarrow(byte_3)$ $(E)\leftarrow(byte_2)$
LXI H	Load immediate register Pair H & L	00100001						10	3	$(H)\leftarrow(byte_3)$ $(L)\leftarrow(byte_2)$
LXI SP	Load immediate stack pointer	00110001						10	3	$(sp)\leftarrow(byte_3)(byte_2)$
MVI M	Move immediate memory	00110110						10	2	$((H)(L))\leftarrow(byte_2)$
MVI r	Move immediate register	00DDD110						7	2	$(r)\leftarrow(byte_2)$
MOV M,r	Move register to memory	01110SSS						7	1	$((H)(L))\leftarrow(r)$
MOV r,M	Move memory to register	01DDD110						7	1	$(r)\leftarrow((H)(L))$
MOV r₁,r₂	Move register to register	01DDDSSS						5	1	$(r1)\leftarrow(r2)$, r1 is the *destination* r2 is the *source*
NOP	No-operation	00000000						4	1	don't do anything except increment (pc) to get the next instruction
ORA M	*Or memory with A*	10110110	•	•	•	0	0	7	1	$(A)\leftarrow(A)$ $((H)(L))$
ORA r	*Or register with A*	10110SSS	•	•	•	0	0	4	1	$(A)\leftarrow(A)$ (r)
ORI	*Or immediate with A*	11110110	•	•	•	0	0	7	2	$(A)\leftarrow(A)$ $(byte_2)$
OUT	Output	11010011						10	2	send (A) to the port specified by $(byte_2)$
PCHL	H & L to program counter	11101001						5	1	$(pc)\leftarrow(H)(L)$, i.e. jump to (H)(L)
POP B	Pop register pair B & C off stack	11000001						10	1	$(C)\leftarrow((sp))$, $(B)\leftarrow((sp) + 1)$, $(sp)\leftarrow(sp) + 2$
POP D	Pop register pair D & E off stack	11010001						10	1	$(E)\leftarrow((sp))$, $(D)\leftarrow((sp) + 1)$, $(sp)\leftarrow(sp) + 2$
POP H	Pop register pair H & L off stack	11100001						10	1	$(L)\leftarrow((sp))$, $(H)\leftarrow((sp) + 1)$, $(sp)\leftarrow(sp) + 2$

mnemonic	description	flags affected Z	S	P	CY	AC	clock cycles	length	meaning
POP PSW	Pop A and Flags off stack	11110001 ·	·	·	·	·	10	1	(status flags)←((sp)), (A)←((sp)) + 1), (sp)←(sp) + 2
PUSH B	Push register Pair B & C on stack	11000101					11	1	((sp)) - 1)←(B), ((sp)) - 2)←(C), (sp)←(sp) - 2
PUSH D	Push register Pair D & E on stack	11010101					11	1	((sp)) - 1)←(D), ((sp)) - 1)←(E), (sp)←(sp) - 2
PUSH H	Push register Pair H & L on stack	11100101					11	1	((sp)) - 1)←(H), ((sp)) - 2)←(L), (sp)←(sp) - 2
PUSH PSW	Push A and Flags on stack	11110101					11	1	((sp)) - 1)←(A), ((sp)) - 2)←(status flags), (sp)←(sp) - 2
RAL	Rotate A left through carry	00010111					4	1	carry A
RAR	Rotate A right through carry	00011111			·		4	1	carry A
RC	Return on carry	11011000					5/11	1	same as RET if (carry) = 1, otherwise go on in sequence
RET	Return	11001001					10	1	(pc) (sp) + 1) ((sp)), (sp) (sp) +2 i.e. jump to address stored on the top of the stack
RLC	Rotate A left	00000111			·		4	1	carry A
RM	Return on minus	11111000					5/11	1	same as RET if (sign) = 1, otherwise go on
RNC	Return on no carry	11010000					5/11	1	same as RET if (carry) = 0, otherwise go on
RNZ	Return on not zero	11000000					5/11	1	same as RET if (zero) = 0, otherwise go on
RP	Return on positive	11110000					5/11	1	same as RET if (sign) = 0, otherwise go on
RPE	Return on parity even	11101000					5/11	1	same as RET if (parity) = 1, otherwise go on
RPO	Return on parity odd	11100000					5/11	1	same as RET if (parity) = 0, otherwise go on

mnemonic	description	op code	Z	S	P	CY	AC	clock cycles	length	
RRC	Rotate A right	00001111				•		4	1	carry A
RST	Restart	11AAA111						11	1	push (pc) on the stack, then (pc)—000000000AAA000 (for responding to interrupts)
RZ	Return on zero	11001000						5/11	1	same as RET if (zero) = 1, otherwise go on
SBB M	Subtract memory from A with borrow	10011110	•	•	•	•	•	7	1	$(A) \leftarrow (A) - ((H) (L)) - (carry)$
SBB r	Subtract register from A with borrow	10011SSS	•	•	•	•	•	4	1	$(A) \leftarrow (A) - (r) - (carry)$
SBI	Subtract immediate from A with borrow	11011110	•	•	•	•	•	7	2	$(A) \leftarrow (A) - (byte_2) - (carry)$
SHLD	Store H & L direct	00100010						16	3	$((byte_3) (byte_3)) \leftarrow (L)$ / $((byte_2) (byte_2) + 1) \leftarrow (H)$
SPHL	H & L to stack pointer	11111001						5	1	$(sp) \leftarrow (H)(L)$
STA	Store A direct	00110010						13	3	$((byte_3) (byte_2)) \leftarrow (A)$
STAX B	Store A indirect	00000010						7	1	$((B) (C)) \leftarrow (A)$
STAX D	Store A indirect	00010010						7	1	$((D) (E)) \leftarrow (A)$
STC	Set carry	00110111				•		4	1	$(carry) \leftarrow 1$
SUB M	Subtract memory from A	10010110	•	•	•	•	•	7	1	$(A) \leftarrow (A) - ((H) (L))$
SUB r	Subtract register from A	10010SSS	•	•	•	•	•	4	1	$(A) \leftarrow (A) - (r)$
SUI	Subtract immediate from A	11010110	•	•	•	•	•	7	2	$(A) \leftarrow (A) - (byte_2)$
XCHG	Exchange D & E, H & L Registers	11101011						4	1	H ↔ D, L ↔ E

flags affected

mnemonic	description	op code	flags affected					clock cycles	length	meaning
			Z	D	P	CY	AC			
XRA M	*Exclusive or* memmory with A	10101110	·	·	·	0	0	7	1	$(A) \leftarrow (A) + ((H)(L))$
XRA r	*Exclusive or* register with A	10101SSS	·	·	·	0	0	4	1	$(A) \leftarrow (A) + (r)$
XRI	*Exclusive or* immediate with A	11101110	·	·	·	0	0	7	2	$(A) \leftarrow (A) + (byte_2)$
XTHL	Exchange top of stack, H & L	11100011						18	1	$(L) \leftarrow ((sp)), (H) \leftarrow ((sp) + 1)$

Note: the newer 8085 microprocessor has all the above instructions plus two more:

RIM	read interrupt mask	00100000						4	1	$(A) \leftarrow$ (interrupt mask)
SIM	set interrupt mask	00110000						4	1	(interrupt mask) $\leftarrow (A)$

APPENDIX H

Bibliography

There are literally hundreds of new titles published each year in the general computer, computer technology, programming, information processing area. At this moment, for example, there are over 80 books in print covering programming in Fortran, and somewhere between 30 and 40 on programming in Basic. In compiling this Bibliography, I've tried to include a good sample of books and magazines that are directly relevant to home computing. By browsing through technical bookstores and college libraries, watching the ads in the magazines, and talking to friends, you can uncover scads more.

Organization of the Bibliography

Hardware
    Books dealing mainly with hardware
    Manufacturers' literature
Software
    Books dealing mainly with software
    Textbooks covering specific languages
General Interest
Periodicals
    Popular magazines
    Trade magazines

Hardware

Books dealing mainly with hardware

C. Gordon Bell and Allen Newell, *Computer Structures: Readings and Examples,* McGraw-Hill, 1971, xix + 668 pages.
> This massive book provides a taxonomy of computer architecture, that is, an orderly classification of computers in terms of their hardware organization and instruction sets. It shows the historical and logical relationships between the designs of a huge number of different machines. It stops short of microprocessors, but all the design ideas used in microprocessor organization are covered many times over.

Thomas R. Blakslee, *Digital Design With Standard MSI and LSI,* John Wiley, 1975, $19.95, 357 pages.
> Updates a number of digital design techniques for use with the new generations of components.

Paul M. Chirlian, *Analysis and Design of Digital Circuits and Computer Systems,* Matrix Publishers, $16.95, 606 pages.
> Starts from scratch, gives general ideas about digital devices, tells how number systems work, develops Boolean algebra as a means of analyzing digital logic, takes you to the point where you can design major components of computers. Includes a separate 82 page booklet giving answers to exercises and problems.

Wayne Green (ed.), *Hobby Computers are Here,* 73 Inc., 1976, $4.95, 11"x8", 95 pages. Reprints (from 73 Magazine) of articles and feisty editorials about getting started in hobby computing.

Don Lancaster, *TTL Cookbook,* Howard W. Sams & Co., 1974, $8.95, 335 pages.
> First 120 pages give descriptions of specific TTL components (official number, what logic is on the chip, what pins connect to what, switching speed, power requirements, special considerations). The rest of the book tells how to use TTL by covering a number of specific projects. Other Sams books by Don Lancaster include the *User's Guide to TTL* and the *TV Typewriter Cookbook.*

E. J. McCluskey, *Introduction to the Theory of Switching Circuits,* McGraw-Hill, 1965, $12.50, xv+318 pages.

The strong point of this book is its development of techniques for minimizing the number of gates required to implement at given logic expression. An old standard text.

Daniel R. McGlynn, *Microprocessors: Technology, Architecture, and Applications,* John Wiley, 1976, about $9, xi+207 pages.

Where Osborne's book (see entry immediately below) may have too fine a focus for the hobbyist, this book's focus may be too broad. Probably aimed at engineering management, it gives an overview of exactly what the title says. Good, understandable treatment of applications, interesting data on trends in microelectronics.

Adam Osborne, *An Introduction to Microcomputers,* Adam Osborne and Associates, 1975, $7.50, xix+397 pages.

If you have some familiarity with computers, and want to learn about microprocessors, this is an excellent book. If you're starting into computing for the first time, the particular slant of the book (it's aimed at people who want to use microprocessors in design, not as microcomputers), its fast pace, and its occasional typos will make it tough. On the other hand, there's not much else available. Now out in revised form as Vol. I and Vol. II — the second volume contains specifics about particular microprocessors.

Charles J. Sippl, *Microcomputer Dictionary and Guide,* Matrix Publishers, 1976, $17.95, approx. 700 pages.

More than just a dictionary for all the quirky acronyms you come across, this book contains a wide variety of useful information (despite its occasional tendency to lapse into descriptions of specific products instead of covering the broad meaning of the word being defined). For instance, entries beginning with **TTL** take up almost two full pages and include such topics as **TTL; TTL applications; TTL compatibility; TTL input/output; TTL logic; TTL logic features; TTL low power Schottky (LSTTL); TTL, Schottky; TTL vs. CMOS.**

Branko Soucek, *Microprocessors and Microcomputers,* John Wiley, 1976, $23.

Manufacturers' Literature
Each manufacturer provides some kind of descriptive material telling how to use its product. Here are some that were used in writing this book.

Microcomputer Handbook, Digital Equipment Corporation (DEC), 1976.

8080 Microcomputer Systems User's Manual, Intel Corporation, 1975.

M6800 Microprocessor Applications Manual, Motorola Semiconductor Products Inc., 1975.

TTL Data Book for Design Engineers, Texas Instruments Inc., $3.95, 640 pages.

Software
Books dealing mainly with software
C. William Gear, *Computer Organization and Programming,* McGraw-Hill, 1969, $14, xiv+397 pages.

Lots of good material at an understandable level. Unfortunately, most of the specific examples are written in IBM 360/370 assembly language. But that may not be as big a problem as it seems at first glance — the people who designed the 808ʳ were no strangers to the 360's architecture, and with just a little extra effort, yo can figure out what's going on. Covers a very wide range of basic programmin techniques.

Brian W. Kernighan and P. J. Plauger, *The Elements of Programming Style,* McGraw-Hill, 1974, $3.95, x+147 pages.
This is a nice book to look at once you've assimilated the basics of programming in a higher-level language. It's filled with good tips for making your programs cleaner, easier to understand, and easier to debug.

Donald E. Knuth, *The Art of Programming,* Addison-Wesley, $29.95 per volume,
Vol. 1 *Fundamental Algorithms*
Vol. 2 *Seminumerical Algorithms*
Vol. 3 *Sorting and Searching*
De rigueur among academics, widely used by all manner of professional programmers, this multi-volume (eventually there are to be seven), master work covers the ins and outs of programming technique. An excellent source for a long term study of specific algorithms, ways of devising algorithms, and the analysis of algorithms.

Jurg Nievergelt, J. Craig Farrar, Edward M. Reingold, *Computer Approaches to Mathematical Problems,* Prentice-Hall, 1974, xiii+257 pages.
Provides a solid introduction to a number of advanced programming techniques. Especially suited to those who have a background in mathematics. Useful annotated lists of references. Anyone who plans to write a championship chess playing program should be familiar with the techniques covered here.

101 BASIC Computer Games, Digital Equipment Corporation, $7.50 and the companion

Understanding Mathematics and Logic Using Basic Computer Games, $4.50.
The first popular book of computer games.

People's Computer Company (with Hewlett-Packard), *What To Do After You Hit Return or P.C.C.'s First Book of Computer Games,* 1975, approx. $7, 11''x15'', 158 pages.
Fanciful descriptions and fun introductions to 48 computer games. Full listings (in Hewlett-Packard's version of extended Basic) for 37 of the games. A good place to start if you're looking for tips on designing your own games. Listings for two of the most popular of the games that are left out of the listings here (Hunt the Wumpus and Startrek) may be found in *The Best of Creative Computing, Vol. 1.*

Jean E. Sammet, *Programming Languages: History and Fundamentals,* Prentice-Hall, 1969, xxx+785 pages.
Gives history, syntax, example programs, discussion of merits for over a hundred programming languages. Virtually every language that saw the light of day before 1969 is covered. Contains an extensive section on all the languages I've seen covered in hobbyist publications except for Wirth's language PASCAL which is a more recent creation. Extensive bibliography.

Scelbi software books:
Scelbi's First Book of Computer Games for the 8008/8080, $14.95.

Scelbi's Galaxy Game for the 8008/8080, $14.95.

Scelbi 8080 Software Gourmet Guide and Cook Book, $9.95.

An 8080 Assembler Program, $17.95.

An 8080 Editor Program, $14.95.

etc.

All include program listings you can copy for use on 8008 or 8080 based systems. More on the way!

Harold S. Stone, *Introduction to Computer Organization and Data Structures,* McGraw-Hill, 1972, $13.50, 320+pages. If you're getting tired of feeling slightly lost as you attempt a major program, but you have a good grasp of programming basics, going through the last half of this book (Chapters 6-11 on Data Structures) will yield a quantum jump in your programming abilities. Tells how and why to use **arrays, stacks, queues, lists, plexes, trees, heaps**—all manner of data structures.

Dennie Van Tassel, *Program Style, Design, Efficiency, Debugging, and Testing,* Prentice-Hall, approx. 250 pages. This book is crammed with helpful hints, tips, and ideas, all of real pracitcal value. Putting them in practice will make your program cleaner, easier to read, de-bug, and use. Also includes 101 programming problems—a good source of ideas for useful programs.

Gerald M. Weinberg, *The Psychology of Computer Programming,* $9.95, 288 pages.
This is a fascinating book—it looks at the behavior of and patterns of interaction among computer programmers. Although it may be intended more for people who have to manage teams of programmers, it contains a number of ideas which are of direct practical value to the individual programmer. See especially the sections on **ego-less programming.**

Textbooks covering specific languages
Basic
Robert L. Albrecht, LeRoy Finkel, and Jerald R. Brown, *BASIC,* John Wiley, 1973, $4.95, 325 pages.
In a programmed instruction format. Patient and gentle.

Michel Boillet and Lister Horn, *BASIC,* West Publ. Co., 1976, xii+273 pages.
Good coverage, lots of good problems at the end of each chapter, many business oriented.

John G. Kemeny and Thomas E. Kurtz, *Basic Programming,* John Wiley, 1971 (2nd. ed.), $7.75, 8'' x 11'', 150 pages.
The "old standard". Moves quickly, has lots of really clever examples.

Robert E. Lynch and John R. Rice, *Computers: Their Impact and Use: Basic Languages,* Holt, Rinehart, and Winston, 1975, xi+398 pages.
The first half gives a broad overview of computing, the second half covers programming in Basic. Moves fairly rapidly, includes a number of nice, real world examples.

Paul W. Murrill and Cecil W. Smith, *Basic Programming,* Intext Educational Publishers, 1971, $6, 8'' x 11'', 155 pages.

Anthony P. Peluso, Charles R. Bauer, and Dalward J. Debruzzi *Basic BASIC Programming,* Addison-Wesley, 1972, $7.50, 8''x11'', 274 pages.
In a programmed instruction format, broad coverage.

People's Computer Company, *My Computer Likes Me (When I Speak in BASIC),* DYMAX, 1972, $1.50, 64 pages.
Nice, mellow, friendly, very brief introduction in Basic. Good place to begin if you're starting completely from scratch.

etc.,etc.,etc.,etc.

Fortran
Rich Didday and Rex Page, *Fortran for Humans,* West Publ., 1977 (2nd: ed.), 1974 (1st ed.), approx. $9,xv+430 pages.
etc.,etc., etc., etc., etc.

LISP
John McCarthy, et. al., *LISP 1.5 Programmer's Manual,* MIT Press, 1962, $3,106 pages.

PASCAL
K. Jensen and N. Wirth, *PASCAL — User Manual and Report,* Springer-Verlag, 1976, $5.90, viii+167 pages.

PL/I
Frank Bates and Mary L. Douglas, *Programming Language/One*, 2nd. Ed., 1970, 432 pages.

SNOBOL4
R. E. Griswold, J. F. Poage, and I. P. Polonsky, *The SNOBOL4 Programming Language*, 2nd Ed., 1971, 8''x11'', 256 pages.

Note: before you rush out and buy any book on programming, stop in at a college library and look through the ones they have.

General Interest
David H. Ahl (ed), *The Best of Creative Computing, Vol. 1*, Creative Computing Press, 1976, $8.95, 8½''x11'', ix+317 pages.
> If you want to get caught up with what *Creative Computing* (see entry under Popular magazines) did in their first six issues, this is the only way — they're sold out of back issues. Includes programs in Basic for a number of games, including the ever popular Hunt the Wumpus and Star Trek. (Note: Star Trek is a large program, and will have to be altered before it'll run on most home systems. A small version of Star Trek called "Star Trek Trainer" is given in the September 1976 issue of *Byte*.)

Robert Baer, *The Digital Villain: Notes on the Numerology, Parapsychology, and Metaphysics of the Computer*, Addison-Wesley, 1972, approx. 190 pages.

Stewart Brand, *II Cybernetic Frontiers*, Random House, 1974, $2, 96 pages.
> Reports from two frontiers. The first, in the form of a conversation with anhropologist/cybernetician Gregory Bateson, asks what happens when you take the basic principles of the information sciences and use them to analyze the human condition. The second, in the form of a tour of late night activities at the Stanford Artificial Intelligence Lab, asks what happens when you take the techniques of the information sciences and let people play.

Rich Didday, *Finite State Fantasies*, Matrix Publishers, 1976, $1.25, 8½''x11'', 48 pages.

Charles and Ray Eames, *A Computer Perspective*, Harvard University Press, 1973, $15, 9''x9'', 175 pages.
> An astonishing slice of computer history, shown in photographs, private notes, letters, circuit diagrams and early flowcharts of the founding fathers and mothers, pictures of early equipment, etc.,etc. It's historically accurate, incredibly well thought out, and absolutely fascinating. The book consists of materials gathered for a major display at the IBM Exhibit Center in New York City, and covers the rise of computing from Babbage up to the early 1950's. The snapshot (p. 133) of Goldstine and Eckert standing like proud papas holding a memory unit is worth the price of admission by itself. The unit is wider than the both of them, about a foot high, and stored *one* decimal digit!

John G. Kemeny, *Man and the Computer*, Charles Scribner's Sons, 1972, $1.45, 152 pages.
> A non-technical piece done by one of the co-inventors of Basic. Develops the notion that humans and computers are symbiotic; presents and predicts their co-evolution.

Theodor H. Nelson, *Computer Lib/Dream Machines*, Hugo's Book Service, $7, 10''x14'', 128 pages (of course).
> Welcome to the wonderful, wacky, zany, rib tickling, sloganeering, crusading world of Ted Nelson's mind. Full of useful information, funny anecdotes, gossip, diatribes against the powerful, nifty slogans ("Stamp Out Cybercrud! Computer Power to the People!")

Dennie L. Van Tassel, *The Compleat Computer*, SRA, 9''x12'', 216 pages.
A very tasty collection of news articles, cartoons, fiction, poetry, full color reprints of early computerish scific cover art, thought provoking articles, and references to other literature. All with the goal of giving the Big Picture of how computers fit into our society and our daily lives. Goes down easy — fun to read.

Joseph Weizenbaum, *Computer Power and Human Reason*, W.H. Freeman and Company, 1976, $9.95, 300 pages.
This widely read book explores the edge between computer technology and human values. For my money, it's said better in R. Pirsig's *Zen and the Art of Motorcycle Maintenance*.

Periodicals

Popular magazines

ACM Computing Surveys, published quarterly by the ACM (the computing world's professional society). The "Survey and Tutorial Journal of the ACM". Expensive if you don't belong to the ACM, contents frequently not relevant to home computing, but every so often, there's an invaluable piece. Browse at your local college library.

Brail Theory Newsletter, published 4 times a year by the Center for Systems Neuroscience, University of Massachusetts, Amherst, Massachusetts 01002, $5/year. Contains brief reports of current research, reviews of books and papers, controversies. If you have an interest in applying your knowledge of computers and information processing to the study of biological information processing systems, have a look here to see what's going on in this challenging field of study.

Byte (the small systems journal), published monthly by BYTE Publications, 70 Main St., Peterborough, New Hampshire 03458, $12/year. The first glossy, professionally conceived and carried out magazine exclusively aimed at the computer hobbyist. Articles to date have run ¾ hardware, ¼ software.

Communications of the ACM, published monthly by the ACM.
Reports on theoretical advances in computing. Currently undergoing a re-evaluation, may shift toward the practical end. Check it out at your local college library.

Computer, published monthly by the IEEE Computer Society. Articles tend to be practical (as opposed to theoretical), informative, and non-threatening. Each issue is usually organized around a central theme. Issues covering microcomputerish topics are available at most computer stores.

Computerworld, published weekly in Boston, is a tabloid/newspaper which covers the commercial computer world. Useful if you want to follow what the big manufacturers are up to, want to follow court decisions related to computing. Buried in the middle is an occasional article on computer hobbyists.

Creative Computing, subtitled "the magazine of recreational and educational computing", published bi-monthly, P.O. Box 789-M, Morristown, NJ 07960, $15/year.
Fun and informative reading on general topics. Good source of references to other literature. Each issue contains listings of games programs.

Dr. Dobb's Journal of Computer Calisthenics and Orthodontia, published 10 times a year, Box 310, Menlo Park, California 94025, $10/year. Each issue contains program listings (almost all in assembly language, very machine specific), teasers about upcoming hardware products. Main idea is to provide a source of free software products to computer hobbyists—has presented a number of different programs which implement subsets and variants of Basic (lumped under the name Tiny Basic). New projects are afoot. Good source of software ideas.

Interface Age, subtitled "microcomputing for home and small business", published monthly by McPheters, Wolfe & Jones, 6615 Sunset Blvd., Suite 202, Hollywood, CA 90028, $10/year. Introductory articles, product reviews, and a substantial Software Section.

Kilobaud, published monthly, Peterborough, NH 03458, $15/year. Main thrust is applications, i.e. What Can You Do With It? Wide range of solid articles relevant to the hobbyist as well as small businesses.

Microtrek, subtitled "the microcomputer magazine for the hobbyist & professional", published monthly, $10/year. — Now merged with Personal Computing

People's Computer Company is a bimonthly newsletter published by the People's Computer Company, Box 310, Menlo Park, CA 94025, $6/year, tabloid style. The PCC newsletter started out (I think in 1972 or so) bringing the word about computing to school aged people, is now shifting more into the computer hobbyist sphere. It must feel good to the people who started PCC to see what's happening—they're no longer a voice crying in the wilderness.

Personal Computing, published bimonthly by Benwill Publishing Corp., 167 Corey Road, Brookline, MA 02146. Premier issue was Oct/Nov 1976, $8/year.

Popular Electronics, published monthly at One Park Avenue, New York, NY 10016, $9.98/year. For the last couple of years, about one fifth of their material has been relevant to home computing. Some manufacturers use Popular Electronics articles to introduce new products. MITS's Altair 8800 and 680 microcomputers, Cromemco's TV Dazzler, and others have appeared first as Popular Electronics construction articles. Lots of good hardware info, no software to speak of so far.

Radio-Electronics, published monthly, subscriptions are $8.75/year from Radio-Electronics Subscription Service, Boulder, CO 80302. *Radio-Electronics* was the first major magazine to run articles on building a home computer (the Mark-8 microcomputer, 1974).

73 Magazine, published monthly by 73, Inc., Peterborough, NH 03458, $10/year. An amateur radio magazine at heart, with a dynamic section on microcomputers called I/O. The I/O section is edited by John Craig (who also edits *Kilobaud*), and has articles providing introductions to hardware (and some software) techniques. Good source of ads if you're shopping for circuit components.

SIGART Newsletter, published bimonthly by the ACM Special Interest Group on Artificial Intelligence, $12/year. Contains brief reports of current AI work, ongoing arguments, occasional bibliographies, reports of computer chess tournaments. Lively, fun to read.

Trade magazines
   There's a tremendous number of magazines which make their living by getting computer and electronic manufacturers' ads on the right people's desks. Usually they include timely, well-written articles. If you are in the right category (your "professional profile" matches the image they want to portray), you can get some of them for free. Good way to get tips on what's about to happen, keep track of trends. Here are a few. If you think you might qualify, write for a subscription form.

Computer Decisions, "distributed computing for management", Hayden Publishing Co., P.O. Box 13802, Philadelphia, PA 19101.

Computer Design, "the magazine of digital electronics", PO Box 302, Winchester, MA 01890.

Datamation, 35 Mason St., Greenwich, CT 06830.

Data Processing, 134 N. 13th St., Philadelphia, PA 19107.

Digital design, "the magazine of digital systems", Benwill Publ. Co., P.O. Box 335, Winchester, MA 01890.

Electronic Design, Hayden Publishing Co., P.O. Box 13803, Philadelphia, PA 19101

Electronic Design News,

Mini-Micro Systems, 5 Kane Industrial Drive, Hudson, MA 01749. (Formerly called *Modern Data.*)

APPENDIX I